COMMON SENSE CHRISTIANITY

COMMON SENSE CHRISTIANITY

C. Randolph Ross

 OCCAM PUBLISHERS

The Scripture quotations used in this book are from the Revised Standard
Version Bible, copyright 1946, 1952, 1971 by the Division of Christian Education of the National Council of Churches of Christ in the USA and are used by
permission.

Other acknowledgments p. 244.

ISBN 0–929368–00–2

LIBRARY OF CONGRESS CATALOG NUMBER 88–61552

Occam Publishers
18 Frank Street
Cortland, NY 13045

Printed in the United States of America

Publisher's Cataloging in Publication Data.
Ross, C. Randolph.
    Common Sense Christianity
    Includes index.
1. Theology. 2. Christology. 3. Christian life. I. Title
ISBN 0–929368–00–2 Hardbound

I wish to extend my deep appreciation to all those individuals who encouraged me during the ten years of the writing of this book. In particular, I wish to thank those - parishoners and others - who shared with me their questions and their faith; the Rev. Loren G. House, Jr., for his continuing moral support over the long course; and Mrs. June House for her faithful rendering of hand-scrawled pages into a typed manuscript. I also need to mention my family: my daughter Rachael, who has shared much of her growing up with the growth of this book, and my wife, JoAnne, whose support for the carrying through of this project has been invaluable.

COMMON SENSE CHRISTIANITY
TABLE OF CONTENTS

APPENDICES

INTRODUCTION

"You will know the truth, and the truth will make you free."
(John 8:32)

I am a heretic. I am stating this right at the start so nobody feels misled.

I am a heretic. In many of our churches this no longer has any meaning, but in centuries past this name would have brought disgrace, banishment, and all too often death.

What do I mean today by applying this word to myself? Two things: (1) that I place myself firmly and staunchly within the Church and the Christian faith; and (2) that I am firmly and staunchly convinced that much of what the Church has taught as doctrine for most of its twenty centuries, and much of what constitutes orthodox belief today, is just plain wrong.

This is a bold statement. But I do not make it boldly. I make this claim in fear and trembling, driven by my love for the Church and by the fact that what is at stake is nothing less than the future generations whom we are in danger of losing. I am driven also by the clear conclusions of reason and a careful reading of the Scriptures. It has been said that the four foundations of our faith are Scripture, tradition, reason, and experience. This formulation makes sense, but I find myself compelled by Scripture, reason and experience to disagree with much of what constitutes traditional doctrine.

Before I begin my argument, I would ask the reader to keep in mind three points: (1) In many respects, I am simply reclaiming for us today the freedom and diversity found within the New Testament itself. Most of our official Church doctrine was developed in the Greco-Roman world in the several centuries after Jesus of Nazareth, and does not necessarily represent the Biblical position; (2) For me to claim that my position is right and (therefore) that all others are wrong does *not* mean that I claim that the others are not valid Christian beliefs. This is a distinction of utmost importance (see Chapter 8); (3) Theology, as the conceptualization and explanation of our faith, must in any case be recognized as secondary to the living of this faith. (See Chapter 8 on this also.)

1

With these points in mind, I am going to argue against an archaic belief system which has become a harmful and unnecessary obstruction to many honest seekers for whom Christianity might otherwise be an option. Furthermore, as official doctrine this orthodoxy instills self-doubt in many thinking Christians and serves to keep them out of the mainstream of Church thought and life. It is against these traditional doctrines that I will be arguing, not God. I am arguing *for* God, I am arguing to free our understanding of God from the prison of these doctrines—doctrines from a particular time and place that are too often considered to be our final destination, instead of guideposts along the way; doctrines that are too often used to stop questions instead of to help find answers.

I will also attempt to outline a viable and faithful alternative for modern Christians. I call this alternative "common sense Christianity".

I do not mean to suggest by this that Christianity should be "reasonable". I doubt that the life and teachings of Jesus the Christ will ever seem reasonable to a majority of our society. My purpose, rather, is to remove the *unnecessary* obstructions and stumbling blocks in order to enable people to confront the central and ultimate stumbling block: the call to commitment that confronts us in the message of Jesus of Nazareth, in the understanding he gives us of God and of love, of truth and reality. It is vital that people reject or accept Christianity because of this central message and challenge, and not because of a secondary and unnecessary theological framework which many of us find outdated and incomprehensible.

By "common sense" I mean the shared world-view, or basic assumptions, with which we approach and understand our universe. I mean a common sense as to how this universe works.

This common sense does not remain static. It changes from age to age and from culture to culture. And all too often the precepts of our faith are presented in words and concepts that reflect a common sense that is very different from ours today. Yet the insights and validity of Christianity are not confined to any one age or culture. So the challenge for us is to conceptualize our Christian faith in a way that is not dependent on the common sense of a different time, in a way that is understandable to us today.

One final note: my intention has been to present my case in language accessible to lay people. I have avoided numerous footnotes and references, and have tried to avoid technical language and theological jargon. The discussion of basic doctrine is too important to leave to scholarly journals and seminary graduates. It belongs to all the people who are trying to follow Jesus the Christ.

PART ONE

COMMON SENSE, FAITH AND THE GOD WHO GOES "ZAP"

In these first four chapters we lay the groundwork. In Chapter One we demonstrate how our common sense has changed over the years.

In Chapter Two we look at why we cannot simply assert the truth of the Bible over our modern common sense and show that Biblical literalism/inerrancy is an approach to the Scriptures that is acceptable neither to our reason nor to our faith.

In Chapter Three we examine the question of whether we can conceive of God as going "zap"—intervening in the physical processes of the world in particular instances. This forces us to confront the problem of suffering, for this is where this question matters the most. We conclude that neither our reason nor our faith in a loving God can allow us to conceive of God as acting in this way.

In Chapter Four we consider different ways of "explaining" miracles, but point out that miracles are in fact not religiously significant—a point apparently recognized by Jesus himself.

With this preparation, in Part Two we then proceed to address traditional Christian doctrine.

CHAPTER 1: COMMON SENSE

"Come now, let us reason together."
(Isaiah 1:18)

What do I mean when I say that our common sense is different now than it was in (for instance) first century Palestine or the fourth century Roman Empire? How is our common sense different now than in the days when the Bible was written and our doctrine was formulated?

For illustration, consider the example of a thunderstorm. A thunderstorm is a common enough occurrence. But suppose you wanted to know why a particularly severe and destructive storm had hit your locality—what would you do? Would you draw straws among your family and neighbors to see who was to blame? Would you kill a goat and examine its innards, or consult an oracle to see what the mayor had done wrong, or pray about it and await divine inspiration?

Of course not. You would want meteorological data. You would want to answer your question with reference to such things as high pressure and low pressure systems, cold fronts, prevailing winds, humidity, and barometric pressure. You would probably just consult the weather report in the newspaper or on TV, complete with satellite photographs of the entire nation. This is just common sense.

It does not matter that there are very few of us who actually understand what all this means, who understand how some air can be heavier than other air, or what ionization is, or why weather fronts cause wind to blow and rain to fall in one place instead of another. It is our common sense that the weather is explained by the kind of information provided by meteorology. Even if we don't trust the weatherman's forecast for tomorrow, we have no doubt that he or she can explain yesterday's weather, including why the original forecast turned out to be wrong.

We all know that this has not always been the case. In Biblical times it was the common sense of people that the weather was to be explained by reference to a very different set of facts. The severe storm in question, for instance, might be explained by referring to the anger of the God (or gods) who controlled it.

Thus in the Book of Jonah, when Jonah tries to sail to Tarshish to escape the call of the Lord and the ship runs into a violent storm, the crew assumes that the storm is caused by the anger of a god towards someone on board. So they draw straws (cast lots, actually) to determine who is responsible for bringing this upon them. This is assumed by the book's author to be a proper and sensible approach to the problem. The procedure works and Jonah is correctly discovered to be the culprit. He confesses and is thrown overboard at his own suggestion, causing the storm to abate, the ship to be saved, and the sailors to believe in Jonah's God.

This common sense of how to explain the weather is not confined to the Book of Jonah. From the great flood, to the drought inflicted on all Israel because of the sins of King Ahab (I Kings 17), to the great wind that killed Job's children, the weather was assumed to be explainable by reference to God (or gods, in other religions) and to divine pleasure or displeasure with people. Consequently it made sense to explain a severe storm by casting lots to determine who had angered the gods, or by trying to figure out what the king had done wrong, or by consulting a prophet or perhaps an oracle who would read the entrails of a sacrificed goat.

Obviously, our common sense of how to explain the weather has changed since then. In fact, how we understand the world has undergone a great transformation over the centuries. Our changed understanding of the weather is just one example of an underlying and thorough-going difference in our common sense of how to understand and explain the world around us. There is no way to escape the fact that our common sense approach to the universe, our common sense of how it works, is very different in some important ways from the common sense of the Biblical authors and the formulators of orthodox Christian doctrine.

In general, we treat our world as a "closed system" universe. Our shared assumption is that the events which happen in our world are caused by other events and circumstances in our world. The explanation of a thunderstorm is to be found in meteorology, not theology; by studying humidity and air pressure, not by casting lots or seeking oracles. The winning or losing of a battle is explained by the comparative strengths of the armies, by the tactics of commanders and the actions of troops, not by the favorable or antagonistic intervention of God. The prosperity of a country is explained in terms of natural resources, a healthy and productive population, and sound economic policies, not in terms of supernatural blessing on a deserving or chosen people.

All this is just common sense. But it is not the common sense of the Bible. The Bible assumes a "two storey" universe: that is, there are events which happen here in the natural world, which we can know and examine, and events which take place in the supernatural realm, usually beyond our direct knowledge. Furthermore, there is open communication between these two realms, so that events in the natural world are sometimes explainable by causes in the supernatural realm.

To get a picture of how the relationship between the two storeys was conceived, imagine a solid rubber ball. Geographically, of course, God's activities were thought of as being centered in the heavens above a flat earth. But we will use this solid rubber ball as a metaphysical metaphor to illustrate how natural and supernatural were thought to interact.

The surface of this ball represents the finite natural world. The ball as a whole, including the surface, represents the realm of the activities of God. All that is below the surface represents the bulk of the supernatural that is out of our sight and not directly knowable. But there is no firm boundary that separates the natural surface from the supernatural whole of which it is a part. Actions on the surface can be expected to cause reactions within, which in turn have effects on the surface. Visible events on the surface can have invisible supernatural causes, and in fact we can reasonably infer such supernatural causes from what we see happening around us.

With this view of the universe, this common sense of how it works, it is entirely reasonable to explain a thunderstorm as the anger of God, or a victory in battle as caused by favorable divine intervention. And this creates a problem for us. How do we go about understanding the Bible when it assumes a common sense different from our own? How do we approach a Holy Scripture that not only explains events differently than we would, but that also has a very different understanding of what even counts for a reasonable explanation?

Before we try to address this problem, however, we ought in all fairness to respond to those who deny that this problem even exists. I am claiming that the Bible has a different common sense than we do, and that therefore there is a problem as to how to relate the teachings and stories of the Bible to us today. The assumption here is that we are not going to change our common sense, and this in effect sets up this modern common sense in judgment of the Biblical accounts.

There are several arguments that can be advanced against this position: first, that there is no need to adapt or interpret the Bible this way because this "modern common sense" is quite *un*common; second, that the current popularity of a belief or point of view is no guarantee of its truth, so the Bible ought not to be adapted to suit the understanding of a particular time; third, that the Bible *cannot* be adapted to this common sense, because this common sense excludes God; and fourth, that if our common sense disagrees with the Bible, then we must change our common sense after all, because the Bible is true.

One: This Modern Common Sense is Uncommon

I agree.

By "modern common sense" we mean the basic understanding that in order to explain the events and circumstances of this natural world we must look to other events and circumstances within this natural world. We do not explain weather or prosperity with references to the supernatural.

In the world as a whole those who have this understanding are no doubt a minority. And those who have this understanding and are always consistent with it in all aspects of their lives are a very small portion indeed.

Does this mean we can ignore it? Does this mean we don't have to worry about interpreting the Bible to these people? No. Not only is it not in keeping with our faith to write off any group of people, but to ignore this common sense would be to write off the future. Those who now share this common sense are those who have best absorbed the modern scientific understanding. As this permeates through education systems to more and more people, an ever-increasing percentage will have this modern common sense. If Christianity remains tied to a common sense from the past and does not adapt and reach out to the common sense of the future it will become a mere historical relic.

Two: Popularity Is No Guarantee of Truth

I agree again. Wholeheartedly. The widespread popularity of any belief is no guarantee of its truth. We have been wrong before as an entire species, and no doubt we shall be again. The fact that more of us will have this modern common sense in the future does not necessarily mean it is right.

If this is so, then why must Scripture spanning a thousand years, and Christian doctrine that goes back almost two thousand years, accommodate themselves to the common sense of any particular time?

The great truths of the Christian faith are timeless, but the way in which those truths are expressed must fit the understanding of a particular time and place. Furthermore, we are convinced that our common sense of how the world works is right. Until we are convinced otherwise we must stick with this understanding. To do otherwise would be dishonest. And to deny our common sense would be to deny an important aspect of who we are.

I am a person of my age and my world-view. I accept myself and even celebrate myself as such, and cannot accept a system of beliefs which would force me to deny what I am. And if we follow this common sense in our every day actions and beliefs, as so many of us do, then it is intellectually dishonest to suspend this common sense when we happen to consider the realm of religion. We do not serve God by abandoning our intellectual integrity.

And the fact remains that specific events in this physical world are simply not explainable as caused by supernatural beings sticking in their thumbs from somewhere else and going "zap"!

Three: This Common Sense Leaves No Room for God

If our modern common sense of how the world works is that it is essentially a closed causal system, with finite physical events to be explained by finite physical causes, is there then any room left for God? Or have we fallen victim to the insidious encroachments of atheistic scientific thought and secular humanism?

If this latter is the case, if our modern common sense rules out God, then indeed it would appear to be an impossible task to try to interpret the Bible or the Christian faith to this understanding. But our common sense does *not* rule out God. I will explain later how modern science, and a common sense informed by it, provide a framework for understanding the presence of God. First, however, we must take a look at how we arrived at our present situation in which the advance of science can be interpreted (albeit wrongly) as the retreat of God.

Let us return to the common sense of the Bible. We represented this by picturing a solid rubber ball, the surface being the finite world, the whole being the realm of God, with no distinct dividing line between the natural and supernatural. For the last thousand years, however, Western Christian thought has been drawing a distinct and rigid dividing line and then backing God into a corner with it.

Different factors contributed to this. One was the classical idea of the perfection of God, which held that since God was perfect God must be unchangeable (and therefore unaffected in any real sense by the affairs of this world). This also implied a very definite separation between this perfect being and our messy, imperfect world.

Another factor was the time-honored custom of turning to God to explain all that we don't understand. When we understand the natural causes of something we explain it through science; when we don't understand its natural causes we explain it by attributing it to God. The underlying assumption here is that an event can be explained *either* by natural laws *or* by reference to God. The problem with this, of course, is that the more we understand about our natural world, the less room we leave for God.

So there developed a common sense that there was a natural world and a supernatural world, and that although the former depended upon the latter, there was a definite line between the two that was not normally crossed. We might represent this understanding by picturing two separate balls: one representing the finite, natural world, dependent for its existence on the other ball that represents the supernatural world, but spinning along quite nicely on its own according to its own set of natural laws. Between the two spheres is a gap that is bridged only by an "unnatural" act.

This, for some centuries now, has been our understanding of a miracle: it must be an event that cannot be explained by science, that can only be understood as a breaking in of the supernatural. Some Biblical authors were able to see certain events as the result of understandable natural causes and *also* as miracles, such was the intermingling of supernatural with the natural. For some time, however, it has been generally assumed that an event must be *either* the result of worldly causes *or* a miracle, either natural or supernatural. A real honest-to-goodness miracle has to be an exception to the normal workings of nature, otherwise it's not a miracle. It has to be the result of God intervening and going "zap".

It is this understanding of how God acts—by miracles—which leaves no room for God when combined with our advancements in scientific knowledge and our modern common sense. It should not be surprising that a theology which grew out of one common sense should not fit with a different common sense. What we have here is (1) a sense (from years gone by) that physical events which we don't understand can be attributed to God's special action, and (2) a common sense that all physical events are understandable as the result of finite causes. It is the combination of these two that seems to leave no room for God.

By itself, then, this modern common sense does not rule out God. What is needed is a theology that explains God's presence and workings in a way that is consistent with this common sense, a theology that doesn't leave God in the unexplained fringes of our ignorance. And this is what I will try to develop later in this book, a theology that is in some ways more akin to the Biblical concept of the intermingling of natural and supernatural than is the recent tradition of two separate spheres. Instead of conceiving of God as acting through miracles (in the traditional sense) we will conceive of God as being present in the processes of our world, in the context within which we live.

Four: If Our Common Sense Disagrees With the Bible, Then We are Wrong

This last objection is a familiar one. "The Bible is right, so anyone who disagrees with it is wrong." Period. End of argument.

As difficult as it sometimes is to address this point of view, it is a widespread one and an important one, and certainly constitutes the majority view over the last two thousand years. The real question here is: what does it mean to approach the Bible faithfully? And can we do this in keeping with our common sense? But this key question deserves a separate chapter.

CHAPTER 2: THE BIBLE

"Thy word is a lamp to my feet and a light to my path."
(Psalm 119:105)

What is the Bible? What is its proper use? What is its authority for us, and why? What does it mean to approach it faithfully?

To begin with the few statements that everyone would agree with: the Bible is a collection of dozens of books, written by a number of different authors over a period of more than a thousand years. This collection of books went through a long and sometimes complex process of selection (and in many cases, editing) before arriving at its present form. It contains a variety of material, including some of the traditions, history, customs, laws, stories, teachings, psalms, and prophets of a small Near Eastern people called the Hebrews or Jews. It also includes some early writings of the followers of Jesus of Nazareth. These include accounts of his ministry and teaching, reflections about who he was, and reflections about the proper beliefs and practices for his followers.

This collection of writings also serves as the foundation of the Christian religion.

Source of Our Religious Truths

This is our starting point: the Bible as source for our religious truths. This is not to say it is the only source, but Christians have always recognized the authority of the Bible for our religious beliefs and practices, even though we may not always act accordingly. We look to the Bible for insights about the nature of God, the nature of humans, the nature of our relationship to God and the world and each other, and the kind of life that is appropriate to these. We look to it for basic attitudes and values. These are all the proper concerns of religion.

But if we look to the Bible for religious truths such as these, that doesn't mean that we also look to it for authoritative answers in the realm of the physical sciences or medicine or astronomy or geography.

We don't look to it for answers in home repairs, or modern technology, or economic theory, or the laws of the State of New York. And while it can sometimes be helpful to people studying history or archeology or sociology with respect to a certain period in a small region of the Near East, it is hardly the place we would look for a summation of the current knowledge in these areas.

We claim that the Bible is the source of our *religious* beliefs. We do not need to claim that is authoritative in every branch of human knowledge.

But we also call it the "Word of God". What does this mean? Doesn't this mean the Bible must be perfect? Mustn't it then be error-free and infallible on the topics it does address?

By saying that the Bible is the Word of God, do we mean that God wrote these words down with quill and ink? Of course not. By "Word of God" we mean truths about God and from God that were grasped and recorded by the Biblical authors.

But some people mean something very different than this when they talk about the "Word of God". There are in fact several ways of delineating just what constitutes the Word of God, and why. All have a place in the tradition of the Church, and all can point to a basis in Scripture itself. But not all are adequate for dealing with the broad diversity of the Bible, and not all fit with our common sense. One traditional view that is very popular today, and that we must deal with before proceeding, is Biblical literalism or inerrancy.

Biblical Literalism (Inerrancy)

Biblical literalism maintains that the whole Bible is the Word of God because it is divinely inspired. Every writer of every book in the Bible was divinely inspired and guided in what he wrote, so every statement on every subject in the entire Bible is literally true, without error.

There are four serious problems with Biblical literalism: (1) it denies the centrality of Christ; (2) it requires a concept of divine inspiration that denies the authors' humanity; (3) it requires that we believe that the Bible doesn't mean what it says; and (4) it stands in opposition to faith in God. Certainly the Biblical literalists do not intend all of these. But this is where their misdirected devotion and their misguided efforts for security lead them.

1. Biblical Literalism vs. the Centrality of Christ

Biblical literalism denies the centrality of Jesus the Christ. If we are Christians, then surely this means that we believe that the life and teachings of Jesus the Christ give us the truest understanding of God, and that this understanding is the benchmark against which we measure other interpretations. But if everything in the Bible is divinely inspired truth then it is all equally true. Statements in the Old Testament about God or about how to treat our neighbors are all just as true and authoritative as those in the Gospels.

To pick just one example, we must then be willing to say that God actually told Joshua to kill all the men, women and children in the cities of Jericho and Ai (Joshua 6–8). Is this the same God preached by Jesus, who commanded us to love our enemies? Even if you believe that God spoke to Joshua, how could a Christian believe that God would order wholesale slaughter? Don't we have to say, at the very least, that Joshua mis-heard, that he mistook the cultural custom of "holy war" for divine command? But the Biblical literalist cannot do this, and has to insist that the words of Joshua and Elijah, Ecclesiastes and Job, are as true as anything Jesus said, and therefore presumably just as important. This negates the centrality of Christ and removes the possibility of his being our benchmark.

Many people address this problem with the idea of "progressive revelation". This is the belief that we have in the Bible a revelation of God—by God—that grows progressively more complete. Thus the earliest books reflect the least complete and least accurate revelation of God, with a progression to a much more complete revelation in the great prophets, and culminating in the final and complete revelation in Jesus Christ.

It does seem that there is in general an advancement in the understanding of God as the Bible progresses. But this is not uniform; I would be hard put to pick Proverbs or Ecclesiastes over Isaiah. And even if there is generally an improved understanding of God, to say that this is because of a progressive divine revelation rather than because of our own increased understanding through the years is tantamount to saying that our earlier ignorance is God's fault for not revealing more sooner. It hardly seems necessary to blame human ignorance on a divine coyness, or to picture God rationing out carefully increased doses of self-revelation.

In any case, "progressive revelation" would also mean that the earlier understandings of God were inaccurate to some degree. This leaves us needing criteria by which to decide what in the Old Testament is really God's Word. While I think this is proper and necessary, it is hardly an option for the Biblical literalist, for whom all parts of the Bible are equally true.

2. Biblical Literalism vs. the Humanity of the Authors

Biblical literalism requires an understanding of divine inspiration that denies the humanity of the authors and defies common sense.

The people who wrote the different books of the Bible were human beings. They had prejudices, they shared most of the views of their particular place and time, and they made mistakes. Yet we are asked to believe that when they wrote about the capture of Ai or the life of Jesus they suddenly ceased to be affected by these prejudices and presuppositions. How is it that a person who is just as human as you or I should suddenly become error-free when writing a book which later on was to be included in the Bible? (Remember, these books were not recognized as Scripture until some later date.)

The only way that this could happen would be if some infallible power took over these writers, suppressed their humanity, and used them as writing instruments just as you and I would use a pen. I cannot see how this idea of using people can fit with the Christian view of God. Neither does it fit with our common sense.

Furthermore, part of the great attractiveness of the Bible is precisely in the human diversity it shows. One need merely approach it with an open mind to see that its authors were no mere robots, but human beings endowed with their own particular insights, virtues, customs, faith, and—as with all people—their own misconceptions and misunderstandings. The value and wisdom and charm of the Bible lies in no small part in seeing its people and its authors struggling with their faith just as you and I do. To claim that what these people wrote is perfect as it stands is to remove them from this shared human struggle.

It is possible, of course, to understand divine inspiration in such a way that it does not make robots of us. But such an understanding cannot serve as a basis for Biblical inerrancy.

3. Biblical Literalism vs. the Bible

Biblical literalism requires that we believe that the Bible doesn't mean what it says. Not only is this not a faithful approach, but it also means that Biblical literalism denies the very literal truth of the Bible which it purports to defend.

Let us look at an example of this: The first (of many) contradictions in the Bible is right there at the beginning, in the first two chapters of Genesis. Genesis 1 tells us that people were created by God *after* all the plants and all the other animals. Genesis 2 tells us that Adam was created *before* all the plants and animals. What are we to do with this?

Personally, I am not troubled by this in the least. The time and place of the origin of the human species is not a religious question. It is not a question for which I look to the Bible for answers. Rather, it is a question for science, to be answered by paleo-anthropologists, if and when they are able to come up with enough information.

What we do with this difference in the two creation accounts is, first, acknowledge it, and second, explain that they are both there because each was a part of one of the two or three sacred traditions put together by an editor to make up the book of Genesis. Each was sacred tradition; neither could be discarded. Furthermore, each makes very important—and different—*religious* points. These are the aspects of the stories which are authoritative for us. Chapter 1 tells us about the goodness of creation (the world is neither to be avoided nor worshipped) and our relationship to God. Chapter 2 tells us about our need for each other, about our stewardship of the earth, and that the knowledge of good and evil is what separates us from other animals and makes us human.

So the contradiction as to the order of creation in Genesis 1 and 2 does not affect the religious points at all. But the Biblical literalist cannot admit to this contradiction. He or she must insist that both the statement that people were created *after* all the plants and animals, and the statement that people were created *before* them, are true. This, of course, is manifestly impossible.

The Biblical literalist is, however, quite willing to admit that there are apparent contradictions in the Bible. In many cases the contradiction is indeed only apparent, and a closer study of context and meaning will show this to be the case. But in many other cases the contradiction is not so easily resolved. Undaunted, the literalist takes on the challenge of showing that opposites can agree. This is done by resorting to the "higher understanding" argument, which goes as follows: "If you think that these two passages disagree, then you don't really understand them. In our feeble human understanding they may *appear* to be contradictory. But in the true understanding, a 'higher understanding' than ours, which our limited minds may never attain, there is no contradiction within the Scriptures."

I readily admit that my own understanding is not perfect. Nevertheless, my limited comprehension is enough to know that "after" is the opposite of "before". To say that "after the plants" is not the opposite of "before the plants" is to say that "before" and "after" do not mean "before" and "after.". To say that the creation account in which humans were created last does *not* contradict the account in which Adam is created before the plants and animals, is to say that the Bible doesn't mean what it says. This, of course, is to deny that it is literally true. Thus, to defend their view, the "literalists" actually have to *deny* the Bible's literal truth!

Confronted with undeniable contradictions if we take the words of the Bible in their normal understanding, many advocates of Biblical literalism choose to defend the Bible's inerrancy by abandoning its literal meaning in this way. This is an abstract sort of inerrancy that maintains that the Bible is true, not that it means what it says, and it makes unrestrained use of the "higher understanding" argument. In the case of apparent contradictions and errors, we are assured that the true interpretation of these passages, this higher understanding, will eliminate these.

There are several problems with this. The first, as we have just noted, is that this involves denying the literal meaning of these passages. If two apparently contradictory passages are both true in the higher understanding, this means that at least one of them doesn't mean what it says, which means it is true (in the higher understanding) precisely because it is false (in the literal sense).

The second problem is that in many cases we have to admit that our limited minds cannot discover the higher understanding that resolves the contradictions. This means that we are defending the truth of the Bible at the cost of its having any meaning at all. But if we don't know what it means, how can it matter whether it is true? Do you know what "xbvlg" means? Does it then make any sense to be concerned about its truth? And is this not where we are if "before" is not the opposite of "after"?

The third problem is that this "higher understanding" gives people free rein to reinterpret the Bible to mean whatever they want, so long as they can argue that this is the true and higher understanding. This is precisely to use the Bible to fit our own notions, to twist it to justify our own preconceived ideas instead of being open to the message it brings. And it is yet another way that this defense of the Bible's "truth" is possible only by sacrificing the integrity of its meaning.

A number of people who lean towards literalism/inerrancy recognize that these problems exist. After all, how can one *defend* the Bible by insisting it doesn't mean what it says? Some of these people avoid this by postulating that the original version of every book was divinely inspired and was indeed literally true and without error. Any errors or contradictions are due to mistakes by the editors or scribes who transmitted this material.

However, every verse in the Bible went through multiple scribes, and in some cases editors, before even our oldest existing copies were made. Therefore we are left to decide about each passage in its present form just as if divine inspiration had not been claimed in the first place. This leaves us to wonder why someone would claim divine inspiration for an original "untainted" version which they admit no longer exists.

4. Biblical Literalism vs. Faith in God

In the final analysis Biblical literalism stands in opposition to faith in God and worship of God, for it replaces these with idolatry of the Bible.

The real reason that so many people insist on the divinely-inspired infallibility of the Bible is a very understandable and very human one: they are trying to fulfill their need for security. If you have a perfect book in your hand or at your bedside, it certainly must relieve some of the anxiety in dealing with this imperfect and often confusing world of ours. Some people add to this the comfort of having all the answers right there in this book, which saves them the acute discomfort of having to think for themselves or make their own moral decisions. Surely it is more secure to have God perfectly in a book than to have to seek God in the gray areas and uncertainties of the world! But is this not our age-old desire to possess God, to capture God in some kind of man-made cage (or statue, or book) to guarantee our security?

The Biblical literalist will claim that he or she trusts God more than I do. In fact the opposite is true, for they are willing to trust God only if these millions of words written over a period of centuries from two to three thousand years ago are all literally true, whereas my faith in God does not depend on this.

Their argument goes like this: "The Bible is God's Word. If God is trustworthy, then God's Word must be free of error. The Bible then constitutes the only sure and perfect guide in a world of uncertainty and imperfection. On the other hand, if God's Word is not trustworthy, not only then is there no sure guide in this world, but also then God is not trustworthy, and so not deserving of our faith."

But what they are *really* saying is: "I claim that the Bible is God's Word, and I mean by this that the Bible is literally true and without error. And if I'm wrong, then I can't trust God."

Of course, this makes no sense at all. If *we* make a particular claim about the Bible, and we are wrong, this casts doubt on *our* knowledge, or *our* trustworthiness in this field. Our being wrong in no way affects the trustworthiness of God. But all too often we insist on believing what we want to about God, and treat any threat to our own set of beliefs as a challenge to God.

In fact, we often need to have our own beliefs challenged precisely in order to free our understanding of God from preconceived notions, in order to open our minds and hearts to the real greatness of God. So a challenge to *our* beliefs may in fact be very much in support of God, not an attack on God. This is a possibility which we must keep in mind if we are not to become intolerant, self-righteous, and closed to the possibility of growth in our understanding.

All the same, we can surely sympathize with the yearning that motivates the literalist, the yearning for security and a sure guide. Who among us has not felt this deep need for something eternal and unchanging to cling to? Who has not longed for the perfect and undoubtable answer?

This yearning is not easily satisfied, and misses its true goal if it settles on anything less than God. To settle on anything else is to fail. To attribute perfection or eternal verity to anything in this finite universe, much less anything made by humans or possessed by humans, is the height of foolishness. Furthermore, to claim this kind of perfection or infallibility for anything is to worship it, to claim divinity for it. And to worship *anything* besides the one God is idolatry. No matter how great our felt need for this kind of security, God is too great to be possessed by us.

To claim that the Bible is perfect and infallible is to substitute it for God, to engage in idolatry, and to close ourselves off from real faith in

God. Our call is to seek God, using the Bible as a guide. Our call is not to seek the Bible or worship the Bible. We must seek God on the open seas of everyday life, with all its uncertainties and confusion and gray areas, confident that the greatness of God is present in all life's situations.

The Faithful Alternative

What is the alternative to Biblical literalism as a way of approaching the Bible? One alternative, of course, is to go to the opposite extreme and reject the whole book outright as unworthy of our attention. For those who prefer black and white choices, who prefer not having to think things through and make decisions, it is certainly easier to either unquestioningly accept or reject the whole Bible. But the whole area of reasonable approach for thoughtful, searching people lies in between these two extremes.

In fact, the most faithful approach to the Bible is also in keeping with our common sense. It is most faithful and most honest and most likely to result in proper understanding to accept the Bible for what it is, rather than to claim it to be what we want.

What then is the Bible? A common sense answer would be that it is a collection of books written by people who, like we, were people of their times, and who like we were capable of misunderstandings and mistakes as well as great insights. And they were, like we, struggling with the meaning of their faith and with their understanding of God in the midst of triumph and defeat, happiness and despair, stability and chaos. We find that our own faith is informed and inspired by their struggles and faithfulness. And since one of our aims in approaching the rich and diverse resources of this book is to understand it better, then we will want to know how these writings came about, and what the authors originally meant, and how they were affected by the beliefs and events of their times. To do this we will welcome all the tools that are available to us to help shed light on the Bible: studies of archeology, ancient history and customs, and other Near Eastern religions, as well as the various types of Biblical "criticism" that can inform us about the background, development, and meaning of the text itself.

This still leaves unanswered the question of Biblical authority. For Christians the answer to this depends upon the role and the authority that we ascribe to Jesus of Nazareth. In fact the primary question is not about the authority of the Bible but about the authority of Jesus the Christ.

So the task is to develop an interpretation of Jesus' centrality that is in keeping with our common sense. Before we do this we must first consider how God does and doesn't act, and what this means for miracles and other forms of divine intervention. We will then examine the traditional formulations of Jesus' centrality which are rooted in a different common sense. Only then can we attempt a reconstruction appropriate both to our faith and to our reason that will give us a way to explain Jesus' centrality. In the light of all this we can then return to consider the authority of the Bible as canon, but because of the somewhat more technical nature of this discussion it will be found in Appendix A.

At this point we turn to the question of a God who goes "zap"—does God intervene in the world on specific occasions?

CHAPTER 3: THE GOD
WHO GOES "ZAP"

"And behold, the Lord passed by, and a great and strong wind rent the mountains, and broke in pieces the rocks before the Lord, but the Lord was not in the wind; and after the wind an earthquake, but the Lord was not in the earthquake; and after the earthquake a fire, but the Lord was not in the fire; and after the fire a still small voice." (I Kings 19:11b–12)

Certainly we would all agree that we need a way of speaking about what God is and does that is both sensible and faithful. This is one of the primary goals of this book. But before we can arrive at this we first have to clear the way by understanding what God isn't and doesn't. And it is neither consistent with our common sense nor in keeping with our Christian faith to speak of God as a God who goes "zap". That is, it is neither sensible nor faithful to conceive of God as "meddling", as intervening on specific occasions for specific purposes in the finite physical events of our world.

Many sensible and faithful people believe that God does exactly this, either on occasion or by controlling every particular thing that happens. Therefore it is incumbent upon me to show how this is inconsistent with our reason and our faith. This is a relatively simple matter in connection with our common sense. But the question of consistency with our Christian faith will lead us to confront the darker areas of life as we deal with the problem of suffering.

Common Sense and the Zap

Let us return to our old friend the thunderstorm. Assuming that you agree that our common sense is that this phenomenon is to be explained by meteorology and not by referring to the wrath of God—why? Why do we think this way? Why do we not consult oracles as well as weathermen?

Aside from the sociological answer that we think this way because we have been taught to by our society, there is also an important principle at work here. It is known in philosophy as the "principle of economy" or "Ockham's razor".[1] The principle is this: that any event or state of affairs should be explained in the simplest way possible, and that once you have explained it one way, you don't go explaining it yet again by postulating other "deeper" causes for it.

"Simplest" explanation does not mean simple in the sense that it is simpler to say, "God caused the thunderstorm," than it is to try to understand ionization and humidity and the like. Instead, we mean that we should first try to explain finite physical events by looking for finite physical causes, by looking to the kind of cause that we know exists and operates in our world. These natural and human causes are "simpler" than any supernatural causes we might suggest. Thus, for instance, if we can come up with natural physical causes sufficient to explain an event, then we need not and ought not to postulate magic, miracle, or mystery.

Likely, you would say that this is just common sense. Quite so. But this was not always the case. Furthermore, besides being aware that part of our common sense is endowed with the fancy philosophical name of "principle of economy" (which doesn't really matter), it is important that we are aware of the principles of reasoning with which we operate so we can ensure our own consistency (which does matter).

Now, Ockham's razor in hand, let us return to the thunderstorm. We explain it as the result of physical atmospheric conditions. This is sufficient. There is no room for Thor, no need to guess at the anger of God.

But suppose during this storm someone is struck by lightning and killed. When this happens a large number of us drop our razors. We seek another kind of explanation. We may talk about fate or the will of God.

If a tree is standing alone in a field and is struck by lightning we are satisfied with a simple explanation of physical causes. But if a person happens to stand in the middle of a field or take shelter under this tree during this same thunderstorm and is struck by lightning, many of us suddenly require a very different kind of explanation. When personal suffering is involved, and especially when a person dies, we need to feel that there is a purpose for this, that there is "more" of a reason than just mere happenstance or bad luck. Often we reassure ourselves with the belief that God is in control, so this must be God's will, and so (we conclude) there must be a good reason for it. The greater the impact on our own life, the greater our need to feel this.

But electrical charges do not distinguish between a tree and a person, so if you can explain the tree getting struck by lightning in a simple way, then the same explanation will hold for the person—except you might wonder why they *didn't* have enough sense to come in out of the rain—

---

[1]William of Ockham was a 14th century philosopher/theologian who said, "Essentia non sunt multiplicanda praeter necessitatem," whatever that means, and who argued that theology should be reasonable and logical whereas faith is a matter of faith and ought to show in your way of life. To which I say, "Right on, brother William!"

even if this person is your spouse or your child. To look for another reason here, a "deeper" reason, is to try to find motives and goals in natural processes just as we would look for these in people.

Our common sense is that finite physical events have finite physical causes. If this is so, it does not make sense to suddenly postulate supernatural causes or metaphysical purposes when these events happen to have a strong impact on our lives. This is true whether we're speaking of storms or floods or fires or wars or automobile accidents. It does not make sense to ask "why" of a storm or a fire. It does not make sense to ask why your child died when hit by a ton of steel moving at sixty miles an hour. We cannot expect that the laws of nature would make an exception in our particular case, or that they have a particular goal in mind.

It does, of course, make sense to ask "why" when it comes to the actions of human beings. This is one of two major exceptions allowed by our common sense to the general rule that finite physical events are explainable by finite physical causes. In a way, this does not constitute an exception: it is still the *physical* action of a human that brings about a physical result. But it does make sense to look for purposes and motives in a way that is not true of natural phenomena, and the cause in which we are interested is likely to be found in the thinking or feeling of another person. We want to know why the assailant shot at us, not why a hammer detonates gunpowder or how this causes a lead projectile to travel at high speed.

The second major exception to the general rule that physical effects have physical causes is in the area of health and illness. We recognize that our mind and body are interconnected, and that a person's mental and emotional state can affect their physical health in a number of ways, and can even make a life-and-death difference under some conditions. One cannot get hepatitis without physical exposure to the virus, but we know that our recovery would depend in part on our own mental attitude. We also know that emotional stress or depression greatly increases our chances of developing a serious illness. The wise among us know that people really do die of broken hearts.

Our common sense is not tied to the purely mechanical. It definitely recognizes these two categories of possible non-physical causes for physical events. We shall address at a later point the question of how God may or may not act in connection with these two categories. However, with the possible exception of these two areas, we do explain finite physical events with finite physical causes. Therefore we must conclude that it is not consistent with our common sense to speak of God going "zap" in the physical world.

Our Faith and the Zap

Neither is it in keeping with our Christian concept of a loving Deity to speak of God as acting this way.

It is possible to think of God intervening in worldly affairs and physical happenings according to two different models: as a constant cosmic string-puller who controls each and every event of any importance (either by causing it or by consciously allowing it to happen), or as an occasional meddler and zapper, limited (perhaps by self-restraint) to intervening in a certain number of instances.

The first of these two conceptions, that God exercises control over at least all those events that are important, is commonly the underlying assumption for those who believe there are "deeper" reasons or purposeful explanations for those events that cause us joy or sadness. Consequently we will address this idea first. The problem we confront here is really the problem of suffering, for it is our hurts for which we most need some sort of justification, some satisfying explanation. I call this the problem of:

Pain, Honesty, and Faith

Pain, honesty, and faith. Separately, each one can be a problem for us. I know they have each been a problem for me. Together they have constituted a special problem. If you are neither blind nor self-deceived, together they constitute a special problem for you, too.

First, there is the problem of pain. At one time or another we are all hurt, and hurt badly, physically or emotionally or both. (I hope all your hurts are small ones. I doubt they will be.) And this presents a problem for us: how do we cope? Why did this happen to me? How do we make sense out of it?

Second, there is the problem of honesty. I mean honesty with yourself: you could also call it intellectual integrity. It means not denying what your eyes see or what your ears hear or what your heart feels or what your mind reasons. Even harder, it means not denying your eyes for the sake of your heart, or your ears for the sake of your mind, or either your mind or your heart for the sake of the other.

Third, there is faith. Perhaps if you do not bring in pain and honesty, if you do not insist that your faith face pain squarely and honestly, that it be consistent with what your mind reasons and your heart feels and your eyes see, then perhaps faith is no problem for you. But if we would have a faith that neither denies pain nor hides in dishonesty, then we must take a long, hard look at the fact of suffering. Let us begin by examining the desire we so often have for a justification or a "deeper" reason for our suffering.

"There Must Be A Reason"

There must be a reason. When disaster strikes, when tragedy tears the normal fabric of our lives, we demand a reason. We demand to know how this could happen, why it was allowed to take place. We want, and perhaps need, to know that there was a reason, that it was not merely senseless happenstance.

Why did the river overflow its banks? Why right here? Why weren't we warned? Why was our house washed away? Why did Uncle Harry die?

Sometimes it's enough to have the simple, causal, often mechanical answers that the razor allows as sufficient: the river overflowed because heavy storms dropped ten inches of rain in a forty-eight hour period just as the snow was melting. It flooded right here because of the contours of the valley. The weather service did issue warnings, but you refused to believe that the levee wouldn't hold, that this could really happen here. Your house washed away because that is the natural result of two fathoms of water flowing against a frame house. Uncle Harry died because he never learned how to swim and so couldn't make it through the water to safety.

Sometimes this kind of answer is adequate. When tragedy happens to someone else, when you're not caught up in the immediate effects, when neither you nor those close to you suffer any great personal loss, this kind of answer is probably all you need. When the same disaster strikes many others as well as you, when you do not feel singled out by it, this kind of answer may well eventually seem adequate.

The crunch comes when you are singled out for pain and suffering: when *your* family is struck with cancer, when *your* child is hit by a drunk driver, when *your* spouse has an emotional breakdown, when *you* are paralyzed from the waist down for life. When anything like this happens the kind of simple causal answers we gave above are likely to seem totally and obviously inadequate. We may ask, "Why?", and in fact we may scream, "Why?", but we are not interested in hearing about the limits of modern medicine or the inevitable result of two thousand pounds of steel impacting on skin and bones. To a large extent our cry of "Why?" is not a question at all, but rather a cry of protest and anger and anguish. To the extent that it *is* a question, we are asking, "Why me? Why did this happen to *me*?"

A couple of factors contribute to our feeling that this question of "Why?" is a legitimate one that demands more of an answer than can be provided by matter-of-fact physical causes. For one, we seem to have the feeling that well-being is normal, that it is to be expected. No matter how often we may speak of counting our blessings, we usually do take them for granted. Though we would deny it, we feel that life "owes" us well-being and even happiness. Therefore suffering is felt as unfair and unjust, and our question of "Why?" takes on a moral tone that seeks an answer that would show us purpose and justice.

We also often feel suffering as a punishment. The reason we feel this way relates back to this same belief that we deserve good fortune, and perhaps also to our childhood experiences of reward and punishment, and to ideas about God doling out good and bad fortune alike. For whatever reason, suffering feels like punishment. And so we demand to know "Why?", though again this is more protest than question, for we know we haven't done anything monstrous enough to deserve to be singled out for this kind of horrible punishment.

But if we cannot explain this suffering as a deserved punishment, most of us still find unacceptable and unbearable the alternative explanation: that there is no deeper reason for our suffering, that it is after all just a matter of happenstance and bad luck, that it is (in a moral sense) senseless. We want to avoid this conclusion. If we cannot avoid it by accepting that suffering is deserved punishment, then we often try to avoid it by saying that suffering is for our own good, or for the good of the world. After all, God works in mysterious ways. As long as we know that God is good and just and in control, then we know that what happens is for the best, even though we may never understand just how or why.

If suffering is either deserved punishment or else is for the ultimate good, then it makes sense to us. It is acceptable to us. And the assertion that all suffering, however great, is one or the other makes eminent sense if you believe that God is good and omnipotent, and that God exercises this omnipotence to control events here on earth. I, myself, cannot believe this. It would be dishonest: dishonest with what my eyes have seen, with what my heart has felt, and with what my mind is able to reason. Nevertheless, it is a time-honored conviction that has been expressed since ancient times.

"The Lord does not let the righteous go hungry, but he thwarts the craving of the wicked."

"What the wicked dreads will come upon him, but the desire of the righteous will be granted."

"The fear of the Lord prolongs life, but the years of the wicked will be short."

"The hope of the righteous ends in gladness, but the expectation of the wicked comes to nought."

"The Lord is a stronghold to him whose way is upright, but destruction to evildoers."

"The righteous will never be removed, but the wicked will not dwell in the land."

"Be assured an evil man will not go unpunished, but those who are righteous will be delivered."

"No ill befalls the righteous, but the wicked are filled with trouble."

"In the path of righteousness is life, but the way of error leads to death."

"Misfortune pursues sinners, but prosperity rewards the righteous."

"A good man leaves an inheritance to his children's children, but the sinner's wealth is laid up for the righteous."

"The wicked is overthrown through his evil-doing, but the righteous finds refuge through his integrity."
    (Proverbs 10:3, 24, 27–30; 11:21; 12:21, 28; 13:21–22; 14:32)

The good are prosperous and happy; the wicked suffer for their wickedness. The Lord who controls the fortunes of human beings doles out good fortune and bad in just portions to those who deserve them. God rewards goodness with a long and happy life and punishes evil with misfortune and suffering.

One has to admit that this is a thoroughly satisfactory system. Who could complain about a world where the good are rewarded and the wicked punished? It is desirable on our part and commendable on God's part. It is everything you could want.

Of course, there is one fairly important problem with all this: the world just doesn't work this way. No matter how desirable and commendable, things just don't always work out according to this plan. You know this as well as I do. And in spite of the impression given by Proverbs many ancient Jews realized this too.

For a while any apparent inconsistencies in divine justice could be explained by making reference to miscreant ancestors. After all, had not the Lord said, "I the Lord your God am a jealous God, visiting the iniquity of the fathers upon the children to the third and fourth generation"? (Exodus 20:5) So if you suffered some undeserved misfortune you could always figure that one of your eight great-grandparents had secretly performed some pernicious iniquity that was only now receiving proper retribution. Not that this would be likely to provide much personal comfort, but you could at least believe that this suffering was in fact deserved by your family and that the system of divine justice still prevailed.

But this sort of explanation could not endure the rise of individualism, the increasing sense of the worth of each individual for his or her own sake. The idea of one person suffering for the sins of another became an affront to people's sense of justice and individual responsibility, and the prophets denounced it:

The word of the Lord came to me again: "What do you mean by repeating this proverb concerning the land of Israel, 'The fathers have eaten sour grapes, and the children's teeth are set on edge'? As I live, says the Lord God, this proverb shall no more be used by you in Israel. Behold, all souls are mine, the soul of the father as well as the soul of the son is mine: the soul that sins shall die." (Ezekiel 18:1–4)

The son shall not suffer for the iniquity of the father, nor the father suffer for the iniquity of the son; the righteousness of the righteous shall be upon himself, and the wickedness of the wicked shall be upon himself. (Ezekiel 18:20. See also Jeremiah 31:29–30)

This is only fair, and returns us to the system of divine justice described in the Proverbs: the good are rewarded and the bad are punished in this life by the all-powerful Lord of human destinies. But if we can't blame obvious exceptions to this system on the sins of our ancestors, then it is left defenseless against the harsh realities of life. The world simply doesn't work this way. It is this problem that is squarely confronted in the Book of Job.

Job

"There was a man in the land of Uz, whose name was Job; and that man was blameless and upright, one who feared God and turned away from evil." (Job 1:1) This was Job, deserving of good fortune if anyone was. But then in the span of one day all his wealth was stolen or destroyed and all his children killed. Soon after he himself was afflicted with sores from the crown of his head to the soles of his feet.

In the prose introduction of this book this suffering is depicted as a test. God, after bragging about Job, grants permission to Satan to do whatever he wants to to test Job's faith. ("Testing" is still a common explanation of suffering which we will consider later in this chapter.) However, the main body of the Book of Job does not try to explain suffering this way. Instead, it gives us a poetic picture of the head-on collision between the facts of life and the belief that suffering is a punishment from God. Job argues on behalf of reality while several of his friends take the side of this traditional belief.

Eliphaz, Bildad, and Zophar come to visit their suffering friend, as friends should. They are good religious men who know that God is just and in control of what happens. They are confident that they understand the workings of God's justice: the good are rewarded in this life and the wicked are punished. So they are convinced that the suffering which afflicts Job can only be the deserved punishment for some evil he has done. And, therefore, they demonstrate their concern for Job by urging him to repent of these sins he must have committed, for only if he repents do they see any hope for their friend.

Job also believes that God has control over what has happened to him, but he knows that he has done nothing to deserve it, as do we the readers. He is innocent. Therefore, unlike his well-meaning friends, he is unable to applaud God's justice. Not only does he suffer without being guilty of any significant sin but he also sees the wicked prospering around him. He knows this is so, and knows it is not just.

Job's friends are not persuaded. They continue to insist that he does deserve this suffering—he must! He has to be guilty, and he had better just quit protesting and repent. Their well-meant admonitions have the look of cruel and callous torment in the light of what we know.

No matter how much we wish that God would ensure good fortune for the good and bad fortune for the wicked, it just doesn't work this way. This is a point of great importance made by the Book of Job.

But then how do we explain Job's suffering? This, of course, is the question that bothers Job himself. He never doubts that his misfortune is under God's control. In fact, he still has enough faith in God's justice that he appeals for a hearing, confident that God will recognize his innocence, and so the injustice of his suffering, and so will revoke it.

As a rule, if someone in a position of power is responsible for the suffering of an upright and innocent person this would seem to provide a reasonable ground for accusing that someone of injustice. In this case, however, by insisting that he is innocent, it is God whom Job is accusing of injustice. So Job comes in for a stinging rebuke.

This is carried out by Elihu, a younger man who first vents his exasperation at the three friends for failing to properly answer Job, and then condemns Job for justifying himself instead of God. He doesn't offer to explain how Job's suffering could possibly be deserved, but simply asserts, "Far be it from God that he should do wickedness, and from the Almighty that he should do wrong. For according to the worth of a man he will requite him, and according to his ways he will make it befall him. Of a truth, God will not do wickedly, and the Almighty will not pervert justice." (Job 34:10–12)

Elihu apparently feels that this assertion is not subject to challenge by mere facts. Furthermore, he insists, whether or not Job may previously have been blameless, he is now guilty of rebellion and pride for challenging God's justice and placing his own wisdom on a par with the Almighty's. Job remains unconvinced, stubbornly holding to the fact of his own innocence and the logical implication that the God responsible for his suffering has acted unjustly. Again he appeals to God, and at last God answers him. But it is not the answer that Job had hoped for:

Then the Lord answered Job out of the whirlwind: "Who is this that darkens counsels by words without knowledge? Gird up your loins like a man, I will question you, and you shall declare to me. Where were you when I laid the foundation of the earth? Tell me, if you have understanding.

Who determined its measurements? Surely you know! Or who stretched the line upon it?

On what were its bases sunk, or who laid its cornerstone, when the morning stars sang together, and all the sons of God shouted for joy?

Or who shut in the sea with doors, when it burst forth from the womb; when I made clouds its garment, and thick darkness its swaddling band, and prescribed bounds for it, and set bars and doors, and said, 'thus far shall you come, and no farther, and here shall your proud waves be stayed?' " (Job 38:1–11)

God goes on in this vein for most of four chapters, describing the wonders of creation and the mighty power, infinite wisdom, and loving providence of the Almighty. Confronted with this awesome display of the majesty and wisdom of God, and suddenly aware of his own insignificance and ignorance, Job backs down:

"I know that thou canst do all things, and that no purpose of thine can be thwarted . . . Therefore I have uttered what I did not understand . . . I had heard of thee by the hearing of the ear, but now my eyes see thee; therefore I despise myself, and repent in dust and ashes." (Job 42: 2, 3, 5–6)

Job's Cop-Out

Yes, Job backs down and repents. It does not matter that he is then blessed with wealth and children again. This was wrong of him. It is not what he ought to have done. It is, in fact, a cop-out, a clear and certain cop-out.

Not that Job or anybody else could reply to God's challenge or answer God's questions. The universe is indeed beyond our understanding. We do not know the beginning and end of it, nor its foundations, nor the God of it all, nor even in any adequate way our own role in it. We cannot presume to meet God's challenge. We can only, with Job, humbly confess our ignorance, our limited view, our failings.

But if Job does not have all the answers, he still knows one important fact, and it gives him a big question that he should not so easily drop. God may know the depths of the universe, but Job knows he has suffered terribly and that he, a righteous man, did not deserve to suffer. So if God can ask, "Where were you when I laid the foundation of the earth?", then Job can ask—and indeed if he is human he must ask—"Where were you, O God, on that day when all my herds were taken and all my servants and even all my children were killed? And where have you been since that day, while I suffered from heartbreak on the inside and a terrible disease on the outside, without aid or comfort? No, I was not there when you laid the foundation of the earth, but where were you when I was hurt and afraid and desperate and cried to you in vain?"

This is what Job must ask if he is to be honest about his pain and his convictions. I don't like this question. It makes me feel uncomfortable and insecure. It reminds me of things I would rather not be reminded of. But the question is there, and if we are honest we must ask it: "If God is a loving and all-powerful God, then why does this God allow so much suffering to happen?"

What answer can God make to this? Or rather, what answer can we make on God's behalf?

If we insist on holding God responsible for fortune and misfortune, health and disease, life and death, and if we also believe that God is loving, then how is it possible to explain undeserved suffering? Whether or not we would claim that any particular suffering *is* deserved, it is obvious that there is a significant amount of suffering that simply *cannot* be called either deserved or just according to any reasonable standard of justice. You cannot justify major suffering by pointing to minor moral failings, which all of us have, especially when many with equal or greater failings suffer less.

Is it possible to reconcile this undeserved suffering with a loving, "in charge" God? It would be, if this suffering could be explained as being in one way or another for the good. If suffering is not deserved, it still could be for the ultimate good, either of the individual or of the world. Only if suffering is for the good can we maintain that a loving God is in control of worldly events.

Before we attempt to explain or justify suffering, we must realize just what it is and what it can do to people. We must make sure that we have an adequate understanding of it. Surely we have all learned something about suffering firsthand. But we are also very good at repressing our memories of pain and agony, so we need to remind ourselves just what it can mean to live in the Valley of the Shadow of Death.

The Valley of the Shadow of Death

This is the valley in which we all live. The shadow cast by death into our lives gives us awareness of our own finitude, the knowledge that we will all die. I will die and you will die. This is your one fling at this thing we call life.

We all have to live with this knowledge. It means that when something happens to mar our one chance, when an accident or bad luck or illness or just circumstances determine that our one chance is to be twisted, or unusually painful, or abbreviated . . . well, that's it. It's once and for all. There is no re-deal of the deck, no court of appeal, no recourse to litigation. That's it.

On the average, of course, the shadow is not as dark as this. But to the young widow with children to raise alone, to the man dying an agonizing and untimely death from cancer, to the person full of life and hope who is incapacitated by multiple sclerosis, or to the child who has to start his or her life with an uncorrectable birth defect, the average isn't what matters. If the suffering that you have known has been the kind which passes after a few months or even—how hard it can be!—after a few years, remember that there are those for whom the cloud never passes.

Remember, too, what pain can do. Plain old physical pain is capable of great destructiveness. Serious pain in just one small part of your body—the kind that sears and penetrates—can act as a great weight on you. It drains your energy, eats away at your ambition, and drags on every movement you make. It wears you down and wears you out until all you want is just to be comfortable, until all you want is for the pain to stop. It eats away at your efforts to live the life you want and sabotages your efforts to pretend you are normal. When it flares up it radiates like poison through your whole system until body and mind alike are infected with it. You can get to the point where all you want out of life is just to be normally healthy, while at the same time you may know this is the one thing you will never be.

This is only simple, uncomplicated pain. We should not be surprised that it is usually complicated—by depression, loneliness, frustration, financial difficulties, and other problems.

Incapacitation, even without any pain, can be just as bad. I doubt if you can really imagine what it's like not to be able to use your body, not to be able to take a walk or play with your children or hold a job or make love, utterly dependent on someone else to look after you, dependent on their being willing to take the time to wait on your wants and needs. It's not easy to imagine this. But there are people around you who don't have to imagine it, who have to live with it as part of their one chance at life.

And then there is emotional suffering and crippling: the unloved, the lonely, the bereaved, the rejected; people with broken dreams and people with shattered psyches. The deep pain in the human soul sometimes caused by that which happens to us can cripple a person and destroy a life just as surely and effectively as any physical ailment.

If a person has difficulty coping with the "normal everyday" problems of life we may call it emotional illness. This may be a result of previous traumatic events in that person's life or may be due to an inherited chemical imbalance in their blood. Too often we think that "emotional illness" means "craziness". It usually does not. What it does mean, more than anything else, is pain: pain somewhere in the depths of our psyches, pain that cannot always be rooted out or covered over, pain that in some cases never gives way to allow a person to live a normal life.

Perhaps only the extreme cases are this bad. If so, there are far, far too many extreme cases. And there are very many more which, if not this extreme, are still undeniable instances of major undeserved suffering.

Of course, we all have our favorite example of the hurt or crippled or deprived individual who through determination and valiant effort has managed to overcome all obstacles and go on to lead a useful and meaningful and maybe even a joyful life. These people deserve all manner of honor and commendation. But they are just a small percentage, the tip of the iceberg, that managed to struggle above water. The many who are not so lucky tend to be hidden away out of our sight.

As for those who are caught by events or stricken by an illness that cannot be overcome by hard work and will power alone, who are condemned to suffer the consequences—yes, like you, I have been surprised and impressed at the good cheer and high spirits that even some of these people exhibit. And isn't it nice how they don't talk about their illness or their pain or their frustration or their despair?

But I learned something about this, learned it the hard way. Perhaps you already knew it. This happy front is not put on for your sake or mine. It is not maintained for the benefit of others at all. And though it is often maintained only with a good deal of effort and energy, it is worth all the trouble it might take. For this front of good cheer represents their pretense of normalcy, not primarily to others, but much more importantly to themselves. It is their defense against constantly confronting the fact of their own deeper misery, a valiant and—thank goodness—sometimes successful effort to deny and hide from the inescapable tragedy of their own lives.

We do not like to confront human suffering like this. I personally find it extremely painful. But if we are to be honest with ourselves we must remember just how dark the shadow is in some lives. We must keep in mind just what this suffering is as we consider the explanations that can be offered to reconcile it with the existence of a loving God who controls worldly events.

The Justifications of Suffering

It is possible to reconcile the existence of undeserved suffering with the existence of a loving God who is responsible for life and death, fortune and misfortune, only if all such suffering can be adequately explained either (1) as a test, (2) as being for the sufferer's own good, or (3) as being for the greatest good of the world, being ultimately for "the best". I will argue that these explanations are inadequate and untenable. This is not to argue against God. This is to argue for God, to free God from some human ideas that do injustice both to God and to us.

1. Suffering as a Test

One possible explanation of suffering is that it's a test. It is a test of our faith, put to us by God.[2] But if this is to fit with a loving God there must be a good reason, in keeping with God's loving nature, for testing us. What could this reason be?

Why do we need to know? Why can't we just say that God tests us with suffering for a perfectly good and loving reason, and we just have no idea what this reason could be?

---

[2]Some would no doubt explain suffering as a test of our faith by "the devil". But if there were a devil who could do this on his or her own, then God would not be all-controlling and not be responsible for this suffering, which is the conclusion I reach anyway. If the devil needs God's permission, then God is still responsible. (See Chapter 15 for more on the devil.)

Of course anyone who wants to can say exactly this. But for one thing, this is tantamount to saying, "I believe that God has a good reason for testing us because I want to believe this, regardless of how it fits with reality or reason." While anyone can say this, they ought not to expect the rest of us to be overwhelmed by their argument.

For another thing, when we have two propositions that appear on the surface to be irreconcilable the burden of proof is on those who would reconcile them. Certainly the evil of the suffering in the world and the loving control of God in the world are not easily and obviously reconcilable. Anyone who asserts that they are should at least indicate how this is possible.

So unless we are to substitute wishful thinking for careful thinking, we need to ask what would be the possible reasons for God to test us with suffering, and are these in keeping with God being good and loving? As far as I can see, there is only one good reason for ever testing anyone: to ascertain whether that person is qualified for, or deserving of, certain rewards or privileges. Thus, students must be tested to see if they have mastered a subject well enough to receive a passing grade. Before anyone is granted a driver's license they have to show both that they are capable of driving a car and that they are familiar with the traffic laws, so they are tested in these two areas. Often a written or oral test is given to applicants for a job. In all these cases the necessary skill and knowledge are tested and the reward is granted or not, according to the results of the test.

So if God tests us, it must be a testing of our faith or our goodness out of a need to know whether we are deserving of certain possible rewards. Certainly this would be in keeping with love and justice as long as the tests were fairly administered and appropriately rewarded. But there are a couple of problems here.

Problem #1: This requires you to say that God would need to test our faith in order to know how strong it is. This means saying that God does not know everything, does not know our innermost selves or how we would react to certain events. If God knew this, the test would not be necessary. Of course, for some people it poses no problem to claim that God's knowledge is limited in this way, but you should be aware that this is the implication here.

Problem #2: The test of suffering is *not* fairly administered and appropriately rewarded. It is not fairly administered because neither is it given equally to everyone, nor is it given only to those whose faith or goodness is seriously questionable. Remember Job.

And how could it be claimed that "passing" the test of suffering could be appropriately rewarded? We all know it isn't always rewarded in this life. In fact, in too many cases it destroys a life. So any reward must come in an afterlife. But those of us who believe in an afterlife also believe that it is available at least to all the faithful. How then are the faithful who suffered more rewarded any more than the faithful who suffered less? Is it conceivable that those who suffered most in this short life are consequently better off for eternity? If so, then it is manifestly unfair that only some of us are put to this test.

Conclusion: for us to explain how a loving God could cause us to suffer as a test, we have to assume that God's knowledge is limited, we have to explain the apparently random selection of people to be tested, and we have to postulate a complicated system of rewards in the life to come in order for the different degrees of severity of the test to be appropriately rewarded. And then we have to explain how it could be fair for some to have a chance at earning these rewards while others do not.

I do not believe that this is possible. It's too cumbersome and too complicated. It forces us to view God as either a schemer or a random chance program. The concept of God that all this requires does not fit with the loving God of our Christian faith.

2. Suffering Is for Our Own Good

The second possible explanation is that suffering is for our own good. That is, while it may not be deserved as punishment it does bring about an over-all improvement so that we are better off because of what happened.

One clear example of this would be the person on their way to the airport for an overseas vacation who gets caught in a traffic accident and ends up instead in the hospital with a broken leg, only to find out that the plane they would have taken crashes and everyone aboard is killed. Obviously, the pain of a broken leg and a ruined vacation are more than offset by the saving of their life.

Another example might be the illness which strikes a dynamic, hardworking business person who has been pursuing material success to the exclusion of their family and other interests, to the exclusion of what is important in life. If a mild coronary or other physical illness forces them to slow down for awhile, and if this gives them the occasion to take stock in themselves and they realize that they have been forsaking the important things in life for the unimportant, then any physical pain and any damage done to their career would be more than offset by their recovery of a proper sense of values, by their recovery of their self.

Things like this do happen. Sometimes a painful experience turns out to be a lucky break for us. Sometimes a particular occasion of suffering clearly produces a very desirable result. Even more often, suffering provides a valuable lesson to us. It can improve our character, give us humility and patience, help us get to know ourselves, and enable us better to appreciate the suffering of others.

All this is true. Suffering can indeed lead to good. It may even be that some good can come out of most suffering. But that isn't the question. The question is, does whatever good comes from suffering balance the bad of it to such an extent that we can honestly attribute it to a loving God?

In some cases it does. A saved life clearly outweighs a broken leg. And certainly there are many cases of suffering in which the pain is outweighed by a significant growth in maturity or sensibility, or by giving rise to a person redirecting their life. But we must be careful here. We must avoid saying that since the good from suffering outweighs the bad in some instances of which we are aware, therefore it must be true that the good outweighs the bad on all occasions. This would be an unwarranted generalization, for there are also instances of suffering in which there is either no discernable good at all for the sufferer or else too little to be worth the steep price.

Consider the all too common experience of losing a spouse through death. It may be that in time the widow or widower develops new abilities or a deeper faith or a better character or at least more sensitivity and compassion for others. Something good may well develop that otherwise would not have. But the loss of a spouse is a tearing, shattering experience, and I doubt that the benefits often outweigh the pain.

Or consider incapacitation of one kind or another. A couple of years of this are usually quite sufficient to teach a person all they can learn of patience and character and compassion. What about after that? What good can come from the additional long years of suffering? What possible good can repay a person for having to spend their one life in an invalid's prison?

Or consider those who die young. What good could possibly come of this to the one whose life is cut short? This could only be for a person's good if otherwise they either would have suffered unspeakably or would have turned evil and missed out on a heavenly reward. But then why would God allow others to suffer so or to turn to evil? And if God is in control, could this not simply be prevented instead?

In the end, I simply cannot believe that each and every young life that is snuffed out would otherwise have suffered great pain or turned to evil. I cannot believe that each and every event of undeserved suffering is outweighed or even balanced by the good that comes of it for the sufferers. Not by a long shot. My eyes, my mind, and my heart all tell me different. And this is just in response to individual cases of suffering, without even considering famine and plague, war and holocaust.

A common response to this runs something like this: "Of course *we* can't see the good here. We don't know everything. We don't see with the eyes of God. We don't know what would've happened to these people if they'd stayed healthy or lived longer. But if we can't possibly know this, God does. With perfect knowledge God sees to it that the way things work out really *is* for the best, even if we don't understand how."

This constitutes the third possible explanation of undeserved suffering for those who would believe that God is both loving and in control.

3. It's For the Best

To say that "it's for the best" is to claim that even though it may not be best for the individual sufferer(s), the consequences of this suffering are such that the world is better off because of it. This claim must be made of each and every case of undeserved suffering. This is easier than might be expected because the proponents of this line of thinking generally do not feel it necessary to suggest *how* this suffering could be for the best, only that it *is*.

As such, this explanation of how a loving, in-control God can be reconciled with suffering is more nearly an affirmation of belief than it is an explanation of anything. It appeals more to our emotional needs than to our logic. We are left to choose between two understandings of the world—one in which a loving God is responsible for the suffering, which we can therefore be assured is "for the best", and one in which it is simply apparent that all this suffering could not possibly be for the best.

No matter how much I would *like* to believe that everything is for the best, I find this impossible to do. How could it be possible? How could it possibly be "for the best" for someone to die a slow and agonizing death from cancer? How can this kind of death be better for that person, or for their family, or for the world, than if they had died a less painful one? And even if occasionally some great spiritual benefit results in one of these cases, what about all the others? Is it really possible that there might be something unspeakably horrible in store for every single person who dies this way, or for the world, that only this kind of suffering and death can avert? Is it conceivable that the future of the world depends on the suffering of each and every one of these separate individuals? Is it possible that the universe is so constructed and is in such danger from some great unguessable horror that it is actually better off because of the traffic death in Iowa and the torture victim in South America and the starving child in Ethiopia? When these are multiplied by the millions?

I just can't believe it.

It is not possible to reconcile belief in a loving God with belief in a God who is in control of events on earth. We must choose one or the other. Since Jesus the Christ ministered on behalf of the God of love and not in service to the God of earthly power, we who would follow Jesus must choose the loving God. We cannot faithfully believe in a God who is a constant string-puller and controller of earthly events, for to do so is to deny that this God is loving.

Can God Be An Occasional Zapper?

But what about God as an occasional zapper? Could not a belief in God as intermittent intervener be in keeping with our faith in a loving God?

I think not. If God intervenes only in some instances and not in others, we must ask why. It would be one thing if it could be shown that God was limited to certain interventions by some important moral principle or by the nature of the events or by God's own limited abilities. If this were the case we could at least say that God does whatever is possible or advisable.

But if some cures or some reconciliations or some narrow escapes are the result of God's intervention, then what do we say of similar cases where there is no cure, no reconciliation, no escape, no intervention? If God could intervene in some cases what could be the reason for not intervening in other cases where it is needed? We cannot say that God *cannot* do this if we are assuming that God has done so at other times. To say that "it's for the best" is to fall back on the unconvincing arguments considered above. Certainly those who benefit from supposed interventions are no more deserving than many people who are not so fortunate.

God as an occasional intervener is as bad as God in full control of everything, giving us a picture of an arbitrary and capricious actor, at times withholding from the most deserving people help that is desperately needed. This is not reconcilable with our concept of a loving God.

Conclusion

In this chapter we have been forced by our honesty and integrity to confront the problem of suffering. This is not a pleasant task, but a faith which cannot do this is not worthy of the name. And we can repeat that usually life is not as dark as this for people. More importantly, we must clarify the role of our faith here. We are not called upon to explain or justify misfortune. What we are called to do is to bring our love to those in pain, to help those in need, to brighten dark days and dark lives with the light of our caring. This is the crucial role of our faith in response to suffering—this, and to suffer with people in our caring about them. The duty of faith here is to be honest about the problem and so to be able to minister to those who hurt. And we *can* bring light and joy and love into people's lives.

We began this chapter by saying that we need a way of speaking of God that is both sensible and faithful, and we have been forced to conclude that to speak of God as either controlling all events in this world, or as sporadically intervening to cause them, is neither. We recognized common sense exceptions in the areas of human motivation and some aspects of health and illness, which will be addressed later. Otherwise, however, we must conclude at this point that to speak of God as determining worldly events, as constantly or occasionally going "zap" into our normal processes, is consistent neither with our common sense nor with our Christian faith in a loving God.

This, of course, raises some questions about the miracles in the Bible. We will turn next to this and then to consequent questions about Jesus of Nazareth and Christian doctrine before returning again to a consideration of talk about God.

CHAPTER 4: MIRACLES AND RELIGIOUS SIGNIFICANCE

"The Pharisees came . . . seeking from him a sign from heaven, to test him. And he sighed deeply in his spirit, and said, 'Why does this generation seek a sign?' " (Mark 8:11–12a)

Our belief in a loving God does not allow us to depict this Being as pulling strings to control events here on earth. Our common sense of how the universe works does not allow us to conceive of God as "zapping" into the normal course of natural laws. What, then, do we say about the Biblical accounts of miracles?

If God doesn't go "zap" then we cannot simply accept all the miracle stories as true at face value. There are three different approaches to miracles generally used by those interpreters of the Bible who don't simply accept them or reject them outright. These alternatives, we will see, boil down to a choice between explaining miracles away or ignoring them. We will begin this chapter by looking at (1) the "classic liberal" approach, which explains them away. Then we will consider (2) Rudolf Bultmann's "demythologization", and (3) "demiracle-ization", both of which ignore miracles under the guise of interpreting them.

1. The Classic Liberal Approach

This first approach to dealing with miracles was especially identified with "liberal" scholars of the nineteenth and early twentieth centuries. It was not confined to this era, however, and still has widespread appeal and usage. No doubt you have either used this approach yourself or have been exposed to it in others. It works like this: the report of a miraculous event is explained as being of a natural, unmiraculous event which was either misunderstood by witnesses or misinterpreted by those to whom it was reported. At the same time it is affirmed that what the Bible reports did in fact happen, or something very similar to it, albeit unmiraculously.

41

Thus, for instance, the stilling of the storm by Jesus is explained as a coincidental or predictable change in the weather following upon Jesus' prayer for calm. The disciples, of course, saw the calm follow upon his prayer and interpreted coincidence as cause and effect. (It would not be unusual for an allusion to be made to the ignorance and superstition of the witnesses. This is both arrogant and not entirely inappropriate.) Similarly, Jesus walking on the water becomes his undetected use of a sandbar or sunken log which no one else knew was there. The feeding of the five thousand becomes a "miracle" of the heart: all those people in the crowd who were selfishly keeping their picnic dinners to themselves were inspired to share with others, as opposed to there having been an actual physical multiplication of the five loaves and two fish.

Another example of this approach was passed on to us by Mark Twain. This was delivered by a certain ship's captain, who, says Twain, "was a profound Biblical scholar—that is, he thought he was. He believed everything in the Bible, but he had his own method of arriving at his beliefs. He was of the 'advanced' school of thinkers, and applied natural law to the interpretation of all miracles, somewhat on the plan of the people who make the six days of creation six geological epochs, and so forth. Without being aware of it, he was a rather severe satire on modern scientific religionists."[1]

Twain overheard and recorded his interpretation of the contest on Mt. Carmel (I Kings 18), which, though perhaps a caricature, illustrates well the shortcomings of this approach. So I pass on to you here a portion of one of my favorite pieces of Biblical exposition. After explaining how Elijah (the captain calls him Isaac), as "the only Presbyterian", challenged all the prophets of Baal to a contest to see whose God could cause an altar to ignite, the captain turns to the contest itself, beginning with the prophets of Baal:

> So they went at it, the whole four hundred and fifty, praying around the altar, very hopeful, and doing their level best. They prayed an hours—two hours,—three hours,—and so on, plumb till noon. It wa'n't any use; they hadn't took a trick. Of course they felt kind of ashamed before all those people, and well they might. Now, what would a magnanimous man do? Keep still, wouldn't he? Of course. What did Isaac do? He gravelled the prophets of Baal every way he could think of. Says he, 'You don't speak up loud enough; your God's asleep, like enough, or maybe he's taking a walk; you want to holler, you know,'—or words to that effect; I don't recollect the exact language. Mind, I don't apologize for Isaac; he had his faults.

> Well, the prophets of Baal prayed along the best they knew how all afternoon, and never raised a spark. At last, about sundown, they were all tuckered out, and they owned up and quit.

---

[1]Mark Twain, "Some Rambling Notes of an Idle Excursion", published with *Tom Sawyer Abroad/Tom Sawyer Detective* by Harper and Brothers. See pp. 234–7.

What does Isaac do, now? He steps up and says to some friends of his, there, 'Pour four barrels of water on the altar!' Everybody was astonished; for the other side had prayed at it dry, you know, and got whitewashed. They poured it on. Says he, 'Heave on four more barrels.' Then he says, 'Heave on four more.' Twelve barrels, you see, altogether. The water ran all over the altar, and all down the sides, and filled up a trench around it that would hold a couple of hogsheads,— 'measures' it says; I reckon it means about a hogshead. Some of the people were going to put on their things and go, for they allowed he was crazy. They didn't know Isaac. Isaac knelt down and began to pray; he strung along, and strung along, about the heathen in distant lands, and about the sister churches, and about the state and the country at large, and about those that's in authority in the government, and all the usual programme, you know, till everybody had got tired and gone to thinking about something else, and then, all of a sudden, when nobody was noticing, he outs with a match and rakes it on the under side of his leg, and pff! Up the whole thing blazes like a house afire! Twelve barrels of water? Petroleum, sir, PETROLEUM! That's what it was!

Petroleum, captain?

Yes, sir; the country was full of it. Isaac knew all about that. You read the Bible. Don't you worry about the tough places. They ain't tough when you come to think them out and throw light on them. There ain't a thing in the Bible but what is true; all you want is to go prayerfully to work and cipher out how't was done.

Now the usual point of this and similar interpretations is to shore up the Bible's believability and to defend its accuracy to people for whom the miraculous has become unbelievable. But as admirable as this intent may be, and as laudable was the good captain's sincerity of effort, the result of this kind of approach is to miss entirely the central point of the miracle accounts. The point of the account of the contest on Mt. Carmel is that the Lord is God and Baal is not. The point is *not* that Elijah could make fire. In defending the truth of this story with his "petroleum" explanation, the captain has changed it from a demonstration of whose God is God to a demonstration of whose prophet is cleverer (or perhaps sneakier).

The point of the miracle stories in the Gospels is to show that in Jesus, God was at work in a special way, and to affirm his unique authority. The point is not to show that Jesus could in fact predict changes in the weather, or appear to walk on water, or perform any other particular trick that might fool his disciples or the crowds.

Miracle accounts in general were not intended simply to relate the specifics of what happened, but to make it clear that God was at work here, intervening in worldly affairs in a special way, such that we should respond with faith and obedience. To interpret these accounts by concentrating on the event itself, and to explain this event as a misinterpreted unmiraculous occurrence, is to remove God from the story and so is to miss the point of it.

This is not to say that this sort of explanation is never valid or helpful. In some cases it seems obvious that we ought to make use of it. But it should be used to help us gain understanding of a passage, rather than being used to interpret it. By this I mean that this "classic liberal" approach can be used to explain the background, origin, or development of miracle accounts. It may give us an idea of what really happened, and so aid in our understanding of the Biblical stories. But we can't assume, as many people have, that this is all that needs to be said in interpreting these stories.

For instance, it is probable that what happened at the Red Sea—actually the Sea of Reeds—had more to do with darkness and an east wind and chariots mired in the mud and the change of the tide, than with the vertical walls of water rendered so picturesquely by Cecil B. DeMille. (These more impressive walls of water seem to be a later elaboration on the Exodus tradition. See Exodus 14:19–29.) Personally, I find it helpful to arrive at this understanding of the event itself.

But we cannot *interpret* this passage by saying that what really happened was a narrow escape in a dark marsh. The point of the story is not just to give the details of how they escaped from Pharaoh's grasp. More important here is the profession by the people of Israel that it was the Lord their God who delivered them out of Egypt. To interpret the Exodus by just "explaining away" God's miraculous intervention is to replace a grand example of God's caring for Israel with a plain old lucky escape, and to replace one of the central formative events of Judaism with an insignificant incident. So while "explaining" a miracle may help us to understand "what really happened", this explanation cannot give us a satisfactory understanding of what the Bible is saying.

2. The Bultmann Approach: Demythologization

While the classic liberal approach concentrates on the physical event and, in explaining what "really happened", ignores any deeper meaning involved in the miracle account, the approach developed by Rudolf Bultmann does just the opposite by ignoring the event in favor of the meaning. Bultmann, a German theologian active in the first half of the twentieth century, developed the aptly named approach of "demythologization". This approach merits our attention both because of the impact it has had and because many seminary graduates believe they use it themselves, though few actually do.

"Demythologization" does not refer to "myth" in its everyday sense of an imaginary legend or fairy tale. Instead, "myth" is used here in its technical sense to mean any story or account that makes reference to

God or to the supernatural in general, especially in relation to events on earth and the affairs of humankind.

Obviously, with this definition of "myth" the Bible contains a substantial amount of material that is mythical. This presents a problem, said Bultmann, for with our different world-view today we cannot understand or believe these mythical accounts. He sought a solution to this problem by examining the Bible—and the New Testament in particular—to see if it presented a truth that did not depend on its mythical content. He concluded that it did, that the true purpose of myth here was to give expression to human self-understanding.

Bultmann's reasoning went like this: he assumed that all statements are either (1) objective statements which are intended to provide information about the world, or (2) existential statements which are intended to confront the reader or listener with a decision about his or her possibilities of self-understanding. That is, all statements are either "this is what is" statements or "this is what you can be/ought to be" statements. Now, religious language in particular is addressed to answer the question of what ought to be rather than what is. Therefore, concluded Bultmann, religious myths are not intended to be objective statements— "what is"—but rather existential statements. So what we need is a translation of these mythical accounts into existential statements—or, if you will, demythologization.

For example, the mythical accounts of Jesus' miracles might be understood as pointing out his special authority and the need for us to respond to his life and message. The meaning of these accounts is obtained by demythologizing them. This is done by taking out the myth and translating the story into a challenge to answer Jesus' call to a new way of life. Thus, Bultmann might say that the miracle accounts can be translated into the existential message that "authentic existence"[2] is a real possibility for you and me.

No one should question the value of demythologization in helping to point out for us the important meaning that is implicit in the miracle accounts. But as practiced in a strict and thorough-going way it has two major flaws as a tool for interpreting the Bible: first, it prohibits us from making any statements at all about God; and second, it fails to do justice to the language of the Bible.

First: Since any reference to God is by definition myth (in the sense of the word we are using here), demythologizing means translating all such language into existential statements without reference to God. By emphasizing the distinction between God-talk and other uses of language Bultmann misses the chance to distinguish between legitimate and illegitimate ways of talking about God, and throws out the former along with

---

[2]"Authentic existence" is a phrase that Bultmann borrowed from the German existentialist Heidegger, and which he believed represented the kind of life to which Jesus called us.

the latter. To say the least, an approach that rules out all speech about God seems somewhat inappropriate as a tool for interpreting a book of religion.

Second: Even without this first defect, demythologization fails to do justice to the language of the Bible. The problem lies in Bultmann's assumption that all statements are intended to be *either* objective information statements *or* existential statements. This assumption fails to appreciate the multifaceted richness of language and leads Bultmann to a false conclusion. Since Bultmann views religious statements as existential, this "either/or" attitude forces him to conclude that they are therefore *not* factual statements. Therefore, to demythologize a miracle story into its existential meaning is not just to give us the existential implications of this miracle account. It is to make a complete translation of this account. Thus, for example, we would have to say that in relating the miracle stories the Gospel writers meant to challenge us with the possibility of authentic existence like Jesus' for ourselves. And this much is certainly true. But if we claim that this is a complete translation, then we are saying that they did *not* also mean to say that Jesus walked on water or stilled the storm.

Certainly the writers meant to point out the authority and specialness of Jesus, and thus to challenge us with a certain response, a certain way of life. But this is not all. They meant just as clearly to say that Jesus did as a matter of fact still the storm and walk on water. The fact is that language is quite capable of making an objective fact claim and giving us existential meaning at the same time, and so demythologization misses half the meaning.

3. Demiracle-ization

A much more common approach is that which I call "demiracle-ization". I am unsure whether the relationship of this to demythologization is that of offspring, parent, or sibling. Many people who have read about Bultmann and who believe that they use demythologization are in fact using this third approach instead.

In fact the thrust of demiracle-ization is much the same as demythologization: to extract and emphasize the *meaning* of the miracle. The difference is that demiracle-ization does not rule out all references to God—all "myth" in the technical sense. Instead, only those passages which are not in keeping with our common sense, such as the miracle accounts, need to be "translated" into different language.

Thus, for instance, the stories of Jesus walking on the water or stilling the storm can be said to be claiming that Jesus is the Son of God, or that he had special authority from God. Demiracle-ization would say that the *point* of these miracle accounts is that God was acting in and through this individual, and also, therefore, that we need to respond to him.

Certainly to this extent demiracle-ization serves a very important purpose. Too often we pay too much attention to the miracles themselves, when the real point of these stories is *not* that Elijah could bring down fire or that Jesus could heal people or walk on water. The point of these accounts is that God is at work in these people and events, that Elijah is the prophet of the true God or that Jesus is the one who can offer us God's forgiveness and a new life in God's love.

Too often we are distracted from the message of these stories by their miraculous nature. Whether or not you believe that the miracle accounts are true, we need to extract their meaning, to understand the religious significance they had for their contemporary audience. Otherwise they may appear to us only as marvelous tricks without any real meaning. So we need to ask, "What is the point of this miracle story? What is it trying to say about God or Jesus or a life of faith?"

The strength of demiracle-ization is that it can convey this meaning to us. Its weakness is that—like demythologization—it ends up translating miracles into other language altogether, and does, in fact, demiracle-ize the Bible. This is for many of us a comfortable way of dealing with miracles, since it allows us to make them disappear without having to come right out and say that we don't believe them, that the Bible is wrong. But this is not quite honest. Furthermore, eventually someone is going to notice that we haven't actually dealt with the miracles themselves, with the claim that God caused the water-soaked altar on Mt. Carmel to burst into flames or that Jesus walked on the water. Yes, the *point* of these is to say something about God, but the writers *also* meant to say that these events did in fact happen in just this way.

At this point we have several choices. Certainly we need to translate the miracle stories so that we today can understand their original significance. But in conjunction with this do we just ignore the miracles themselves? Or do we deny that they happened? Or do we use the "classic liberal" approach and explain them away?

Personally I think that a combination of "demiracle-ization" and the "classic liberal" approach can do justice to many miracle accounts. But there is another alternative that gets to the heart of the matter and avoids disputes over whether a certain miracle did or didn't happen. This alternative is to apply the concept of "religious significance".

Religious Significance

What do we mean by "religious significance"? Religion has to do with our understanding of God, our understanding of our moral and spiritual nature and our relationship with God. It has to do with our understanding of how we ought to live and relate to each other and with how we do in fact live out these various understandings. Therefore, anything which affects any of these understandings or the way we live them out means something to our religion. It has religious significance.

Thus someone who taught that God loves us and that we ought to love even our enemies, and who lived in such a way as to help us see that this is possible, had teachings and a life that are religiously significant. However, if our understanding of God is that God does not act by "zapping" into the finite physical processes of the world, then accounts of events which violate natural laws cannot have any religious significance for us.

Therefore we do not have to argue that this kind of miracle account is completely translatable into a different kind of language or offer non-miraculous explanations. We do not have to take sides with those who claim that they must be true or with those who claim that they are literally incredible, for their truth or falsehood is irrelevant to our religion. They are religiously insignificant.

If a person can walk on water this is very curious and interesting and certainly out of the ordinary. But it is of scientific interest, not religious. It addresses our understanding of natural laws, not theology. The ability of someone to walk on water or ignite an altar gives us not a clue as to their qualification as a moral leader. It tells us nothing about the adequacy of their understanding of God. It does not affect our own understanding of God, or of ourselves, or of the right way to live. Someone walking on water has no meaning, no significance, for our religion.

However, miracles did have religious significance to the people of first century Palestine. It was entirely in keeping with their common sense to explain an event as the result of specific intervention by God. A miracle implied divine authority or approbation.

So it is proper and even necessary to ask, what was the religious significance of this miracle account to its contemporary audience? What is its meaning? What point is it making? But it is also proper and necessary at the same time to point out that the reported miracle can have no such significance for us.

The meaning of the miracle to its contemporaries may be important to us. For instance, the writer may be claiming that Jesus has the authority to forgive sins, or that God is working through this person. We may need to translate the miracle accounts into these kinds of statements to make sure that we do not miss their intended implications, for these implications may in fact be of religious significance to us. But the miracles themselves are irrelevant. They simply are not religiously significant.

Jesus On Miracles

Jesus himself apparently had an attitude towards miracles that had much in common with this. His comments on miracles are otherwise very puzzling, if not incomprehensible:

> The Pharisees came and began to argue with him, seeking from him a sign from heaven, to test him. And he sighed deeply in his spirit, and said, "Why does this generation seek a sign? Truly, I say to you, no sign shall be given to this generation." (Mark 8:11–12)

> When the crowds were increasing, he began to say, "This generation is an evil generation; it seeks a sign, but no sign shall be given it except the sign of Jonah. For as Jonah became a sign to the men of Nineveh, so will the son of man be to this generation. The queen of the South will arise at the judgment with the men of this generation and condemn them; for she came from the ends of the earth to hear the wisdom of Solomon, and behold, something greater than Solomon is here. The men of Nineveh will arise at the judgment with this generation and condemn it; for they repented at the preaching of Jonah, and behold, something greater than Jonah is here." (Luke 11:29–32)

We might remark on several things here. For one, those of us with old fashioned Anglo-Saxon reserve might think it untoward for someone to talk about himself in this way. But Jesus of Nazareth taught "as one who had authority". No one could have followed his course and made his mark without supreme confidence that he was following the will of God. And he was, after all, making a particular point here.

For another thing, we need to point out that Matthew, in his version of this second passage, includes an explanation of the sign of Jonah: "For as Jonah was three days and three nights in the belly of the whale, so will the son of man be three days and three nights in the belly of the earth." (Matthew 12:40) But this is obviously a post-resurrection editorial addition, for besides demonstrating knowledge of the Easter event (albeit with poor arithmetic), it is entirely out of place here. Jesus is arguing *against* signs in this passage. As he pointed out, the only sign to the men of Nineveh was Jonah's preaching, and they repented at this, knowing nothing about the whale incident. The queen of the South came to hear Solomon's wisdom, not to see him perform miracles.

But the really remarkable thing here is what Jesus apparently *did* say. A "sign" is a sign from heaven, a miracle. And he said that no sign would be given to that generation, save only the sign of his preaching. And this is a real puzzle. For on the one hand we have accounts of a large number of miracles being performed by Jesus of Nazareth; on the other hand, we have this same Jesus saying that no sign would be given.

The simple solution here would be to dismiss one or the other, to say either that Jesus didn't perform any miracles or that he didn't really say that no sign would be given. But like most simplistic solutions where one is asked to choose between black and white, this ignores the gray areas that encompass most of reality. The truth is not going to avoid ambiguities just so we can feel comfortable.

We cannot agree with those who would say that since Jesus said this about miracles he must not have performed any signs at all. Admittedly, there is a documented tendency for miraculous stories to grow up around famous individuals. Admittedly, a good number of the miracle accounts may be exaggeration or misunderstanding or legend. But there is a consistency of emphasis on faith healings that is impossible to dismiss. Unlike the walking-on-the-water type of miracle, faith healings appear as an integral part of his ministry. It is clear that many who sought him out came not to hear his preaching and teaching but rather to receive or at least to observe a healing.

On the other hand, we cannot dismiss these sayings in which Jesus says no sign will be given. We cannot explain them away, nor can they be attributed to anyone else. No early follower of Jesus would invent a statement that calls his miracles into question and that implicitly admits that he failed to perform when challenged by the Pharisees.

There is a possible solution to this apparent quandary: that Jesus did in fact perform faith healings, at least early in his ministry, and that he intended them as "signs". For instance, the healing of the paralytic in Mark 2 is specifically intended "that you may know that the son of man [i.e., himself] has authority on earth to forgive sins." However, it developed that people were more interested in the signs themselves than in what the signs pointed to. That is, people were more interested in the apparently miraculous healings than in Jesus' message to which the healings were supposed to bear witness. People came seeking signs, not to hear about repentance and forgiveness and love. They came seeking entertainment, not truth; a spectacle, not a way to live. No observer of humanity can be the least bit surprised at this.

When Jesus realized that most people were rejecting his message, even those who came out to see his signs, he became aware that the healings were not signs at all but were rather distractions from his all-important message.[3] Here he was, bringing the good news of a new life in God, and people turned away from him! How could they hear the call to love and faithfulness upon which their whole lives depended and then demand something more?

Thus in the latter part of his ministry Jesus ruled out any signs. What was important was that people responded to his message. He realized that the faith healings were not of religious significance to people after all, for all they did was distract people from this message. Let them respond to the all-important life-changing truth!

---

[3]Could this also explain some of the secrecy apparent in his instructions to those he healed not to tell anyone?

Faith Healings

After saying that neither our common sense nor our faith allows for a "zapping" God, I have now suggested that Jesus did, in fact, take part in what we call "faith healings". Why this inconsistency?

First: there is no doubt that sudden and inexplicable healings of disease and infirmity do occasionally happen. Almost any physician will testify to that. And sometimes these sudden healings happen in conjunction with prayer and/or the laying on of hands, if not nearly so often as is claimed in Lourdes or by television evangelist healers. (It also needs to be said that this field of endeavor is unfortunately attractive to charlatans.) Nevertheless, the claims of such healings are so persistent that it is difficult to dismiss them all. It seems likely that the heightened excitement and conviction of the "faith healing" process could in fact bring about a physical effect.

Certainly it seems possible that a small percentage of those who are convinced they have been healed are correct, and certainly so strong a personality as Jesus of Nazareth could have elicited this response from people.

Second: this is not an inconsistency after all. In the last chapter we specifically noted that health and illness stand as a common sense exception to the requirement that finite physical effects have finite physical causes. In the case of both illness and healing, we recognize that the state of our mind or spirit plays a very important role. Spirit can affect our physical health.

Nevertheless, faith healings are not miracles in the classic sense. They do not represent an instance of God breaking into our affairs from outside. They are not a case of God's deciding, "I will heal this one," and then going "Zap! Be healed!" (Remember, neither our common sense nor our faith allows for this specific intervention.)

Rather than representing a breaking in of some power from "outside", faith healings represent the tapping of a power that is present in our world and in us. If these healings do happen on occasion, then the potential for them is a part of the context in which we live.

Precisely because this kind of healing does not represent a miracle in the classic sense of a particular case of divine intervention from outside, it just may be of religious significance. Faith healings may inform our understanding of the power of the mind or indicate our connectedness with the spiritual. We may even see them as a part of our relationship with God.

Conclusion

Our conclusion is that miracles in the classic sense of specific divine intervention from outside do not have religious significance for us. We need to understand the religious significance of the miracle accounts to their original audience so that we do not lose sight of the point of these passages. It may also be helpful for us to reconstruct the historical, non-miraculous events that may be at the root of these accounts. And finally, we must remember that Jesus himself felt that "signs" were irrelevant to his message. As far as religion goes, miracles in the classic sense are indeed irrelevant.

PART TWO

TRADITIONAL DOCTRINE

In Part Two we assess the adequacy of traditional Christian doctrine about the resurrection, the divinity of Jesus and the identity of Jesus. We also examine the relationship between faith and doctrine.

In Chapter Five we conclude that we do have a good general idea as to what Jesus said, and we proceed from this to develop two rules of Christian belief to identify when a belief is appropriate for Christians and when a belief may be required of Christians.

In Chapter Six we look at the resurrection and conclude that indeed some special experience took place, but that the resurrection does not have religious significance for us.

In Chapter Seven we consider the question of Jesus' divinity. This doctrine is not Biblical, is logically impossible (as opposed to a paradox), violates our common sense, and is unnecessary and even unhelpful.

In Chapter Eight we pause to highlight the distinction between faith and doctrine. Faith is the way we live our lives, doctrine is the intellectual explanation of this, so one may have a valid Christian belief that is not factually accurate if this belief leads one into right relationship.

In Chapter Nine we continue our consideration of traditional themes by examining the titles used to answer the question "Who is Jesus of Nazareth?" Looking at traditional titles such as "Savior", "Lord and Master", "Son of God" and "Messiah", we find none of them satisfactory. I then explain briefly what I mean by Jesus as "the Christ" understood in a functional way. This leads us into Part Three, my proposal for a common sense and faithful alternative to traditional orthodoxy.

CHAPTER 5: CAN THIS BE CHRISTIAN?

"Not everyone who says to me, 'Lord, Lord,' shall enter the kingdom of heaven, but he who does the will of my father who is in heaven."
(Matthew 7:21)

At this point it seems necessary to pause for an important question. Is it possible to proclaim that the Bible is not perfect, that God does not act in the physical events of this world, and that miracles are religiously insignificant—and still be Christian?

In this chapter we are going to go through several steps that will give us two general rules about Christian belief. These rules are very simple but very important. The first rule will tell us when a belief may be considered Christian. The second will state when a belief may be *required* of Christians.

Part of what we are asking here is what it means to be a Christian. This is a very basic question. To whom do we look for an answer? More important than what Luther or Augustine said, more important than what your pastor or the Pope or Billy Graham said, more important than what your family told you or what your fundamentalist or atheistic neighbor told you—what did Jesus of Nazareth say?

In step one we will examine the question of whether in fact we know what Jesus said. It is necessary that we face this question up front. In step two we will consider the main thrust of Jesus' message. In step three we will draw some conclusions about Christian belief and formulate our two rules.

Step One: Do We Know What Jesus Said?

We must begin by admitting that there is some serious question as to what Jesus *did* say. Whole books continue to be written just on this topic. While some people may think that the red print in their New Testament represents words taken down by stenographers as Jesus spoke, the fact is that the Gospels as we have them were written somewhere from thirty to sixty years after his death. Matthew and Luke both make use of an earlier written record of Jesus' teachings, but we do not know when or by whom this document was written. (It is called the "Q Source", from the German word for source, "quelle".) There is also the fact that each of the four Gospel writers has a somewhat differing interpretation of Jesus, and so each puts a different slant on things. On top of this, Jesus is sometimes quoted as saying things that reflect a little too neatly the needs of the early Church. To give just three examples, there would seem to be legitimate doubts about such passages as John the Baptist's recognition of Jesus as the Messiah, Jesus saying to Peter "on this rock I will build my church," and Jesus' very specific predictions of his death and resurrection. We will take a brief look at each of these to show why.

The story of John the Baptist is found early in all four Gospels. While it does not concern a statement by Jesus, it is a good illustration of the problem at hand. There is no question that Jesus was baptized by John. Jesus' disciples would never have made this up, because it was an embarrassment to them. It was embarrassing because he who baptizes generally has greater authority than he who is baptized, and they had to admit that Jesus was baptized by John, not the other way around. No doubt they were reminded of this by the disciples of the Baptist.

So here was a need of Jesus' early followers: to show that Jesus was the Messiah even though he himself was baptized by another man. They knew that John had said that "he who is coming is mightier than I," and they were convinced that Jesus was this person. And since John the Baptist was a prophet, he must have known who Jesus was, too. So wouldn't it make sense to make this clear by having John say so himself? Thus we have the words attributed to him in Matthew 3:14 and John 1:29–34 (e.g., "This is he of whom I said, 'After me comes a man who ranks before me, for he was before me.' " John 1:30).

But if John knew that Jesus was this person when he baptized him, why did he later on send messengers to ask Jesus, "Are you he who is to come?" (Matthew 11; Luke 7) It doesn't make sense. And the earlier statements attributed to John are just too convenient to believe.

The second example we're looking at is Matthew 16:18, where Jesus says to Simon, "You are Peter, and on this rock I will build my church," in response to Peter's recognition of him as the Christ. We can safely assume that some such incident occurred which caused Jesus to confer upon Simon the name of Peter, or rock. But there is no evidence at all that Jesus had any intention of starting "my church". On the contrary, he was calling Jews back to their God, teaching in the synagogues and the Temple.

Again, however, the early Christians had a need. They had been kicked out of the synagogues and sought justification for the founding of a separate Church. They needed Jesus' authority for it. No doubt Jesus said something about Peter and his other disciples which was later on remembered in this way. But this verse fits the need of the early Church too neatly, while at the same time *not* fitting with what else we know about Jesus, for us not to be skeptical about it.

The third example consists of the very specific predictions that Jesus made of his own death and resurrection. For instance, Matthew 20:18–19: "Behold, we are going up to Jerusalem; and the son of man will be delivered to the chief priests and scribes, and they will condemn him to death, and deliver him to the Gentiles to be mocked and scourged and crucified, and he will be raised on the third day."

There are several reasons to doubt whether this is an actual statement of Jesus. First of all, it's just too precise not to suspect the work of someone who knew exactly how things did, in fact, turn out. Secondly, the disciples give no evidence in their reactions to Jesus' arrest and execution of having ever heard him say this. And thirdly, the early Church had a vested interest here. Crucifixion was an ignominious death meted out to enemies of the state. For this death to make sense to them it had to be seen as part of a divine plan, and as voluntary and intentional on Jesus' part. What better way to show this than by his own predictions of it?

Surely Jesus foresaw danger and possible death in Jerusalem, and surely his disciples would later have read more into any forebodings. "Now we understand what he meant! He was predicting his crucifixion." It would be only natural that by the time it was incorporated in the Gospels a general warning by Jesus had become a very specific prediction of what his disciples knew came to pass.

We have looked at these as examples of specific passages that reasonable people could reasonably doubt the historical accuracy of. There is certainly sufficient reason to believe that the collection of Jesus' sayings presented in the Gospels is not completely accurate. Some scholars, however, have taken this to the extreme. Citing specific examples and the passage of years before the Gospels were written, and the influence of authors, editors, and the early Church, they make themselves opposite counterparts to the Biblical literalists. They appear to follow the rule that if you can't believe all of it, then doubt all of it. It has even been claimed that there is not a single complete sentence that we can be positive was uttered by Jesus of Nazareth.

But this is not very sensible. What may be a good reason to doubt a given verse or set of verses is not necessarily good reason to doubt whole chapters. To doubt for no good reason is as silly as believing for no good reason.

The fact is that the Gospels are not disconnected stories and sayings that could have been chosen at random here and there. The accounts we have of the ministry and teaching of Jesus of Nazareth fit together in a coherent way to portray a remarkable and insightful individual.

It is true that we do not know the precise date of the Gospels or the precise nature of their sources. It is true that it seems likely that Mark, the earliest of them, was written some three decades after Jesus' death.

But we have learned much about the strength of oral tradition in other societies, and how it can convey surprisingly accurate information over years and sometimes even generations. And in the case of the Gospels we are dealing with a time period well within individual lifespans. So while we cannot claim that the Gospels have the accuracy of video tape, and we cannot doubt that there are some errors due to oral transmission, there is also no reason to doubt that they contain a generally accurate picture of a man who made a very strong impression on his contemporaries.

So it is, too, with the influence of the early Church on the Gospels. Certainly there was some impact. And a prudent person can reasonably doubt those sayings which so precisely fit the needs of Jesus' early followers, which do *not* fit with the rest of his message. But this does not give us any reason to doubt all the rest of Jesus' sayings and actions.

We need to keep in mind what the question is. The question is not whether we have a precise record of exactly what Jesus did, and when and where and how he did it. For the most part we do not have all this. The question is, do we have an accurate representation of the kind of things that Jesus did, of the kind of life he lived, and of the main events in it?

And the question is not whether we have Jesus' sayings in the exact words he uttered. There is no way of knowing this, and it doesn't much matter. The question is, do we have the faithfully remembered ideas of this man who made such an impression on those who heard him? And the question is not whether we have his ideas rendered exactly right on every single issue addressed in the Gospels. The question is, do we have a coherent and accurate statement of his central message?

Yes, we do. An unbiased look at the overall picture makes it impossible to conclude otherwise. With what we now know about oral tradition we cannot use the time lapse before the Gospels were written to cast doubt on their general accuracy, even as we cannot guarantee their accuracy in every detail. We have a generally consistent account about an exceptional individual who had a great impact on his contemporaries. If it was not Jesus of Nazareth who taught these teachings and through his life and death gave impetus to this movement, if it was not this Jesus of Nazareth who was revered by the early Church as it passed on his precepts—within the lifespan of those who knew him—then who was it? Does it make sense to invent another person here when all the testimony points to Jesus, and when the Gospels paint a coherent picture of a man who lived and taught his powerful understanding of the love of God? Of course not. The only reasonable conclusion is that we do have a generally accurate picture of the way Jesus lived and of his central message.[1]

---

[1]If one wishes a more detailed study of the question, one can read Schillebeeckx's *Jesus*, in which it takes him 437 pages to come to this point: "All in all, we are led to conclude that

The Exception: The Gospel of John

So: we have a generally accurate representation of the life and the teachings of Jesus of Nazareth. In essence, we are saying that unless you can give a good reason to doubt a particular passage, there is no reason to doubt it. With this guideline we can be generally satisfied with the vast majority of Matthew, Mark, and Luke. These three have much in common, and in fact are collectively called "the Synoptics" because of their similarity.

The Gospel of John is different. Jesus talks differently in John than in the Synoptics. This is apparent even in the English translation. He speaks in a very stylized manner, he uses different concepts than in the other Gospels, and in places he is almost overloaded with symbols like the "bread of life" and "light of the world". It is apparent on even a cursory reading that something has happened here to the sayings of Jesus.

With some study, it is evident that John's Gospel is the end product of significant theological thought. John has done more "theologizing" than the other three Gospels together. This doesn't mean that what John says is necessarily wrong or necessarily right. But it does mean that what he quotes Jesus as saying has been filtered through a particular process, much more so than in the Synoptics. In effect, what we have here is Jesus quoted as saying what John thought Jesus meant to say. Maybe the intent is the same as what Jesus actually said, and maybe it isn't. In either case, Jesus' words here are definitely restructured by John's theology.

What this means, of course, is that there is good reason to be more skeptical of what Jesus says in the Gospel of John. One must look at whether particular sayings are consistent with his teachings as we know them from the Synoptics. One must also look out a little more carefully than in the other three Gospels for the influence of the early Church and of the author's own theology.

Step Two: What Did Jesus Say?

We began this chapter with the question of what it means to be a Christian and decided that we must begin with what Jesus said. We asked first of all whether we know what Jesus said. In step one we concluded that while there are particular reasons for doubting particular passages, we have a generally accurate representation of Jesus' actions and (in Matthew, Mark and Luke) of his teachings. In other words, yes,

the New Testament, not in spite of the diverse kerygmatic projects but because of them, gives substantial information about Jesus of Nazareth." (Edward Schillebeeckx, *Jesus* [Crossroad Publishing Co., 1979.] p. 437) we do know well enough what Jesus said. Now in step two we will consider the question of what Jesus said it meant to be a Christian.

Of course Jesus never answered this question directly. In fact, he never said anything about "Christian" at all. In the first place, Jesus was intent upon reforming Judaism, not starting a new religion. In the second place, this name was not given to his followers until some years after his death.

So we will ask a different question: what does it mean to be a follower of Jesus of Nazareth? But this is not really a different question. This is just another way of asking the same thing, for if it means anything to be a Christian it means to be a follower of Jesus the Christ.

What did Jesus ask of his followers? What did he call people to do? What response did he seek to himself and his message?

There are three passages in the Gospels which serve as particularly good summaries of Jesus' teachings, though each in a different way. Each of them gets to the heart of the matter in a way that rings of authenticity. They are: the Great Commandment, the Sermon on the Mount, and the Great Judgment.[2]

I. The Great Commandment

And one of them, a lawyer, asked him a question, to test him. "Teacher, which is the great commandment in the law?" And he [Jesus] said to him, "You shall love the Lord your God with all your heart, and with all your soul, and with all your mind. This is the great and first commandment. And a second is like it, You shall love your neighbor as yourself. On these two commandments depend all the law and the prophets. (Matthew 22:35–40)

This passage is found with slight variations in Mark and Luke (Mark 12:28–34; Luke 10:25–28). Incidentally, it's a good example of the kind of differences between Gospels that is *not* important. In Mark it is a scribe that asks the question, not a lawyer, and Jesus' phrasing is slightly

---

[2]It is widely accepted that central to Jesus' message was "the Kingdom of God". I have avoided the use of this phrase here for two reasons: (1) The popular understandings of this phrase range from perfection on earth, to heaven, to the millenial rule of Christ after the Second Coming, all of which serve to confuse the issue at question here. (2) For most of this century it was assumed by scholars that Jesus' references to the Kingdom of God referred to a future eschatological event: an imminent end to the world as we know it. But the scholarly consensus is now trending to the opposite viewpoint: Jesus did not preach the end of the world, and those passages which clearly refer to a Second Coming or end of the world are the creation of the early Church. (See Marcus J. Borg, "Jesus and the Kingdom of the God", in *The Christian Century*, April 22, 1987, p. 378–380.)

Therefore, for Jesus, the Kingdom of God is concerned with a life lived now in response to God, in the presence of God. However, because of all the unhelpful connotations of the traditional phrase, the substance of this kind of life is better addressed by examining Jesus' central themes as we do here, and in an expanded way in Chapter 16, rather than by using the phrase "Kingdom of God".

different. In Luke Jesus throws the question back to the lawyer, so it is the lawyer who states the two commandments and Jesus who says he is right.

What is important is that in all three Jesus affirms the central importance of these two commandments. In Luke, he follows up with the parable of the good Samaritan, which gives an important expansion of our idea of who is our neighbor. The indisputable point here is that Jesus' guiding principles were the love of God and love of neighbor.

II. The Sermon on the Mount

This second selection spells out more specifically what the Great Commandment says in general. It is the Sermon on the Mount, Matthew 5 through 7, paralleled in part by the Sermon on the Plain in Luke 6:17–49. In each case, though to a greater extent in Matthew, the occasion is used to pull together a collection of Jesus' teachings.

Certainly it makes no difference whether the setting is a mountain or a plain, and after the Beatitudes there are only slight differences in wording.[3] Many familiar teachings are included here: turn the other cheek, go the second mile, be reconciled with your brother, lay up treasures in heaven, judge not, and love your enemies—not just your friends, but your enemies! Jesus lays out here the kind of attitudes and actions that he is calling for. He does not address doctrines but the kind of life we should live.

As if to confirm this, towards the end of "the sermon" Jesus comments on people who call him "Lord". This is of particular note because of that large faction of Christianity which seems interested only in whether you and I have accepted Jesus as our "Lord and Savior". What Jesus says is, "Not everyone who says to me, 'Lord, Lord', shall enter the kingdom of heaven, but he who does the will of my Father who is in heaven." (Matthew 7:21) This is paralleled by Luke 6:46, "Why do you call me 'Lord', and not do what I tell you?" The point is clear. Jesus is not as concerned with what people call him as with how they live. What he calls for in the Sermon on the Mount, and gives numerous examples of, is a life lived in right relationship with God and neighbor, in line with the Great Commandment.

III. The Great Judgment

The third passage that serves as a good summary of what was important to Jesus is the Great Judgment in Matthew 25. Here he paints a

---

[3]The Beatitudes, on the other hand, show a noteworthy difference in emphasis. Matthew refers to "the poor in spirit:, Luke to "you poor"; Matthew speaks of "those who hunger and thirst after righteousness", Luke of "you that hunger". Luke then follows with a set of woes to the rich and the full. This difference of concern between the poor in spirit in Matthew and the poor in Luke is one which deserves serious study and reflection.

word picture of judgment day, when the son of man will come in his glory to judge the nations and shall separate them "as a shepherd separates the sheep from the goats". Those on his right hand are then told why they are destined for heaven:

"For I was hungry and you gave me food, I was thirsty and you gave me drink, I was a stranger and you welcomed me, I was naked and you clothed me, I was sick and you visited me, I was in prison and you came to me." Then the righteous will answer him, "Lord, when did we see thee hungry and feed thee, or thirsty and give you drink? And when did we see thee a stranger and welcome thee, or naked and clothe thee? And when did we see thee sick or in prison, and visit thee?" And the King will answer them, "Truly, I say to you, as you did it to one of the least of these my brethren, you did it to me." (Matthew 25:35–40)

Those on his left hand are likewise informed that they are destined to eternal punishment because they did *not* do these things for "the least of these".

In his depiction of the Great Judgment, Jesus makes no reference to doctrine or belief at all. He does not mention belief in Biblical inerrancy or salvation by faith. He doesn't even mention any beliefs about himself. The deciding factor as to whether someone goes to heaven or hell is the way they have dealt with other people.

In the second and third of these passages we find confirmation of the first. They are amplifications of the Great Commandment, examples of love in action. In his teachings and in his actions, we find this pervasive central theme of Jesus: love God and love your neighbor. This is what he preached to the crowds and expected of his disciples. This is what he lived for and what he died for. Certainly this is what he wanted most to pass on to his followers.

What then does it mean to be a Christian, that is, a follower of Jesus of Nazareth? First, of course, it must mean that you have made a conscious choice to follow him. This means to place his teachings and his example at the center of your understanding of how to live, of what is important in life, and of what God is like. If Jesus the Christ does not have this centrality for someone, then however good a person they may be, they can hardly claim to be his follower. Secondly, this centrality of Jesus' message in your heart must show itself in your actions, in the way you treat people and in what your goals in life are.

Step Three: What Is A Christian Belief?

We began this chapter by asking whether we can hold certain beliefs and still be Christian. How do we decide whether something is a Christian belief?

What we are really asking here is, when is a belief appropriate for Christians? This brings us to Ross Christian Belief Rule #1: A belief is Christian (meaning that it is appropriate for Christians to believe) if it is (1) in keeping with the thrust of Jesus the Christ (as expressed in the Great Commandment), and (2) is also consistent with the life and teaching of this Jesus being central to our understanding of our relationship to God and to other people.

Can We Separate Jesus from John and Paul?

A multitude of learned and respected Christian voices will object to this. Perceptive people whose opinions I value will fulminate against me. They will point out that I have tried to separate the gospel of Jesus in Matthew, Mark, and Luke from the gospel of John, Paul, and Hebrews. They will say that this is ill-conceived, illegitimate, and impossible.

Many of these people are intelligent, sincere, and faithful. They are certainly defending an important traditional principle. They are also wrong.

They are right, however, about what I have done. As the criteria for Christian belief I have chosen the life and teachings of Jesus of Nazareth, which are best conveyed in the first three Gospels. But they are wrong in saying this cannot be done. It *must* be done. The Church is not "the Church of John" or "the Church of Paul". It is not "the Church of the first century Apostles" or the "Church of the New Testament in general". It is not even the "Church of Jesus and John and Paul." We are the Church of Jesus the Christ.

To be Christian is to follow the Christ. This is why we must distinguish his teachings from the teachings of others. The message of Jesus must form the base, the keystone, for our religious understanding. Certainly the teachings of others may be added to this. Many wise and faithful men and women have passed on important truths to us. But any addition to the message of the Christ must first pass the test of consistency. If it is not consistent with what Jesus lived and taught then it cannot legitimately be a part of our Christianity.

This is true whether we are examining a belief put forward by you, or by me, or by St. Paul. This is true whether it was added today or 2000 years ago to what Jesus said. We cannot assume just because an idea is in the New Testament that it is consistent with what Jesus taught. This would be a lazy and dishonest cop-out on our part. There are certainly some great insights into what it means to be Christian given to us by other New Testament writers and by ancient teachers. But people were as capable of misunderstanding Jesus of Nazareth ten or twenty centuries ago as they are now.

Belief in Jesus Christ

Whatever problems there may be in deciding whether certain particular teachings in the Synoptics are attributable to Jesus, when we come to John and Paul there is a clear and certain difference. People are not just called upon to follow the teachings and example of Jesus. Instead, John and Paul add on to this a particular set of beliefs and insist that these beliefs are necessary to our relationship to God. Our status as Christians and our entry into heaven are made to depend on a particular belief—a belief in Jesus Christ.

But how can this be, when the Christ himself never demanded this of people? "For God so loved the world that he gave his only Son, that whoever believes in him should not perish but have eternal life." So reads John 3:16, probably the most favorite Bible verse of all. Surely we as Christians must believe in Jesus Christ?!

But what are we being asked to believe? What is meant by "belief in Jesus Christ"? Is it like believing in Santa Claus? Does it mean simply to believe that Jesus of Nazareth lived and taught in Palestine? No, this is too trivial. This is accepted by all reasonable people and could hardly serve as the cornerstone of our faith.

What is generally meant by believing *in* Jesus Christ is actually believing certain things *about* him. When an orthodox Christian asks whether you believe in Jesus Christ they mean, "Do you believe that Jesus of Nazareth is the Son of God, the Messiah; and that he and he alone has freed us from the bondage of sin and death; and that he is divine; and that through him and him alone you can enter heaven, by believing all this about him?"

If we look at the words of Jesus of Nazareth as we have them in the first three Gospels we can see that (with the possible exception of being the Messiah) Jesus does not ask us to believe a single one of these.

But does he not demand that people make a decision and respond to him? Doesn't he seem to say, especially in some of the parables and in his relationship with the scribes and Pharisees, that a person's response to *him* determines their relationship to God? And so do not John and Paul and orthodoxy simply spell out the implications of this?

Indeed Jesus does demand a response to himself. And clearly he believes that much depends on this response. But is he concerned about the response just to himself as an individual person, in and of himself? Or does he rather consider this so important because a response to the messenger is a response to the message, because to accept or reject God's messenger and God's message is to accept or reject God?

It is clear to me that it is the latter. The message is what is of prime importance to Jesus. This is his emphasis over and over again in the Gospels. And as in the Parable of the Great Banquet (Luke 14:16–24), to reject the master's servant is to reject the master. So to accept Jesus as God's messenger is to accept the all-important message, and to accept God's message is to accept God. To reject the messenger is to reject

God's invitation, which is to reject God. *This* is the importance of a person's response to Jesus of Nazareth.

Since this is the case, since this is how Jesus pictures the importance of a response to him, any requirements *we* make about belief in Jesus Christ must be in accordance with this. We mean here, of course, beliefs *about* Jesus.

So here is Ross Christian Belief Rule #2: Since it is the message that is important, we can say that a given belief about the *messenger* is necessary, only if this belief is necessary to our acceptance of the message. Therefore, if you want to say that we *must* believe certain things about Jesus of Nazareth, you must show that these things are necessary to his message. These beliefs may be necessarily implicit in the message itself, or they may be necessary for a positive response to the message. But unless a belief about Jesus is one or the other we cannot claim that it is necessary, we cannot say it is a "required" belief in order for someone to be considered Christian. Essentially, we are saying that if you can follow Jesus without a particular belief, if you can answer his call to live according to the Great Commandment without this belief, then this belief is not required in order to be Christian.

Summary

In this chapter we have established two general rules about Christian beliefs. One identifies those which it is alright for Christians to believe, the other those which are necessary for someone to believe in order to be considered Christian. They are:

Ross Christian Belief Rule #1: A belief may be considered Christian (i.e., appropriate for Christians to believe) if it is consistent with the Great Commandment and with the centrality of Jesus of Nazareth to our religious understanding.

Ross Christian Belief Rule #2: A belief may be considered required of Christians only if it is necessarily implied in the life and teachings of the Christ or if it is necessary to accepting his message.

We can now answer the question with which we began this chapter: Yes, the views expressed in this book qualify as Christian. Not as beliefs that can be required of Christians, but as beliefs that are appropriate for Christians. There are no doubt many untraditional ideas that meet the criteria of Rule #1. This is also where many traditional beliefs fall. We must be careful about claiming that beliefs—new or old—meet the criteria of Rule #2. Most do not. And some traditional ones do not even meet the criteria of Rule #1.

Now we are ready to look at some particular traditional doctrines. We shall begin with the resurrection.

CHAPTER 6: THE RESURRECTION: HISTORICALLY PROBABLE, RELIGIOUSLY INSIGNIFICANT

"Mary Magdalene and Joanna and Mary the mother of James and the other women with them . . . told this to the apostles; but these words seemed to them an idle tale, and they did not believe them." (Luke 24:10–11)

This will no doubt be considered a strange combination. Nevertheless, I regard it as historically probable that something happened on that first Easter, something not too unlike the Biblical resurrection accounts. And I also maintain that what happened is not of any theological significance. In this chapter we will examine the case for each of these positions and then briefly suggest some consequences.

I: Historical Probability

Assume for the moment that we are careful, impartial historians, used to dealing only in probabilities. Let us examine the evidence and see what conclusions we can draw.[1]

We should first of all look at the New Testament to see what the Gospels say happened on Easter. Being attentive to detail, as behooves careful historians, we notice that the testimony is confusing and even inconsistent: the post-resurrection Jesus appears and vanishes like a spirit (Luke 24:31, 36–7; John 20:26), yet he can eat solid food (Luke 24:43); he can be touched (Matthew 28:9), and he cannot be touched (John 20:17); it was indeed Jesus, but they do not recognize him at first (Luke 24:15f; John 20:14, 21:4). But we also take note that the Biblical accounts are in total agreement in making the same extraordinary claim: Jesus of Nazareth, who had been crucified, dead and buried, was alive!

---

[1] A more detailed assessment of current scholarly argument about the resurrection may be found in Appendix B.

This is the testimony. What can we conclude from this? Can we say because of the apparent inconsistencies that this testimony is false? No, for as careful historians we would expect an event like a resurrection to cause confusion. We know that disagreement about details does not mean that the main message is wrong. Messengers who observed a battle from different vantage points could differ greatly on how the battle was won, and still all be correct in reporting that the country has been saved by a great victory.

Can we then say because of the unanimity of the testimony that Jesus was indeed raised from the dead? No. As careful historians all we can say is that according to the record these early disciples claimed to believe that Jesus was resurrected.

How do we get beyond this to assess whether this belief was true or not? How can we judge the probability of the resurrection itself?

Not every one wishes to think about the historical probability of the resurrection. There are a number of people on both sides of the issue who dismiss this question, usually in one of three different ways: (1) The Biblical literalist cannot consider the question of the resurrection's historical probability, for this would be to admit that the accuracy of the Bible is open to doubt. So the literalist avoids this by saying, "Of *course* it happened!" (2) At the other extreme there are people who argue that they have never seen a resurrection, and that therefore such things do not happen, and are therefore impossible, and so a resurrection couldn't and didn't happen to Jesus. These people can no more consider the possibility of an event different in kind from what they have experienced than Biblical literalists can consider the possibility that the Bible is wrong. So these people avoid this by saying, "Of *course* it didn't happen!"

(3) A more imaginative approach has been taken by some theologians who have suggested that the resurrection was an act of God and therefore not a part of human history, and is therefore not subject to the judgment of historians. But this is not very persuasive. Either the resurrection happened to a human or it did not happen at all. And we know of it only because of the reported observations of the disciples. If these observations were not a part of human history, open to study by historians, then they didn't happen.

Being careful and objective historians we are unable to take any of these ways to avoid the question. But if we can't avoid it, how do we answer it? How can we assess the probability of this reported event of two thousand years ago? The written testimony is hardly objective—it is all by one group of people with a very definite bias. How can we get behind this testimony to the event itself?

We can't, at least not in any direct way. But does this mean we must give up any attempt to assess its historical probability? No. There is some important circumstantial evidence to consider.

It is not at all unusual for historians to have to content themselves with unobjective accounts of an event and to make use of circumstantial evidence to confirm or disprove these accounts. Centuries later this is usually all we have to go by. And it is often quite adequate to allow us to reach very definite conclusions.

This may surprise us, for we are used to the TV courtroom dramas in which circumstantial evidence is much maligned. But circumstantial evidence can be good, strong evidence. For instance, if Jones the underpaid bank clerk didn't show up for work one Monday and was never heard from again, and a large amount of money was discovered missing in his department, we would all agree that this was a pretty good reason for suspecting Jones of the crime. If we then discovered that he was living high on the hog in Barbados, we would all think this was adequate evidence to consider Jones guilty *unless* he could offer an alternative plausible explanation of these circumstances. If he didn't just come into an inheritance or win the state lottery, we could justifiably conclude that Jones has embezzled, just from circumstantial evidence. No one actually saw him make off with the money, but we don't need that to prove our case. The evidence of the surrounding circumstances is overwhelming.

Thus, if a certain event or fact under question is the *only* plausible explanation of the known facts, of the surrounding circumstances and events, then we should certainly say that this event or fact is at least probable. Generally, we are not so cautious and would consider it proven.

Before and After

We can now consider the evidence. From Biblical passages which there is no reasonable cause to doubt we can draw this general account of the time in Jerusalem:

The disciples came with Jesus from Galilee for the Passover. Their expectations were undoubtedly high. Had not their teacher astounded all of Galilee with his teaching and healing, and drawn great crowds in the Decapolis, and confounded the scribes and Pharisees with his wisdom and authority? Had he not come through it all unscathed and even victorious? The possibilities in Jerusalem must have seemed limitless. Was it not the Holy City itself, with the one great Temple of God? Perhaps it was even time for God to fulfill some of the ancient prophecies and restore the throne of David. At the very least, Jesus would be received as the great prophet he was. This was the unavoidable feeling of Jesus' disciples. If he did warn them of danger it certainly didn't sink in.

Then there was the entry into Jerusalem. They may have spent the night before in Bethany, just a few miles away. Either there or in Bethphage he borrowed a donkey—one might infer from the Synoptics that this was prearranged, complete with a password—and so began his descent down the Mount of Olives in a way that seemed to fulfill the prophecy of Zechariah: "Shout aloud, O daughter of Jerusalem! Lo, your king comes to you . . . humble and riding on an ass." (Zechariah 9:9)

The accounts agree that it was a joyous and triumphant entry. The disciples, and probably a number of fellow travelers from the crowds coming up for the Passover, shouted hosannas. Crowds can easily get excited for celebrities, and they may have cried out such things as "Blessed is he who comes in the name of the Lord! Blessed be the son of David!", and they even spread "palms" in the road before him.

The first few days in Jerusalem must have continued to raise their hopes. He "cleansed" the Temple, enforcing the law by chasing out the money-changers and the pigeon-sellers while the temple police just watched, unable or unwilling to stop him. Again he confounded the scribes and Pharisees and he attracted crowds so large and enthusiastic that the authorities, concerned about him, were afraid to lay a hand on him in public. It must have seemed evident to his disciples that Jesus of Nazareth was bound for new heights of recognition and triumph. Who could guess what he might accomplish next?

Then, suddenly, it was over. The inconceivable had happened. His whereabouts made known to the high priest, betrayed by one of his own inner circle, Jesus was arrested away from the crowds. Tried at the high priest's home that very night and before the Sanhedrin the next morning, taken to Pilate, rejected by the crowd and mocked by the Romans, he was sentenced to the debasing death of crucifixion and by sunset he was dead and laid in a tomb.

The reaction of the disciples was what we would expect. They were shocked, demoralized, and uncomprehending. In a strange city, bereft of their charismatic leader, identifiable as rustic Galileans by their accents, afraid of persecution and arrest to the point of denying Jesus, and most of all suffering grief-stricken shock and shattered dreams and hearts, they clung together for awhile helplessly and hopelessly. But soon they began to drift apart. After all, what purpose did they have anymore? Their hopes and expectations for their beloved prophet had been decisively and cruelly brought to an end in a way that had not seemed possible. They were defeated.

There is no reason to doubt the general accuracy of this picture. But there is also no question that just a short time later this same group of people was proclaiming that this Jesus of Nazareth was the Messiah and had been raised from the dead. And we find them preaching this with enthusiasm, purpose and dedication—and with such conviction that they were willing to risk persecution, imprisonment, and even death in order to make known their message.

Something Happened

Obviously, something happened. Something happened to cause this radical turnabout. There are two possibilities: either the disciples, in their mourning, conspired together to put one over on the world, or else they really believed that Jesus of Nazareth had been raised from the dead.

We have to ask ourselves which of these is more probable, putting aside our preconceptions and keeping in mind what we know of human nature. Can both of these possibilities explain the sudden turnaround of a grief-stricken and demoralized group of people? Can both possibilities explain the enthusiasm and contagious conviction which led to the rapid spread of Christianity? Can both explain the disciples' willingness to suffer and die for the sake of this message?

No. It strains our credibility beyond the breaking point to try to explain all this as the result of an apostolic fabrication. Could you go out and preach with joy? Or risk death for a message if you had any doubts about it? If you had made it up?

In the face of the evidence the impartial historian is bound to conclude that the disciples did indeed sincerely believe that Jesus of Nazareth had been raised from the dead.

Obviously, then, we must also conclude that something happened to cause them to believe this. Something happened. This much is certain. The question is, what happened? What was the nature of this event? Was it really a resurrection?

If we are prudent and objective historians we cannot answer this question. Something happened which caused the disciples to believe that Jesus was resurrected. We cannot say precisely what that something was.

There are a couple of more things that we can say about this event with a fair degree of certainty. First, it is very probable that the tomb was indeed empty. Not only do the four Gospels agree on this, and not only do Mark and John point out that this in itself further saddened the disciples, but Matthew goes to the trouble of discrediting a tale started by opponents of the early Christians that the empty tomb was a result of the disciples stealing away Jesus' body while the guards slept. (Matthew 28:11–15) Certainly no opponent of the Church would try to explain the missing body with a tale like this unless they felt they had to admit that the tomb was empty to begin with.

Secondly, there is little doubt that it was Mary Magdalene who discovered that the tomb was empty, either alone or with other women, and that it was she who first reported an experience of the risen Jesus. This same experience was then repeated by others, and before long there was enthusiastic preaching of the risen Christ.

In the role of objective historians we can conclude only that something remarkable happened on the first Easter, something that was capable of being interpreted as the resurrection of Jesus of Nazareth. We can never know just what his disciples experienced to convince them of this.

Personally—that is, no longer sticking to the role of objective historian—I believe that whatever happened was enough like the triumph of Jesus over death that to call it a resurrection has some legitimacy. And after all, it doesn't really matter if it was an actual bodily resurrection, because a bodily resurrection has no religious significance.

II: Religious Insignificance

After pointing out the impact of the Easter event, we cannot now say that it was *historically* insignificant. Whatever its precise nature may have been, it provided the impetus for the movement that became the Christian Church. It has historical importance of the first magnitude. But this event, and its historical probability, do not have *religious* significance.

This statement flies directly in the face of what is probably the only consensus of Christians and non-Christians alike about the Christian faith: that it stands or falls on the resurrection of Jesus of Nazareth. But this consensus is wrong. We will examine the two areas in which the greatest importance is claimed for the resurrection: (1) the question of our salvation; and (2) the question of the identity of Jesus of Nazareth (which is of course related to the first question).

(1) Soteriological[2] Insignificance

"If Christ has not been raised, then our preaching is in vain and your faith is in vain." So says Paul in I Corinthians 15:14. He repeats this for emphasis just three verses later: "If Christ has not been raised, your faith is futile and you are still in your sins." Paul is saying quite clearly that salvation from sin and death is directly dependent upon the resurrection of Jesus of Nazareth.

This is probably a common belief, but it places more weight on the resurrection than it can logically bear. Even if we were to grant (for the sake of argument only) that God could or would intervene in this way in earthly affairs, God's resurrection of this one person cannot logically support the likelihood of salvation for the rest of us: (A) It cannot prove that God is able to save us from death and grant us eternal life; (B) it cannot guarantee that God is interested in doing this; and (C) it does not even show that God will forgive our sins.

(A) The resurrection of Jesus of Nazareth does not even show that God was able to grant eternal life to this one individual, much less to the rest of us. At the most, it shows that God was able to keep one person alive for a short time after physical death. That Jesus went on to *eternal* life is certainly not proven by his few days or weeks of post-death appearances on earth. This can only be accepted on faith. Of course, if we believe that God is creator/maintainer of the universe then we can have faith that God somehow preserves our lives after death. But we ought to be able to have this faith without demanding a proof—for no proof is

---

[2]Soteriological means having to do with salvation.

possible—and quite independently of whether or not Jesus was raised from the dead. (If there *were* a connection between eternal life and a bodily resurrection shortly after death, this would be of little solace to the rest of us.)

(B) Even if the resurrection of Jesus of Nazareth could show that God could grant eternal life—which it doesn't—it still gives us no indication that God has any intention of granting this to any of the rest of us. After all, none of the rest of us happens to be Jesus Christ. (Again, we could note the apparent dearth of resurrections recently.)

Assuredly, we have faith that God loves us and that therefore God will grant us eternal life if this is possible and is best for us. But again, this is an article of faith. It can neither be proven or disproven by the truth or falsity of the resurrection accounts.

(C) It will be claimed that the resurrection of Jesus is vital to our salvation because the resurrection showed God's acceptance of the sacrifice of Jesus on the cross. This of course ties in with the idea that Jesus died *in order* that God could forgive our sins and so grant us eternal life. This is wrong (see Chapter 14). But even if you believed that since Jesus died on the cross, *now* God can forgive your sins, and you will be saved if you repent and believe—what does the resurrection add to that? If God will forgive you for Jesus' sake, isn't that true whether or not Jesus was raised?

Or to look at it another way: what is there in the resurrection of this one man which implies the forgiveness of anyone? What is there in the Easter event itself that indicates this? Nothing. Only by referring to the preaching of Jesus (and the Church) do we hear about God's forgiveness. We can only accept on faith that God forgives and accepts those who repent and turn. Jesus tells us this before the resurrection and entirely apart from it.

(2) Christological Insignificance

It could be argued that Paul was saying something else. In saying, "If Christ has not been raised, then our preaching is in vain and your faith is in vain," perhaps Paul meant not that our salvation depends on the resurrection itself, but rather that our salvation depends on Jesus being the Son of God, and this is what depends on the resurrection. After all, Paul says that Jesus was "designated Son of God . . . by his resurrection from the dead". (Romans 1:4) Indeed, do we not depend on the resurrection to show us that Jesus of Nazareth is the Christ, the Son of God? Isn't this what makes him the Messiah?

Certainly the Easter event played an important and probably decisive role in convincing his disciples that Jesus was "he who is to come", the promised one, the Messiah. We can understand why this was so. They had a common sense that accepted the idea of a God who intervened in human affairs on specific occasions for specific purposes. The resurrection of a dead person—whatever its precise nature—could be seen as a miraculous act of God. Furthermore, at that time many Jews (though not all) believed that God would effect a general resurrection at the end of the world. So they were prepared to recognize a resurrection as an act of God. And certainly the resurrection of one particular individual in advance of this could indicate this person's importance or merit in the eyes of God.

But would a resurrection naturally prove to Jesus' contemporaries that he was the Messiah? Did it make him the Christ? No. There was no expectation or tradition that would identify a resurrected person as the Messiah. And in many cases Jesus of Nazareth was the antithesis of the messianic warrior-king prophesied by Isaiah and others (see Isaiah 9 and 11). Why then was he given this title by his disciples? Perhaps because he was crucified by Pilate as "King of the Jews", a messianic title. Or perhaps because none of the possible titles fit very well—there were a number to choose from—and "Messiah" was the pre-eminent one.

In any case, we have already acknowledged the great historical importance of the resurrection. And part of this importance was that it convinced his disciples that Jesus was the Messiah. But does this mean that the resurrection *made* him the Messiah? And can the resurrection serve to convince us today that Jesus was the Messiah? These are two separate if related questions. The answer to both is "no".

There is no good reason to believe that the resurrection is what made Jesus the Messiah. There are no prophecies, no rules, that say this is how someone is "made" Messiah. And to say that Jesus was made Messiah by the resurrection is to say that he was *not* the Messiah during his earthly ministry.

Of course, if you wish to believe that it was the resurrection that made him the Messiah, this is your privilege. But you need to be aware that there are no good reasons for this belief.

But what about the resurrection as proof to *us* that he was indeed the Messiah? We have said that it convinced the disciples. But the fact that a bodily resurrection could have certain implications for people of the first century does not necessarily mean it can have these same implications for us today.

The return to life of a dead person today would be a great scientific curiosity. We would marvel at it. Suppose there were physicians in attendance who verified that indeed there were no clinical signs of life, and two days later this individual was alive: we would be amazed, but we would not feel compelled to speak of angels or to wonder if this person were a chosen one of God. It would tell us nothing of the validity of his or her religious teachings.

Our common sense does not allow us to believe that God intervenes in our finite physical processes in this way. Therefore a resurrection cannot be an act of God. And therefore it cannot say anything about Jesus' identity as Messiah. It has no Christological significance, just as it has no soteriological significance.

Is the resurrection then unimportant? I am not saying that. It was of critical historical importance to the genesis of Christianity. It may have this same historical importance in the personal faith of some individuals today if it helps them to understand the nature of God's love or the message of Jesus of Nazareth. And certainly the resurrection remains as an important symbol of God's love and of the triumph of love over death.

But while our belief in a loving God can be symbolized by the resurrection, it cannot *depend* on the resurrection. Neither our belief in salvation through faith, not our confidence in God's forgiveness, nor our affirmation that Jesus of Nazareth is the Christ, can depend on the resurrection. It proves none of these. It is essential to none of these. It simply can't bear the weight that Paul, and so many since him, have wanted to put on it.

III: The Consequences

Thus far we have concluded that the resurrection of Jesus of Nazareth (or something that resembled this) is historically probable and historically of great importance. I have confessed my own belief that whatever happened can reasonably be called a resurrection. But we have also concluded that it is not, and cannot be, of religious significance to us. What are the consequences of this?

1. At the end of the last chapter we concluded that in order for a belief about Jesus to be required for a Christian it must be either implied in his basic message or necessary for a positive response to this message. The resurrection is not implied in his teachings about God and faith. And since it is not religiously significant, a belief in it cannot be necessary to respond to Jesus' message.

2. Therefore, if someone does not believe in the resurrection, neither we nor they themselves can consider them not to be Christian on this basis alone. We can only accuse them of poor historical judgment.

3. Therefore those who cannot believe in the bodily resurrection of Jesus of Nazareth cannot use this as an excuse to reject Christianity. They must respond to Jesus' message the same as anyone else, and either accept or reject his call to turn to God and love their neighbor.

4. Since Christianity does not depend on either the nature or the historicity of the resurrection, this should allow for a less emotional and therefore more fruitful consideration of the subject. And by affirming our common sense view that a bodily resurrection could not be a miraculous interventionist act of God, we can allow for the historical probability of the resurrection without denying our common sense.

5. Finally, while ruling out any religious significance for a bodily resurrection, we leave open the possibility that, to the extent the Easter event was an event of spiritual insight, it just may have had something to do with God.

Now, however, it is time to turn to another belief about Jesus of Nazareth that is often considered to be necessary. In Chapter 7 we consider the question of his divinity.

CHAPTER 7: THE QUESTION OF THE DIVINITY OF JESUS OF NAZARETH

"I do not pray for these only, but also for those who believe in me through their word, that they may all be one; even as thou, Father, art in me, and I in thee . . . that they may be one even as we are one, I in them and thou in me." (John 17:20–23)

In considering the question of Jesus' divinity the first thing we should do is try to state clearly the orthodox doctrine. This is not as easy as you may think. Even among people who consider themselves to have a perfectly orthodox belief in the Trinity and the Incarnation there is a good deal of confusion as to precisely what these mean. This should not be surprising, for the doctrine of Jesus as "God the Son" includes either some extremely fine nuances or (depending on your point of view) a good dose of contradiction and vagueness.

Nevertheless, I need to confess that I stand in awe and admiration of the orthodox dogma, particularly in light of the world-view, the Greek philosophy and the doctrinal debates that served as its background. I do not find it to be necessary or helpful for us today, but I admire it as the best possible answer to the doctrinal needs of its day.[1]

If we extract it from the Greek philosophical language in which it was first framed, we might state the orthodox position as follows: "There is one God, one divine being. This one God, however, has three aspects, or presents itself as three "persons": the Father, the Son, and the Holy Spirit. This is the Trinity, the one triune (three-in-one) God. The second person of the Trinity is called God the Son or the "Logos" (the Greek word often translated as "the Word", as in John 1). As an aspect of God the Logos has existed since the beginning, and at the birth of Jesus of Nazareth became incarnate in this human being. In this one individual

---

[1]The reader is recommended to *The Emergence of the Catholic Tradition* by Jaroslav Pelikan (University of Chicago Press, 1971) or *A History of Christian Doctrine,* Hubert Cunliffe-Jones, ed., (Fortress Press, 1980). John Cobb, Jr., also has a nice summary in Chapter 9 of *Christ in a Pluralistic Age* (The Westminster Press, 1975). None of these individuals should be held responsible for anything I say in this chapter.

there was a truly divine nature and also a truly human nature. The human was not made divine, nor the divine human, nor were the two somehow mixed, but both were in this one person. Nor can we say that the divine nature in Jesus did one thing and the human nature in him another, for all actions and experiences were those of the one individual, Jesus Christ, both human and divine."

This formulation satisfied a number of requirements. First, by the time it was formally adopted there was a long-standing tradition of worshipping Christ. This, of course, required that he be divine.

Second, it met the needs of most of the contemporary doctrines of salvation. These depended either on (1) the atoning sacrifice on our behalf of a perfect being, or else on (2) the incorruptible and eternal having come into our corruptible and finite flesh. The former required that Jesus who was crucified be divine; the latter required that God became human. The Incarnation satisfied both of these.

Third, the Scriptures seem to speak of Jesus in most instances as human, but in some cases as divine. The Doctrine of the Incarnation allows both of these to be true.

Fourth, it was taken for granted by the Greco-Roman philosophical world that God was immutable and could not suffer pain. By postulating the existence of two natures in this one person, the Doctrine of the Incarnation allowed one to say that the suffering of Jesus as reported in the Gospels was experienced by the one human-and-divine person through his human nature, which avoided a run-in with the prevailing wisdom of the time.

Thus the Incarnation met the needs of its day for worship, soteriology, and evangelism in a way not incompatible with the Bible. It represents a remarkable theological achievement.

The Incarnation Reconsidered

This doctrine of the nature of Jesus of Nazareth was not firmly fixed until the Council of Chalcedon in 451. Nevertheless, from the end of the first century it seems to have been generally accepted by the Church that Jesus was divine in one manner or another. On top of this, the Chalcedonian formulation itself now has more than fifteen centuries of tenure. Thus, one of two common reactions to it (when people bother to think about it at all) is this:

"How can anyone doubt the consensus of the Church, developed in the early years of the faith from the Biblical witness, confirmed in the teachings of scholars and saints through the centuries, and tested and proven in the living out of millions of faithful lives?"

However, the other common reaction to the Doctrine of the Incarnation reacts to its antiquity in a different way:

"How can anyone pay any attention to a doctrine that grew out of a

Greek conceptual system being imposed on Jewish Scriptures, that was as foreign to Jesus as it is to us, that depends on concepts and a common sense that have gone the way of the Roman Empire, and that is about as understandable as if it were still written in ancient Greek?"

Both of these reactions are extreme, of course. And both ask too much of us. The first asks us not to think for ourselves, while the second asks us to ignore the past and not even consider beliefs which are still held by many contemporary Christians. Whether or not you share my admiration of the orthodox doctrine, we have to recognize that it represents an interpretation of God and Jesus which not only has had the allegiance of the vast majority of Christians in the history of the Church, but which also has a proven track record as a doctrine which can help people to lead faithful lives following the teaching and example of the Christ. Only for the gravest of reasons, and only with an appropriate sense of awe, ought one to dare to challenge this traditional understanding.

The reasons are grave indeed. So in spite of my trepidation, and in awe of tradition, and knowing that this gives an impression of audacity when what I feel is rather an obligation that I cannot avoid, I am impelled by my understanding (such as I am capable of) to raise this challenge. I find myself a servant or even a prisoner of the truth that I feel, to which I have no choice but to bear witness. In so doing, I find it necessary to challenge the orthodox doctrine of the divinity of Jesus of Nazareth, the Christ. I do this on four grounds:

(1) The orthodox doctrine is no more Biblical than some other interpretations of Jesus' nature, and is in fact less Biblical than some.

(2) Even if this doctrine once made sense to the philosophical heirs of Plato and Aristotle—a question beyond our purview here—it no longer makes sense to us. I am not just saying that it is difficult to understand. I am saying that it cannot meaningfully be said, that it is impossible.

(3) If it could make sense, which it can't, its meaning would violate our common sense.

(4) Last but not least, this doctrine is unnecessary. It is unnecessary to the message of Jesus or the centrality of Jesus. Furthermore, for some people it actually stands in the way of their receiving the message.

1. The Orthodox Doctrine Is Not Required By The Bible

When the Church fathers were formulating their Christology they were constrained by the fact that they were Biblical literalists. Because they took for granted that all scriptural references to Jesus were true, they had to come up with *one* doctrine of his nature that was in harmony with *all* these different passages. Since at times Jesus is spoken of in very human terms, and on occasion is spoken of as divine, the only solution was to conceive of him as somehow combining both the human and the divine.

In contrast to this, the actual (and liberating) fact is that we do not have in the New Testament a single, monolithic interpretation of Jesus. Rather, we have a diversity of interpretations. In this regard the New Testament demonstrates both the unity in essentials and the liberty in interpretation that are appropriate to the Christian Church.

The Gospels are unanimous about the centrality of Jesus the Christ: his central importance to our understanding of God and as our norm for living in right relation to God. But while they all agree on this centrality, the different New Testament authors have different ways of conceptualizing and explaining it. Matthew views Jesus as "super-prophet", the man chosen by God to fulfill the Old Testament prophecies, in the tradition of Moses and Elijah but surpassing even them in importance and authority as the culmination of the prophetic line. Mark and Luke differ from Matthew in emphasis: Mark depicts Jesus as a rather secretive Messiah, chosen by God to inaugurate the Kingdom of God, while Luke highlights more clearly Jesus' mission to bring the gospel to people of all stations and all nations.

John is the only Gospel to portray Jesus as different in *nature* from the prophets, as more than the culminating high point of the succession of people called by God and commissioned with special tasks. Especially in the prologue (John 1:1–18), it is clear that John considers Jesus to be more than human. He shares somehow in divinity, but in a way that is not very clear, and which seems to owe much to Jewish "wisdom literature" (see Proverbs 8:22–31). Jesus was pre-existent as the "Logos", which is translated "word" but which means much more than that. The Logos is divine ("was God"), but is not *the* Deity ("was with God"). Jesus himself is quoted as claiming oneness with God, but when he is alive he always claims this same oneness with his disciples. So in sum, while it is clear that John considers Jesus to be more than human, it is not clear exactly what he has in mind.

Paul, as usual, says different things in different places. In Romans 1:4 he says that Jesus was "designated Son of God . . . by his resurrection from the dead". This implies an "adoptionist Christology"—that is, that Jesus was a mortal man who after his faithful obedience to the cross was *then* designated (adopted) Son of God. In Philippians 2:5–7, however, he says of Jesus that "though he was in the form of God, did not count equality with God a thing to be grasped, but emptied himself, taking the form of a servant, being born in the likeness of man". This has many possible interpretations, but all point to a pre-existent Jesus who was more than human and somehow like God. In Colossians 1:15–16 Paul reaffirms Jesus' pre-existence in words that (like the prologue to John) echo wisdom literature, as he through whom all things were created.

The non-Pauline Letter to the Hebrews also affirms this of Jesus, and goes on to say that he "bears the very stamp of [God's] nature". (Hebrews 1:3) But the author speaks of Jesus not as God, but as son and heir, as higher than the angels. What we have here is a "ladder of being" not uncommon in ancient times: there is God at the top, with human beings below God but above all other animals, and there are also beings above humans. Angels, for instance, would fall in here. They are more divine than we but less divine than God. What Hebrews does (and perhaps John and Paul do as well) is to place Jesus next to the top of this hierarchy, below God but above angels and everybody else.

Now if you were to ask which of those is *the* Biblical position on the nature of Jesus of Nazareth, the answer would be "none of them". Instead, each of them represents a Biblical alternative for explaining the central importance of Jesus. And since we are not burdened with the need to come up with one good interpretation that incorporates all of these—as is the literalist—we are free to choose for ourselves the one which best helps us to understand Jesus and to respond to his message. In fact, we can go further than this. Since the constant in the New Testament is the centrality of Jesus and his message, and not any particular explanation of why and how he is central, we are then free to interpret this centrality in a way that meets the needs of our own day and our own common sense, so long as we remain compatible with the basic thrust of Jesus' teaching.

In fact, *only* if we allow for the introduction of other non-Biblical conceptualizations can we accept the orthodox doctrines of the Trinity and the Incarnation as legitimate Christian options. It may be argued that these doctrines represent the development of Biblical ideas, but neither of them can be found in Scripture in their orthodox form. Obviously, if we allow one set of interpretations that is developed from positions found in the New Testament then we must allow others as well, so long as they are compatible with Jesus' message.

2. The Orthodox Doctrine Is Impossible

The doctrine of the Incarnation, that Jesus of Nazareth was fully God and fully human, is simply impossible. It does not make sense. The words cannot be put together this way without doing violence either to their meaning or to the rules of logic.

To be human is to be finite, limited in knowledge, fallible, and imperfect. To be human also means to be aware of one's finitude, and of one's separation from others and from God—sometimes painfully aware. If Jesus was human, then he was all of these—and indeed this is how the Gospels portray him, experiencing anger, fatigue, uncertainty, reluctance, pain and even death.

To be God—not just to share a spark of the divine, nor to be in God's image, nor to be a lesser divine being like the angels, nor any of the other possible subversions of the orthodox doctrine,[2] but really to be God—in any Christian understanding, this means to be eternal and un-

[2]Those who speak of God as immanent in all of us but *fully* immanent in Jesus of Nazareth present an alternative which escapes some of the problems of the orthodox explana-

limited, to be perfect in love and understanding. Now, either Jesus of Nazareth was limited, fallible and imperfect, or else he was unlimited, infallible and perfect. These two sets of attributes are opposites of each other. You can't have it both ways; he was either one or the other. You can't say of one person that he was both.

"Ah!" some will say. "That's the paradox!" No, it isn't a paradox. This is a very important point, so please take special note: a paradox is something which seems impossible but which is demonstrably true. Thus, it was a paradox when some scientist carefully analyzed bumblebees and concluded that according to the laws of physics they couldn't fly. There was contradiction and apparent impossibility, but bumblebees kept on flying.

However, for an individual to be both perfect and imperfect is the reverse of this: it may seem true to some, but it is demonstrably impossible. And not just impossible according to our understanding of the laws of nature, which can be wrong (as with the bumblebee), but impossible according to the rules of logic upon which all our reasoning is based.

To say someone is both perfect and imperfect is like saying that you saw a square circle. This is an impossibility. Are you saying the circle was not round, in which case it was not a circle? Or are you saying the square was circular? This is not a paradox; this is meaningless nonsense, however imaginative it might be.

To say someone is both perfect and imperfect at the same time is to say that "X" and "not-X" can both be true. This is either to abandon the meaning of these words or else to abandon logic, and in either case this means we are speaking nonsense that can have no meaning for us.

The orthodox will reply that Jesus was limited, fallible and imperfect with regard to his human nature, but unlimited, infallible and perfect in his divine nature. This sounds nice, but what does it mean to have two natures? If it means having two minds and two wills and two characters, one perfect and the other imperfect, then it means there were two separate persons occupying this one body (or else Jesus was schizophrenic). On the other hand, if this was really the one person Jesus the Christ, as orthodoxy claims, then either this person was perfect or he was not. Either he was capable of sin or he was not. Either he had limited knowledge or he did not.

For instance, either he knew—not believed, but *knew*—that he would be raised on the second day after his death, or he did not know this. If he knew this then he did not face death as any other human, and he was not taking any real risk in allowing himself to be caught, tried and crucified. So in this regard he could not be considered fully human. If, on the other

tion of Jesus' centrality. But one must keep in mind that this is *not* the orthodox doctrine of the Incarnation, which represents Jesus as different from us in kind, not just in degree, and which does not say that God was *in* Jesus but that God *became* Jesus.

hand, he did not know he would be raised, and faced death in faith but without this knowledge, then how could he also be God? If the divine nature in him knew he would be raised, but *he* did not know this, then it was not *his* divine nature. If the divine in him knew something he did not, we are back to two persons.

So to say that Jesus was fully human and fully divine is not a paradox. It is instead like talking about a round square: it sounds good, and makes an interesting combination of images, but it is in the end without discernable meaning. Some people have tried to alleviate this by saying that his person was constituted by God the Son and his humanity was "impersonal". But this does not help much. Impersonal humanity is like a square without four corners: it might do better at being round, but it is no longer a square.

Others would respond that the problem here is that I am using words in their human meanings, whereas I ought to realize that when applied to God these words gain a different and deeper meaning. Let me say this: if you wish to redefine some of these words, that's fine, as long as you can tell us the new meanings that you are using. The usual practice, however, seems to be to say that while one cannot say precisely what these new meanings are, one is nevertheless sure that they fit together in a way that makes sense. This, of course, is simply an effort to duck the requirements of logic. But if you do not know the meanings of the words which you are applying to Jesus, then you are merely saying "Jesus is X" and "Jesus is Y", X and Y being unknowns. This, of course, is to say nothing at all.

Even if this little matter of logic were surmountable—which it is not— and we were to admit that it is *possible* for Jesus, a human being, to be fully divine, we would still have to point out that he would not be fully human in the same sense as you and I. You see, I—and, I suspect, you— do not happen also to be God. I have the feeling that this is not simply a minor point, but that a central fact of the human predicament is precisely that of being and feeling separate from the infinite and eternal God. If this is so, then also to be God is not to experience the human predicament. And if Jesus did not experience our predicament, not only was he not fully human but his teachings and example are of questionable relevance to us.

3. It Violates Our Common Sense

You probably know what I'm going to say. Even if it were logically possible for Jesus to be fully God and fully human, it would still violate our common sense. If our common sense cannot conceive of God as an interventionist zapper then we certainly cannot conceive of God as somehow zapping in and *becoming* a particular human being. This might be appropriate for Zeus or Apollo, but not for the God of the Universe.

Mind you, I'm not saying that Jesus wasn't more in touch with God or more receptive to God than most. I think he was, as I'll try later to explain. And I'm not saying that God wasn't in him, working in him or through him. All I'm saying is that if I can't believe that someone being struck by a thunderbolt is an act of God, then neither can I believe that the man Jesus was God in person. It's the same common sense.

4. It Is Unnecessary and Even Unhelpful

We have already seen that the orthodox belief in the divinity of Jesus of Nazareth is (1) only one of the possible ways of explaining his centrality that can be developed from the New Testament; (2) does not fall within the limits of what is logically possible; and (3) is contrary to our common sense. Besides all this, it is also quite unnecessary.

In Chapter 5 we established our two Rules of Christian Belief. Rule #2 states that a belief can be considered necessary for the Christian faith only if it is strongly implied in Jesus' message or else is necessary to the acceptance of this message. Is either of these the case here?

Regarding Jesus' message, there is a very impressive consensus among Biblical scholars that (whatever John and Paul might say) Jesus did *not* claim that he himself was God, either explicitly or implicitly. I can find no reason to challenge this consensus, and much to support it. So a belief in Jesus' divinity cannot on this account be considered necessary.

Could it be necessary, then, to believe that Jesus is divine in order to accept his message? Perhaps. If you believed that the love and forgiveness and new life in God that Jesus offered would not be possible unless a perfect being suffered and died for us, or unless the incorruptible Deity entered the sphere of corruptible human flesh, then for you a belief in Jesus' divinity might be necessary before you could respond positively to his message. However, not everyone believes one of these, so not everyone finds it necessary to believe in Jesus' divinity. Jesus didn't preach that it was necessary; his disciples (according to Matthew, Mark, and Luke-Acts) didn't find it necessary; I don't find it necessary; and many committed Christians through the centuries have not found it necessary. If *you* find it necessary then you are certainly welcome to believe it. Belief in Jesus' divinity is certainly a Christian alternative, even though it is mistaken. (See the next chapter for the distinction between being right and being Christian.) But please don't jump to the conclusion that because you find this belief necessary for *your* acceptance of Jesus' message, it must therefore be required of all of us. This does not follow.

Indeed, there are many people who will be able to accept Jesus' message only if it is *not* attached to a claim of his divinity. If we tie his message to a particular, unnecessary and illogical interpretation of his centrality, we are preventing this message from being a live option for people who might readily accept another, just as Biblically authentic, interpretation. As Christians we do not have the right to withhold the gospel from people in this way. Many centuries ago the Church used Greek philosophical concepts to evangelize the Greco-Roman world. Does not evangelism now call for an interpretation in keeping with our *own* common sense?

Furthermore, by regarding Jesus as fully human and therefore as *not* divine, we make it possible for his life to serve as an example for us. You see, if this person who sought out sinners, loved the unlovable, and forgave his enemies even as he died on the cross—if he was divine, then I can shrug off his example as possible only for people who happen also to be God, and dismiss his teachings as fitting only for those who do not share my own predicament, that of being only human. On the other hand, if this man was human as I am, if he was a limited, feeling, fallible creature like myself, and he was able to live in this way and love in this way and give of himself in this way—then so can I! And his teachings are then relevant, for they come from someone who shared my predicament. For me, and to many, Jesus' relevance as an example and teacher is much more important to our acceptance of his message than is his divinity.

Where Do We Go From Here?

If Jesus is not divine, then where does his authority come from? How do we give him such a central place of importance? Who then do we say that he is? These are the questions we must take up next.

First, however: I have now stated the most serious of my differences with orthodox doctrine. I have said that with regard to the Incarnation it is inadequate, senseless and unnecessary, but also that I believe it is still a valid Christian alternative. This, then, would be an appropriate place to explore the relationship between doctrine and faith, and to explain the difference between being right and being Christian.

PART THREE

THE COMMON SENSE AND FAITHFUL ALTERNATIVE

In this section I put forth my proposal for a new interpretation of our faith that is in keeping with both the message of Jesus the Christ and our common sense. In Chapter Ten we pursue the theme of Jesus as the functional Christ, as he through whom we focus our understanding and faith, he whose life and message are central to the way we choose to live. We see that this is not only indisputable, but also that since Jesus is the answer to our deepest question—the question of meaning—this is also to claim for him the most that could possibly be claimed, a special role that can only be called sacred.

In Chapter Eleven we prepare for our discussion of God. We ask whether our common sense allows for this at all and demonstrate that in spite of a few extremists, it does indeed. Then we look at the straightforward rules of language for talking about God or anyone else, and at what kind of verification is appropriate.

In Chapter Twelve we finally talk about God. We note some wondrous aspects of reality that point towards God— we are not looking for a magical "proof"—and we describe how we can speak of God acting. We briefly address a few questions about the nature of God before suggesting a few images that might help to communicate our understanding of God.

In Chapter Thirteen we are then able to consider the question of Jesus' authority. We put forth several reasons which support the choice of Jesus of Nazareth as our compass, but we recognize that in the final analysis it is a question of values, of the heart.

In Chapter Fourteen we begin a look at some more traditional doctrinal themes to see if we can offer a positive reconstruction for their use today. We conclude that we must continue our use of the concept of "sin", but that the ideas of "original sin" and "salvation" are too tied up with an unchristian view of God and must be discarded.

In Chapter Fifteen we continue reconstruction by proposing the category of Christian Myth as a positive category for those aspects of the Christian story which exemplify or reinforce Christian values but which can no longer be taken as true. There is no reason for this to be seen as a negative classification. We then look at various aspects of the Jesus story to see what would qualify.

Then we move on to Part Four, a consideration of the real stumbling block: living as a Christian.

CHAPTER 8:
BEING RIGHT vs. BEING CHRISTIAN
or
THE DISTINCTION BETWEEN
DOCTRINE AND FAITH

"Master, we saw a man casting out demons in your name, and we forbade him, because he does not follow with us." But Jesus said to him, "Do not forbid him." (Luke 9:48–49)

I have by now dismissed as wrong the beliefs of a vast number of Christians. But please note: I have *not* said that these beliefs are unchristian. All too often, lacking the charity and wisdom of him whom we call the Christ, we have labeled as unchristian those who do not believe as we do. We call into question the faith of those who do not follow with us, those who do not echo our particular doctrinal line. But it is very evident in the lives of those around us that there is no necessary connection between believing correct doctrine and living a life of faith. You know as well as I do that the two cannot be equated.

In this chapter I will try to do two things: first, examine the difference between faith and doctrine; and second, show why saying a belief is a valid Christian belief is not the same as saying it is "right" in the sense of being consistent with truth. This will show why the wrong beliefs do not necessarily make a person unchristian, and why believing all the right things does not necessarily make someone faithful.

I. Doctrine vs. Faith

A. Faith
In an important way our faith can be said to be parallel to our common sense. This common sense is made up of the presuppositions which we use as we try to understand the world, the assumptions we make as

we explain the workings of the universe. So, too, does faith consist of certain basic assumptions: assumptions about meaning and value, certain attitudes about the proper way to relate to people and to the world, and certain presuppositions about what is most important and most valuable in life.

Thus it is our faith that informs us that the most important goals in life are to love God and to love other people as ourselves. It is our faith that tells us that right relationship with others is more important than personal gain, and that honesty, integrity and kindness are more important than comfort, pleasure and wealth. These and similar presuppositions are obviously of crucial importance in determining our actions and our other beliefs.

Our faith generally also includes some assumptions (or "primary beliefs") about the metaphysical nature of the universe. These are assumptions about ultimate reality that support our presuppositions of meaning and value. We might, for instance, believe that there is a God who holds the same basic values as we do. Beliefs such as this give coherence to our value system and reinforce our faith-attitudes towards others and towards life. As such, these beliefs are "primary beliefs". They are included in the basic presuppositions that constitute our faith.

However, while faith can include certain basic beliefs and can express itself in beliefs, faith can never be *equated* with any particular set of beliefs. Faith is *not* just intellectual assent to a set of propositions. Faith is deeper than this, providing the underlying direction to one's life.

Faith also includes trust. Like faith, trust includes certain beliefs. It implies certain statements about whatever or whomever you trust. But trust, too, is more than this. Again, it is an attitude, a way of relating to people and to the world, a basic orientation that cannot be adequately captured in any group of statements.

Christian faith is the complex of attitudes and approaches that leads one into right relationship. It is the understanding of the heart that leads one to forgive instead of seeking vengeance, to love instead of hate, to be open to others instead of closed, to seek the good of all instead of just one's own well-being, to give of one's self and one's property for the good of others, and to feel that a God of love is pulling for all of these.

You have *Christian* faith when these basic attitudes are consciously and pre-eminently drawn from, based on, or focused by the teachings and example of Jesus whom we call the Christ or the body of the faithful that we call the Church, and when there is a deep commitment to living out these basic attitudes in your life.

Finally, we must note that even though our faith is primary—underlying our beliefs and actions—it is still subject to change. Just as with common sense, when our faith turns out to be inconsistent with our experience of reality, when the beliefs implicit in our faith just don't fit, then our faith must undergo some adjustments. These may be minor or they may be major, but they must be made. The only alternative is to sacrifice the honesty and integrity of our intellect.

B. Beliefs

The distinction I make is between "faith" and "doctrine". The former can include beliefs, the latter consists of them. But those which are a part of our faith I call "primary beliefs". These are not derived from other beliefs or values. They are generally not debatable; one either accepts or rejects them as the presuppositions for other beliefs. Examples of this would be our presupposition that it is better to do right than to do wrong, or a general assumption on how to distinguish one from the other.

Suppose one person believes that the right course of action to take is that which increases their own power or wealth, and another believes that the right course is that which helps others and advances the common good. When they disagree as to what it is right to do, any discussion they have about this would probably be very frustrating. There is no common ground to which to appeal—at least, none that is easily found. What we have here is a difference of faith, a clash of presuppositions or primary beliefs.

The beliefs that make up doctrine are not these primary beliefs. Instead, they either derive from these primary beliefs or else are constructed to explain them. It is this category of beliefs that we are contrasting to faith.

C. Doctrine

Whenever we try to explain our faith and put it into general concepts, whenever we put into words our other beliefs about religion, we have doctrine. And this is also where we run into common sense again. For when we use language and logic to state our beliefs and talk about our faith, we are applying our reason to our religion. We must be consistent with the common sense that underlies our reason just as we must be consistent with the faith that underlies our beliefs. Only then can our doctrine make sense and our reasoning be faithful. And the faith and common sense must be consistent with each other if we are to have continuity and integrity of self.

Thus, for instance, the central importance in our lives of the life and teachings of Jesus of Nazareth is a matter of faith. This importance is not an award we bestowed after a lengthy reasoning process nor a conclusion we reached by deduction. It is not subject to debate. As a result of upbringing, experience, relationships, learning, etc., it is a primary part of our system of value and meaning, of the way we orient our lives. The importance of Jesus of Nazareth in our lives is not subject to the rules of logic. It just is, as a matter of value.

On the other hand, the way we choose to *explain* this centrality of Jesus, the way we conceptualize it and put it into words—this is a matter of doctrine. This explanation—whether it refers to the nature of Jesus, or his role, or something else—is subject to all the requirements of logic, consistency and factuality that apply to any statement. Its implications and assumptions must be examined and are open to challenge and debate. And, not least in importance, we look for any such statement of doctrine to make sense, to fit with our common sense.

Thus it is that we can question whether doctrine is right or wrong, true or false, in a way that is quite different from the way we might question somebody's faith. We might challenge a doctrine if we didn't think that it represented the truth. But if we wondered about someone's faith, it would be because of the way they acted. We would approach the two in quite dissimilar ways.

With this in mind, let us now make another distinction by examining how the question of whether a doctrine is right or wrong is different from the question of whether it is a valid Christian belief.

II. Being Right vs. Being Christian

We said earlier that the purpose of religion is to orient us toward right relationship with God and with our neighbors. Consequently, we cannot judge the validity of religious beliefs by asking whether they are true or whether they are consistent with some other beliefs or principles. Instead, we must judge the validity of religious beliefs by asking whether they help fulfill this purpose. If a belief helps lead to right relationship with God and neighbor then it can be considered a valid religious belief.

What is this? Am I saying that we cannot judge the validity of a religious belief by its truth or falseness? Did we not just say that doctrine is subject to the requirements of logic and truth and common sense?

Indeed we did, for indeed it is. But by examining a doctrine's consistency with reason and truth we can only judge whether it is right in the sense of being factual or truthful. What I am saying now is that the question of its validity as a religious belief is an altogether separate question.

Do I, the champion of reason and common sense, maintain that reason, believability and even truth cannot judge the validity of religious tenets? Exactly so. Beliefs that appropriately fill the proper function of religious beliefs, that promote right relationship, must be considered to be valid religious beliefs regardless of their truth.

For an example, let us look at the Book of Mormon. If one examines it objectively there is no way to escape the conclusion that it is a pious fraud. It consists of cheap imitation King James verbiage about events that never happened in places that never existed, all supposedly translated from a mysterious book of gold that conveniently disappeared. Nevertheless—now that I've alienated several million Latter Day Saints—I must admit that I am impressed by the number of Mormons who have a faith that leads to right relationship. Since for many this faith is accompanied by a set of doctrines that includes belief in the literal truth of the Book of Mormon, we have to say that this can be a valid religious belief. Even though a belief in the Book of Mormon is mistaken, it is a valid religious belief so long as it is an integral part of a set of beliefs that promotes the right relationship which is the purpose of religion.

Similarly, the belief in the literal truth of the whole Bible is just plain wrong. But if this particular belief helps someone to take seriously the words of Jesus of Nazareth, and so helps orient them toward a life of love and service for others, toward right relationship, then I have to say that for this person this is a valid Christian belief. Remember Christian Belief Rule #1: a belief is appropriate for Christians if it is consistent with the message of Jesus the Christ and with the centrality of this message. It can be appropriate in this way without necessarily being true.

The Question of Truth

Does the truth or falseness of a religious belief have no bearing at all on its validity? Once all the disclaimers have been made—that many religious beliefs are supremely difficult to test for truth because they refer to the supernatural or to that which it is beyond our mental powers to discern, or because (in the case of faith) they are values and not truth-claims—once all this has been said, we still have to admit that yes, of course the question of truth enters in here. But it does so in a restricted, very personal way. A religious belief can only be valid for you, can only serve to orient you to right relationship to God and neighbor, if this belief has the ring of truth for *you*.

This has an equally important corollary. What does not seem true to one person may indeed seem true to another. Therefore a belief which we are convinced is false can be a valid religious belief for someone else, if indeed it helps to lead them into right relationship. Thus the question of truth is limited to this function here: a religious belief can only be valid for someone who perceives this belief to be true.

One Faith, Many Doctrines

Each of us, of course, considers our own opinions and beliefs to be right. Otherwise they wouldn't be our beliefs. Naturally, then, we have to maintain that anyone who believes differently than we do is wrong. Nevertheless, I am quite convinced that many of these "wrong" and mistaken people, past and present, were and are dedicated Christians. It does not matter that we and they disagree on minor or even major aspects of Christian doctrine. Nor does it matter if you and I disagree in this way. What matters is whether a person lives a life directed towards right relationship with God and neighbor, with attitudes and understandings drawn from Jesus the Christ. This is what it means to have Christian faith.

If we were to say of someone that they are not Christian, we would mean specifically that their lives are not ordered in this way. This need not mean that they are better than anyone else or worse than anyone else. It means only that they do not have the values and attitudes of Jesus the Christ self-consciously at the center of their lives. To say that someone is Christian or not Christian is descriptive, not pejorative. The exception to this, of course, is the person who professes to be a Christian. If we say they are not, they will feel judged. Whether or not you profess to be Christian is up to you. But if you profess this without living accordingly, then you will be judged—not by anyone else, but by your own life—to be a hypocrite.

Since it is the faith that marks us as Christians, the life self-consciously lived in love of God and neighbor according to Jesus' precepts, then we can disagree on doctrines and still share this faith. What matters most is the centrality of the Christ in our lives, not the doctrine with which we explain this centrality.

So let us disagree and argue about doctrine. We can do this and still admit that the other person's mistaken doctrines are valid religious beliefs. And certainly doctrine is important enough to deserve our study and debate, for it is the way we try to understand and explain our faith. But at the same time we need to recognize that doctrine is *not* faith, and that the faith which unites us is more important than the doctrine which divides us.

After considering some of the traditional answers to the question of "Who is Jesus?" we will now move on to my conception of the centrality of Jesus of Nazareth. This is my explanation, my doctrine, of this distinguishing mark of our faith.

CHAPTER 9: WHO IS JESUS OF NAZARETH?

"He asked his disciples, 'Who do men say that I am?' And they told him, 'John the Baptist; others say Elijah; and others, one of the prophets.' And he asked them, 'But who do you say that I am?' Peter answered him, 'You are the Christ.' " (Mark 8:27–29)

If we do not claim that Jesus is God, then how do we explain his importance? How do we interpret the fact of his centrality to our faith? What concepts or images do we use? Who then do we say that he is? Having rejected the title of "God the Son", it is appropriate to begin by examining the other commonly used traditional titles: Savior, Lord and Master, Son of God, Messiah, and Christ.

1. Savior of the World

But when Christ appeared as a high priest . . . he entered once for all into the Holy Place, taking not the blood of goats and calves but his own blood, thus securing an eternal redemption. For if the sprinkling of defiled persons with the blood of goats and bulls and with the ashes of a heifer sanctifies for the purification of flesh, how much more will the blood of Christ, who through the eternal Spirit offered himself without blemish to God, purify your conscience from dead works to serve the living God. (Hebrews 9:11–14)

This passage contains the combination of Jesus' nature (as sinless) and role (as sacrifice) that is central to the traditional idea of Jesus as Savior: he was a person without sin, and by offering himself up in our place as a perfect sacrifice he has secured salvation for those who join themselves to him by faith. We are saved from sin and death by his blood, so he is our Savior.

We can see that this might make sense to someone brought up in the ancient Jewish tradition in which an unblemished animal was sacrificed to God to make atonement for the sins of the people, and in which the

iniquities of Israel were all put on the head of a goat which was then
driven out into the wilderness, taking the people's sins with it. And
certainly we are familiar with this view as a traditional Christian theme:
Jesus died for our sins. He did this so that we might be forgiven and
reconciled to God. The implication of this is that without Jesus' death
we could *not* be forgiven. Sometimes this is made explicit: God could
not or would not forgive us until the blameless Jesus took our sins upon
himself and suffered in our stead.

This may not make much sense to those of us who don't sacrifice
other living things to atone for our sins. Entirely aside from this, however, this view that Jesus is the Savior because he saved us from eternal
punishment by dying for our sins is untenable for three reasons.

First and foremost, it gives us a repugnant and unchristian picture of
God. If God demanded the death of an innocent and blameless person
before forgiving anybody, if God turned away even from those who repented until someone *else* suffered for their sins, if God demanded the
pain and blood of the cross before admitting anyone into right relationship . . . what kind of blood-thirsty, sadistic being would this be? This is
not a God of love or even a God of justice. This is a picture of some
demonic pagan deity, not the God whose love and forgiveness were
preached by Jesus of Nazareth, who reached out first and foremost to
those who were sinners.

Secondly, this idea of Jesus as Savior presents a despicable and unbib-
lical view of humankind. It maintains that as sinful men and women we
are so fallen and degenerate and unworthy as to be totally without hope
of reconciliation with God, unless God in a gracious act of divine imagination pretends that our sinfulness has disappeared, that it has somehow
been removed by the execution of Jesus of Nazareth. (This, when you get
right down to it, is the meaning of justification through grace.) Now, we
must certainly admit that people are capable of great evil. But just as
certainly, to think of people as worthless in the eyes of God is directly to
contradict the insights of the great prophets, the teaching that "God so
loved the world", and Jesus' understanding of the great worth of each
and every human being.

Thirdly, the idea that there could be no forgiveness until Jesus saved us
by dying as a sacrifice on our behalf is contradicted by the simple fact
that Jesus himself proclaimed forgiveness during his own lifetime. He
didn't tell people that they were forgiven "as of Passover the year after
next" or that they were worthless and without hope until the divine
bloodlust had been satisfied. He simply said, "Your sins are forgiven."
Right then and there. And I suspect he knew what he was about.

Now it is no doubt true that there are people who call Jesus "Savior"
who do not think of him as substituting for us on the cross to propitiate
a bloodthirsty deity. But for me the title of "Savior" is so tied up with a

repugnant picture of God and with an unchristian view of humanity as totally worthless, that I just cannot accept this as a suitable title for Jesus of Nazareth.

2. Lord and Master

"Lord" and "master" are both terms that were widely used in society until recent centuries. Students would address teachers this way, slaves their owners, and servants their employers. Those of lower social status would address those of higher status this way, whether a serf to a local landowner or a duke to a king.

These titles have virtually disappeared from use in the modern democracies. I doubt that any American would ever call *anyone* "lord" or "master". So besides having a certain antiquarian charm, applying these titles to Jesus would have two benefits: it would attribute a unique status to Jesus, since we no longer use these of anyone else. And it would give us a little humility on our own part, which we must confess would do many of us Americans some good.

I have a trio of qualms, however, which prevents me from being comfortable with this pair of titles (and also from speaking of Jesus as "king"). The first qualm is based on our need to encourage our own servanthood. We can do this by lifting up and emphasizing the servanthood of Jesus. But we cannot emphasize his servanthood by calling him lord and master! These are titles which connote power and status and domination of others, not the loving gift of oneself for these others.

The second qualm has to do with how we think of ourselves if we call Jesus—or anyone—our lord and master. The implication of having a lord or master is that you must obey this person. You act out of obedience, with little or no real choice in the matter. To surrender your will in this way is to surrender your decision-making and so also your responsibility. But this we cannot do. In spite of all the hymns which laud the surrender of our wills to God, we ought to do what is right not just because some outside power makes us, but because of a decision on our own part to do so, because of inward conviction and principle and faith. (Is it just my imagination or do many people who call Jesus "lord and master" shy away from discussions with those of other views because—acting in obedience to someone else's interpretation of Jesus—they have no reasoned convictions of their own?)

My third qualm has to do with the suitability of these two titles for our modern day and age. We think today in terms of democracy, while the Bible uses the imagery of tyranny (this is, after all, what we would call a ruling monarch). We think in terms of liberty, equality, representative government, popular elections, and office holders as public servants.

The Bible often couches its message in the metaphor of kingship, hierarchy, obedience, masters and slaves.

Assuredly, we need to speak of the authority of Jesus of Nazareth. But it does not seem appropriate to speak of this as the authority of a "lord" or "master", imposed from above us and outside us. Rather we need a way of speaking of Jesus' authority that recognizes that this authority is based on the position we give him in our internal value system. We need to give due credit to our part in giving him this authority, and so explain it in a way in keeping with our democratic heritage.

3. Son of God

I am rather fond of this title for Jesus. It has an amiable vagueness about it because of the wide range of meanings that have been given to it. "Son of God" can mean "God the Son", that is, the second person of the Trinity, God incarnate. It can also mean (as it is used at times in the New Testament) anyone who is a faithful follower of God. Or it can mean anything in between. Which is what most people seem to mean by it: to call Jesus the son of God is to say that he is somehow special, without specifying too precisely in just what way. So we can all happily agree that Jesus of Nazareth is the son of God, each of us with our own different idea of what this means.

However, while this gives us a vague common denominator which we can all use, by virtue of this same vagueness it isn't much help in saying who Jesus is. Since we have chosen not to claim that Jesus is divine, it isn't clear that being a son of God distinguishes him from a number of other people.

4. Messiah

This is the title that was recognized by his followers early on—though probably not until after Easter—as the determinative answer to the question, "Who is Jesus of Nazareth?" The other titles might be seen as appropriate, and they might contribute to the understanding of Jesus, but the Messiah is who he was. This became such an integral part of his identity that only a few decades after his death this Jewish title was used in its Greek translation—Christ—as part of Jesus' proper name.

Identifying Jesus as the Messiah seems only natural to many of us. We have assimilated the common view that the whole of the Old Testament points to the coming of the Messiah, and that its predictions and expectations were completely and obviously fulfilled in the person of Jesus of Nazareth. This view, however, is overly simplistic on some points and just plain wrong on others.

For one thing, the Messiah was not the only person expected or hoped for by first century Jews. There were other titles available, other comings prophesied both in the Old Testament and more recently. Some looked for the coming of "the Son of Man", others for the return of Moses or Elijah, others for someone else altogether.

For another thing, those who did look for the Messiah expected a very different kind of person than Jesus of Nazareth. The Messiah was supposed to accomplish different things than Jesus did. The Messiah was not only to be the son (that is, descendent) of David. He was also to occupy the throne of David and re-establish David's kingdom. For example, look at Chapters 9 and 11 of Isaiah. We tend to ignore certain parts of these when we read them around Christmas.

> For to us a child is born, to us a son is given, and *the government* will be upon his shoulders . . . Of the increase of *his government* and of peace there will be no end, *upon the throne of David* and *over his kingdom.* (Isaiah 9:6–7. Italics added.)

> There shall come forth a shoot from the stump of Jesse, and a branch shall grow out of his roots. And the Spirit of the Lord shall rest upon him . . . and *he shall smite the earth* with the rod of his mouth, and with the breath of his lips *he shall slay the wicked.* (Isaiah 11:1–2a, 4b. Italics added.)

And later in Chapter 11 it speaks of the return of all the Jews from foreign lands and their revenge on their neighbors.

Jesus, you recall, had neither throne nor government. He did not slay the wicked. He did not rally people to the battle cry of "liberty, empire and vengeance!" No wonder the vast majority of his contemporaries couldn't accept him as the Messiah. He didn't even drive out the Romans! Worse yet, he didn't even hate them. And he ate with tax collectors!

The wonder isn't that most people didn't accept Jesus as the Messiah. The wonder is that his disciples decided that this is, after all, who he was. They were convinced that Jesus was beyond a doubt the one who was to come. If he didn't meet people's expectations, then these expectations were wrong. The reality of God's messenger would naturally burst beyond the bounds of human expectation. And the disciples knew the impact of Jesus was so great that titles could not define him, but rather his reality would determine the true meaning of any titles used of him. So if the Messiah was pre-eminent among those who were prophesied, then Jesus must be the Messiah, giving new meaning to this title in his person and ministry[1].

---

[1]One interesting hypothesis as to how this particular title came to be attached to Jesus gives the credit to Pontius Pilate. Pilate, from what we know of him, was arrogant and hateful even for a Roman governor. Apparently in order to insult the Jews, he had a sign put on the cross that read "Jesus of Nazareth, King of the Jews". Now "King of the Jews" was a title

In spite of this conviction on the part of his disciples that Jesus of Nazareth was the Messiah, this does not seem to me the most suitable identification for him. "Messiah" is a title with a long history that we cannot ignore. The "Son of David" was to be a king, a warrior, and triumphant in worldly terms. Jesus of Nazareth was none of these. Far too often we forget this. Whenever we identify him with the lordly and powerful of this world, whenever we think of him as king, we cloud our understanding of the man from Galilee whose greatness lay in his giving of himself and his being a servant to others.

5. The Christ

"Christ" is the Greek word used to translate the Hebrew word "Messiah". Nevertheless, it does not have the same connotation for us. Because in our translations of the Bible we find "Christ" only in the New Testament, we do not identify it with the Old Testament warrior-king. In fact, "Christ" became so closely identified with Jesus of Nazareth that it became in actual usage a part of his proper name. It has for most people no other meaning than to name this particular person[2], though there may be an awareness that this part of his name means that there is something special about him.

"Christ" is also the title that gave us Christians our name. Because of this, and because of its unique association with Jesus, and because of the fact that it is relatively free of traditional meaning, this is the title that I choose to identify Jesus of Nazareth. He is the Christ.

I do not wish to call him Savior, Lord, Master, or Messiah. I do not find these to be appropriate or helpful. Instead, I acknowledge him to be the Christ. And I recognize that in so doing I am taking what had become in practice a name and am rehabilitating it as a title. I also freely admit that one of my reasons for doing this is that, because of a long lapse in its use as a title, "Christ" is more open than the others to being given new meaning.

I acknowledge Jesus of Nazareth to be the Christ. What do I mean by this? I do *not* mean that I believe him to be divine, or that he was without sin, or even that he was necessarily the wisest and best of all people. Rather, I define "the Christ" in a functional manner. That is, I identify Jesus as the Christ by the function or role that he plays for me. As long as he fulfills this function I don't need to claim that he was born

identified with the Messiah, and since Jesus was crucified as the Messiah, this theory goes, his disciples concluded that he was raised as the Messiah.

[2]This was not always the case. At one point early in Church history "Christ" was equated with the divine Logos, and there was some disagreement as to how this was related to the man Jesus. But this has long since ceased to be a common understanding.

of a virgin or was specially chosen by God, that he healed the sick or was raised from the dead. I may believe one or more of these—and in fact I probably do—but they are not necessary in order to identify Jesus as the Christ.

When I say that Jesus is the Christ, I mean to claim that this person is the one through whom we as Christians focus our understanding and our faith. He is the one whose life and message are central to our understanding of God and reality, the one whose teaching gives direction to our lives, and the one whose example of love and right relation and concern for others informs our attitudes and actions.

In the next chapter I will explain how the identification of Jesus as the Christ through this functional interpretation is indisputable, sufficient, and even sacred.

CHAPTER 10: JESUS AS THE (FUNCTIONAL) CHRIST: INDISPUTABLE, SUFFICIENT, AND SACRED

Jesus answered . . . "For this I was born, and for this I have come into the world, to bear witness to the truth." (John 18:37)

Indisputable

When I say that Jesus of Nazareth is the Christ I mean that he is central to my understanding of God, of reality and of life. Jesus is the Christ because he plays this particular function or role for me. The question of a different "nature" or "being" has no interest. We do not have to appeal to a supernatural birth or a divine commission. We refer instead to simple historical fact.

For the fact of the matter is that the basic attitudes that make up my faith are based either directly or indirectly on Jesus of Nazareth. This is true for my understanding of religion and of the purpose of life. It is true for the principles with which I address questions of public and private ethics. These are all the result of my exposure to (1) the life and words of Jesus of Nazareth as contained in the Gospels; (2) the Church whose purpose and intent (if not whose actual accomplishment all of the time) is to promote and live according to his teachings and example; and (3) individuals who have tried to live out their lives according to the precepts of Jesus. These three sources shaped my basic attitudes. This cannot be disputed. And this makes Jesus of Nazareth and his heritage the most important focus to my whole approach to life. If, in addition, I recognize and embrace this fact, and commit myself to strengthening the efficacy of this focus and putting my whole life in line with it, then I accept Jesus as the Christ and I am a Christian.

Of course, it could be said that all of Western culture is pervaded by the direct and indirect influence of Jesus of Nazareth simply because of the dominant role of the Christian Church in shaping our heritage. Simply to acknowledge this historical fact does not make anyone a Christian. But to claim Jesus and his message as the central focal point of one's own life—not by default but by free and serious personal choice—is to confess him as the Christ, and is what distinguishes a person as a Christian. Please note: we must claim Jesus' message as our focal point not only with our words. There are far too many people who consider themselves Christians but whose lives are obviously focused on serving mammon or serving themselves. We must claim Jesus as our focus by the way we order our priorities and make our decisions and live our lives.

To the extent that we practice what we profess and that we profess the values of Jesus the Christ, it is beyond dispute that Jesus plays this role of focus for us as Christians. But is this sufficient? Is this adequate? Can it be enough to claim that Jesus is the Christ if by this we mean only that he is the one we choose to follow? What reason is there to follow someone whose status depends on our choosing to follow him, someone for whom we claim neither divinity nor infallibility nor pre-selection by God?

Sufficient

To answer this we must first of all consider what we are asking in the question, "Who is Jesus?" Throughout the centuries the Church has maintained, sometimes in so many words, that "Jesus is the answer." So when we say who Jesus is, we are saying what the answer is. And when we say what the answer is, we are saying what we believe the *question* to be.

For his immediate disciples the question was how to explain this man who made such an impact on their lives and who was obviously (to them) on a mission from God. They naturally looked to their Scriptures (the Old Testament) both to try to understand this man and also to meet their need to show that he was indeed the one who was prophesied to come. This last was soon taken for granted by Christians, but in each succeeding era the Church emphasized that aspect of Jesus of Nazareth which answered the most deeply felt questions of their age.

Thus for those whose primary concern was how to escape their bondage to sin, Jesus was the Savior who offered forgiveness. For those trapped in serfdom or slavery, it was belief in Jesus that offered the promise of a better afterlife. For those oppressed by the evil and finitude of this world, Jesus was the perfect and infinite God coming into our midst. To be the answer for people whose most deeply felt need was release from sin or escape from the evils of the world—people whose common sense was different from ours—it was fitting that Jesus should be sinless and divine.

But times change. The dominant questions with which we address life now do not have to do with how to save ourselves from sin or how to ensure ourselves the best destination after death. Not that these are inconsequential! I, for one, believe they are still extremely important. But they have become secondary to the question that consciously or unconsciously pervades our society: the question of meaning. Our most pressing and tormenting questions have to do with the discovery of meaning, meaning and purpose in the midst of the joys and sorrows, hopes and fears of *this* life.

So, back to our original question: is this functional manner of identifying Jesus as the Christ—as he who is the focus of our basic attitudes and understandings—sufficient? One might ask in return, "Sufficient for what?" The answer to this is perhaps obvious, but it is very important: it must be sufficient for *our* needs and *our* faith and *our* common sense, not for the needs and faith and common sense of some other people or some other time.

To some people it may seem to be claiming "more" for Jesus to claim that he was divine or perfect or atoned for our sins. But none of these makes sense to us, and to claim things which make no sense is not to claim more, but to claim nothing at all. Furthermore, none of these speaks to our deepest question. If we were hungry and someone offered us a work of art, saying it was worth more than food, our hunger would not be satisfied. Likewise, if we were seeking beauty but someone offered us a meal, saying food is worth more, we would not be satisfied. Food is not "more" to someone seeing beauty; art is not "more" to someone who is hungry. In this same way, to claim a special nature for Jesus of Nazareth or to say that he was sinless is *not* to claim more for him if what we are seeking is purpose and meaning. In fact, these claims miss the mark and are of no value to us at all.

On the other hand, if we were able to claim (in a way consistent with our common sense) that Jesus of Nazareth provides the answer to our deepest question and provides the center of our faith, then this would be to claim for him the most that could possibly be claimed for anyone. And this is precisely what we do when we claim that Jesus is the Christ, meaning that it is he, in the main thrust of his life and message, that serves as the center point of our faith and the focus to our understanding of the meaning and purpose of life.

Now if someone were to make the observation as a sociologist or historian that Jesus is the Christ, they would be making the objective (and basically indisputable) statement that he is the one whom Christians claim to follow. But for us to make the claim *as Christians* that Jesus is the Christ is to claim much more than this. It is to say that we orient our approach to life according to his message. And this is to claim that Jesus of Nazareth is *right*, that his perceptions are correct and his teachings true. In so doing we are making the audacious and even outrageous claim that the essential nature of God is love, that loving God and loving one's neighbor as oneself are the basis for all right action, that returning love for hate and forgiveness for injury is a greater victory than vengeance or conquest, and that giving of oneself for others is the highest achievement. We are saying that these insights of Jesus of Nazareth are the Truth, and that by this Truth we define the purpose and meaning of our own lives.

Whatever may have been the case in past centuries, the question of meaning is the most important question in our lives today. Therefore to claim that Jesus of Nazareth, as the Christ, provides us with the answer is to claim the most that could possibly be claimed on his behalf. In fact, to say that Jesus is the Christ and to mean by this that he provides the compass, the focus, by which we find the meaning and purpose in our life, is to claim for the Christ a special role and value that can only be called sacred.

The Sacred

What is "the sacred"? What does it mean to be sacred? This is one of those concepts that is difficult to define but for which we have a reasonably good feeling. We know how we feel towards that which is sacred for us: it is special and set apart. It is "tabu", untouchable, not subject to being questioned in the same way as other things. It is of such value that it inspires awe and reverence.

Sometimes it is a place that is sacred: a temple or a mountain. These were originally places that belonged to God or where God was thought to dwell. Later these were places that were dedicated to God, to the service or worship of God. These places were often approached in certain specified ways that indicated reverence and awe.

For the Biblical literalist the text of the Bible is sacred in much the same way. It derives from God in a special way and shares somehow in the divine attribute of perfection. It is thus to be approached with awe and worship, not with analysis and criticism.

Certain objects are often considered sacred. This is generally due to their use in worship or to their association with holy people considered to have a special relationship to God. These objects are handled with special care and honor, treated with reverence.

Certain obligations are considered to be "sacred duties". These may or may not be duties to God. They are obligations that are unquestionable, that supersede all others, that must be honored even at significant hardship and cost.

I will not essay a definition of the sacred here. I do not know of one that I consider adequate; this may be a task for poetry rather than prose.

Nevertheless, we have pointed to the ineffable height and depth of what it means to be sacred. And when I claim for Jesus of Nazareth the role of the Christ, the role of focus or compass for my understanding of God and of the purpose of life, I am claiming for him a role that is nothing less than this.

The fact that Jesus is right in his understanding of God and life would not in itself give him a sacred position. Something cannot be sacred unless it is sacred to somebody. It is our recognizing and embracing his message as giving us the deepest truths about God and reality that establish his as a sacred office. If our greatest question is one of meaning, then the one who provides the answer has a role that inspires awe, reverence and mystery. (We may take it for granted until we lack it, but the presence of meaning in our lives is a far greater mystery than is its absence.) In his role as the Christ, Jesus is set apart just as much as Mt. Sinai or the Great Temple, though his sacredness is in some ways more like that of a sacred obligation in that it cannot be located entirely outside of us. In the importance of his role, in his set-apartness, in the way we incorporate him into our value system, the Christ is clearly in the category of the sacred.

Why Bother With The Sacred?

Why bother with the sacred? It has been going out of fashion for several centuries now. We tend to associate it with superstition or with such things as the sacred cow or a sacred volcano. We expect to encounter it only in anthropological reports about "primitive" people.

Certainly we do not think of God as being located in a particular object or place. In fact it often seems that quite literally nothing is sacred anymore.

Why, then, do I—the apostle of reason and common sense—seek to revive this concept? Is this not one world? Is not God everywhere, in everything? How, then, can we give special distinction to anything by calling it sacred?

At one time it made sense to claim that certain places or objects were sacred. There was the Mountain of God, the Temple of God, the Ark of the Covenant. But—again—our common sense has changed, and this understanding of the sacred could not survive this change.

But if we cannot locate the sacred in particular places or objects outside of us—what about finding it within us? In fact we all need the sacred to give our lives direction. Certain things must be set apart from and above everything else.

It is true that many people give this primacy to such things as comfort and security, to their physical appetites or to a desire for pleasure, fame and fortune. But these cannot support the weight we put on them. If we allow them to direct our lives they lead ultimately to spiritual emptiness and moral bankruptcy.

If we would give our lives a shape and meaning that is worthy of us we must guide them with higher values. We must recognize that that which gives direction to our lives is the "sacred" for us, and we must give this status only to that which is worthy of it.

But the sacred is not entirely within us. It is rather in the focus-giving relationship between Jesus of Nazareth and us who are Christians, in the role that he plays for us, that makes him the Christ. Reviving the concept of the sacred is the only way that we can do justice to the importance of this function of Jesus the Christ. (And since we can adequately describe Jesus' functional role only by using the concept of the sacred, can we doubt that this role is a sufficient way of identifying who he is?)

At this point we need to say more about places and objects. It is true that they cannot be sacred in the sense of God being in them in a special way. But if they cannot be sacred in and of themselves, in this older sense, they *can* share in the sacredness of the meaning-giving role of the Christ. If a certain object or place is especially connected for us with the Christ function, if a place of worship highlights and strengthens this role for us, if a certain book such as the Bible originates and supports and elucidates it, then these participate in the sacredness of the Christ. This is a derivative sacredness, but a true sacredness nonetheless. Those places and things which for us are associated with the Christ function share in the sacredness of this role.

What About Revelation?

We have seen in this chapter that to identify Jesus as the Christ in this functional way is not only indisputable and adequate, but is also to give him the greatest distinction possible. We have turned aside from Christologies that were suitable to different ages and different questions. And we have put in their place a way of identifying Jesus that addresses our questions of meaning and that ties him once again with the sacred.

We ought to consider one more question here. It is common for theologians to speak of God as revealed (or self-revealed) in Jesus of Nazareth. How does this fit with our functional identification of Jesus as the Christ?

If to say that God was revealed in Jesus implies that God intervened in the world in a special way, that God went "zap", then we cannot go along with this. Our common sense will not allow it. But this does not rule out saying that God was revealed in Jesus in a special way if we mean by this that the special action was on Jesus' part. And in fact this is just what we claim when we say that through his life and teaching we learn the deepest truths about the nature of God. We are claiming that in Jesus we find these truths revealed. That is what makes him the Christ.

There is a further possibility here. It may be that Jesus lived in such a way as to allow God, who is always striving for the actualization of certain goals, to achieve self-revelation. To put this another way: perhaps by acting in consonance with God's intentions—obeying God's will, in traditional language—Jesus provided the vehicle for God to reveal these truths to us. But this gets us back to the question of how God acts, which is the subject of the next two chapters.

CHAPTER 11: TALK ABOUT TALK ABOUT GOD

or

Prolegomena to any Future Metaphysics

"Shall windy words have an end?" "I have uttered what I did not understand." (Job 16:3, 42:3)

Time to talk about God, I said. But no—alas! First we must talk about talking about God.

It is frustrating to have to stop every few steps to examine our presuppositions and ground rules. But the alternative is worse. To charge ahead without a road map will only lead us to confusion. So before we proceed to talk about God we must consider several questions:

I. First, does our modern common sense even permit God-talk? We will (A) look at the extreme viewpoint which suggested that it does not, (B) look at some of the developments which make it clear that it does, and then (C) draw some conclusions about common sense and God-talk.

II. Once we have established the possibility of talking about God we need to look at (A) how the rules of logic apply to this use of language, and (B) what kind of verification is appropriate.

III. Finally in this chapter we will touch briefly on the difference between speaking conceptually of God and speaking in images, and the appropriate use of each.

I. Does Modern Common Sense Allow for God-Talk?

Let us begin by repeating our basic common sense of how the world works. We share a sense that we live in a closed causal universe. Events in this world are explained by reference to causes in this world. God does not go "zap," intervening from "someplace else" into the processes of this world.

This is not to say that there are no phenomena beyond our powers of explanation. Indeed there are. But we assume that there *is* an explanation for each of these which fits our common sense, which we just don't know yet.

Does this common sense that the world is a closed causal unit allow room for God? Some would say that our "modern scientific" common sense doesn't allow for any reality that we can't touch, weigh and measure. Have we, in fact, found ourselves carried inexorably to this extreme?

IA. The Road to Logical Positivism

There has certainly been an element of this in our culture in the last couple of centuries. There has been a tendency to try to explain every possible phenomenon in terms of the physical sciences. During this time physics and chemistry and biology amassed one discovery and conquest after another. Intelligent people got swept up in the feeling of triumph and declared not only that we could explain all *physical* processes this way, but that we could explain *all* of reality with these sciences. This led to a circular redefinition of reality. Once people accepted as an article of faith that modern science could explain the totality of our world, they had to say that anything which fell outside the scope of science isn't real. This is the attitude that says, "If it can't be studied and analyzed by chemists or physicists or biologists, it doesn't exist."

It is very understandable that some people would be led to this extreme. Modern science is the basis of our technology, the basis of our material way of life. It depends on precise measurements, repeatable experiments and strict controls—none of which is applicable to the spiritual realm. If you adopt this kind of science as the appropriate way of investigating all of reality, then you also close your eyes to anything not open to this sort of approach. Which may be quite a bit.

The question we have to answer is whether this attitude has permeated our common sense. Certainly we must admit that elements of it have crept in. But this is far different from saying that our modern common sense has adopted wholesale the view that only the material world is real. It has not. This view has had only a temporary sway over a minority of people. And in fact its high water mark was already past by the third quarter of the twentieth century, having reached its zenith at different times in different disciplines.

We have a strong urge to try to explain all of reality in one way, so it was probably inevitable that the methodology of the physical sciences would be carried into inappropriate areas. If we had to pick one symbolic high point of this invasion it would be the publication of A. J. Ayer's *Language, Truth and Logic* in 1935. In this work Ayer propounded "logical positivism"[1] with his "principle of verifiability". He maintained that for a statement to be either true or false—and thus, for it to have any meaning at all—it must be verifiable. That is, we must be able to test any statement, must be able to prove it right or wrong. (Here is a principle right out of the classical physical sciences.) If it can't be tested, said Ayer, it doesn't have any meaning for us.

It was quickly pointed out that this would mean that a statement such as "the moon is made of green cheese" is meaningless. But while "the moon is made of green cheese" may have been unverifiable—remember, this was in 1935—and may be an altogether silly thing to say, we all know perfectly well what it means. That's how we know it's silly. It is *not* meaningless. So Ayer decided that a statement need be only verifiable "in principle". That is, we do not actually need to be able to verify it at the present time with our present technology, but it must be possible that we *could* do so if we had the necessary capabilities, just as we found out for sure several decades later about the moon (for those who had lingering doubts).

But there are still a lot of statements that are not testable or verifiable even "in principle". Ayer would rule out as meaningless such statements as "God is good", "God is responsible for the evils in the world", and "God loves you". Now each of these three statements is debatable. Each has been subject to fuzzy thinking at times. Each has proven to be of interest to people and has in fact been the subject of intense debates. They are all impossible to prove or disprove empirically. They are, in fact, unverifiable. So logical positivism would say that they don't mean anything.

But are they meaningless? What do you think? Do you have an idea as to what any of these three statements is saying? If you do, then Ayer is wrong.

Or, to give another example: a philosophy professor of mine claimed to have an invisible, weightless elf that lived inside his watch. As unverifiable—and as silly—as this statement was, you and I both know perfectly well what he meant. Which was precisely his point. It is simply not true that unverifiable statements cannot have meaning for us.

As for A. J. Ayer, within a couple of decades his book was relegated to the ignominious lot of a classic example to show undergraduates how not to reason. (See J. L. Austin's *Sense and Sensibilia* [Oxford University Press, 1962].) Even in the skeptical world of modern analytic philosophy, common sense could not be dragged into adopting a world-view based on the physical sciences alone. Here and there, of course, different

---

[1]For those interested in fine points, Ayer distinguishes between his own "logical empiricism" and the positivism of the "Viennese circle". The difference is little enough in any case, and is certainly not germane to our discussion. For that matter, I can't remember why it was ever called "positivism", but that isn't germane either.

individuals reached this point (and some still do). But the tide had already turned, not least in the sciences themselves.

IB. Signposts on the Road Back

We will note three areas which serve to highlight the journey back from logical positivism and which also show that our underlying common sense does not itself rule out the spiritual.

(1) Modern (or "Post-Newtonian") Physics[2]

In the orderly world of Victorian physics there were particles and there were waves, and the two quite properly refrained from fraternizing, and all physical processes were at least in principle predictable. Since then our understanding of the basic pieces and forces that make up the world has undergone a revolution.

Without going into unnecessary detail let us just note two of the cornerstones of modern physics. First: the basic building-blocks of the universe cannot be neatly classified as either waves or particles in the traditional sense. Instead they behave sometimes as one, sometimes as the other. Our neat traditional dichotomies of matter vs. energy, body vs. mind, cannot be maintained at the most basic level.

Second: the result of a given action on a particular individual atomic particle cannot be predicted. That's right, the certain predictability of cause and effect also disappears at the subatomic level. We are left with probability. On a large scale it can be a very strong probability, but it is probability nonetheless.

Our view of the physical world can no longer be what it once was. The neat certainties and easy distinctions of Newtonian physics turned out to be too neat and too easy and too naïve. Even if we don't remember—or never learned—what Einstein meant by general or specific relativity, we need to understand that theoretical physics has drastically changed our understanding of reality. In fact, physics now resembles metaphysics more than anything else, with its theories to explain how realities unobservable by us produce the visible world. More importantly, mechanical certainty has given way to probability and the matter vs. energy distinction has faded away.

---

[2]A necessary note on the word "modern": some people use "modern" physics to mean physics from Newton up to—but not including—Einstein. I suppose this is the influence of all those college courses entitled "Modern Philosophy" or "Modern European History" which never get past 1850. One would then have to call the physics of today "post-modern". This is an intriguing adjective. But then what would you call the theories of the next century? "Post-post-modern"? Come, now. Are we so cowed by the last generation that we have surrendered "modernity" to be ever theirs? Or are we so taken with ourselves that we have to find a new word to fit us? This is silly. If modern physics must be called "post" anything, it is post-Newtonian.

Why does this matter? For two reasons: it takes away the simple, mechanistic understanding that hard, physical, certain reality was the paradigm by which we must understand the world. We can't even understand the *physical* world this way! And secondly, it points to deeper realities underlying the visible world. If our common sense can accept this for physical forces then surely it does not rule this out for spiritual forces and entities.

(2) Holistic Medicine[3]

The medical sciences made such great strides in the past century that some physicians, concentrating on the vast amount of knowledge about our physical processes, forgot that there are other factors which affect human health. And some preferred to avoid such an "unscientific" area as human emotion. But this could not last for very long. The connections between our mental/emotional health and our physical health were just too apparent, with cause and effect running in both directions.

So the lesson was relearned. In the 1970s two movements in this direction made significant progress. The first is "holistic medicine", a general movement towards treating the whole patient instead of just physical symptoms. Unfortunately, in some areas "holistic medicine" came to mean anything that wasn't part of Western scientific medicine. Thus it came not only to mean a concern for a person's psycho-social (as well as physical) well-being, but it came also to include some practices which remain untested and which strike some as quackery. However, regardless of whether "holistic medicine" means to you the broader movement or the questionable fringe, the fact is that it has helped re-establish what many folks never forgot: that if we limit our attention to the strictly physical aspects of a person's health, we limit our ability to adequately treat many physical conditions. The emotional/mental realm has power to affect the physical. Did anyone seriously doubt that people can—and do—die of broken hearts?

The second movement, much more specific, represents the inclusion of a more holistic approach in the medical establishment. It is the creation of the "new" physician specialty of "family practice". While a number of factors combined to establish this as a specialty—complete with three-year medical school residencies and national boards and certification—it represents a definite move away from treating human beings piecemeal. Family physicians are trained to consider the whole of an individual's psycho-social situation in treating a problem.

Both holistic medicine and family practice represent a renewed recognition that our emotional health has a real impact on our physical health. This is important to our current argument because it shows that

---

[3]If I had not just expounded upon the use of the word "modern" I would have something to say here about the missing "w" in this word.

our common sense—and even our medical science—recognizes that even our physical health, much less reality as a whole, cannot be reduced to physical processes alone.

(3) Parapsychology

Under the rubric of parapsychology is grouped the study of such things as telepathy, clairvoyance, communications with the dead and other exotic phenomena and pseudo-phenomena. Personally, I do not believe in demons or magic or Ouija boards. In fact, I'm rather convinced that they are bunk. I am not so sure about ghosts, but have never (to my knowledge) seen one myself—which state of affairs, I hasten to add, I have no urge whatsoever to alter.

Surely the only attitude to take towards claims in this area is a healthy skepticism. Of what possible relevance, then, is parapsychology?

If we are *honest* skeptics, and if we bother to acquaint ourselves with even a small portion of the available evidence, we will find—even after we dismiss a lot of reports as pure rubbish—that it is impossible to deny that there are some strange sorts of communication going on. (Or perhaps they only seem strange to those of us who were in danger of surrendering too much to the physical sciences.) The plain fact is that there are a number of people who have known immediately when a relative has died, or who were able to lead their families to their great-grandfather's grave in the dark in a cemetery they'd never been to before, or who have sensed approaching danger in a very specific way. There may not be a great lot of people with these experiences, but there are far too many to deny or ignore. And some of them are very credible witnesses. The two people who I have known who had experiences of this type were rather skeptical sorts.

I would personally be much more comfortable if we could just deny that this sort of thing happens. But we cannot. The evidence is too compelling. These phenomena are even beginning to receive serious study at respected academic institutions.

The point here is not that ghosts may exist. The point here is rather that some people have experiences that involve a reality beyond our known physical world. And whether or not we choose to believe these people, we are willing to grant that it is *possible* that this happened to them and that it is worth our while to investigate some of these phenomena. Our common sense recognizes that reality is not limited to the physical universe.

IC. Conclusions on Common Sense and God-Talk

We began Section I of this chapter with the question of whether our common sense today allows for talk about God at all. I have briefly noted some aspects of modern physics, medicine, and parapsychology to point to what you probably already knew: there is nothing in our modern common sense itself which rules out our consideration of a spiritual reality.

It needs also to be said that common sense is not a single, monolithic way of thinking without variability or flexibility. It has been in some degree of flux for at least the last five centuries. But while there are times when the geography of our common sense may alter suddenly and drastically in one area of thought—the earthquakes of Copernicus and Darwin, for instance—it is more often like a glacier. Movement isn't noticeable at all. You can only tell movement has happened by looking at the marker of its position a year or a decade or a century ago.

It is not unusual for a small segment to try to carry the mass of common sense with it to one extreme or another. But glaciers are not easily convinced. While a section of ice may lead in a new direction or to new limits, making the most noise and gaining the most attention, these peninsulas are also the most likely to be those that break off and fall into the sea as icebergs, floating away and disappearing.

The surrender of the whole universe to the physical sciences, represented by A. J. Ayer in philosophy (and by others in medicine and psychology) was a loud, daring little ice floe that tried to pull the glacier with it, failed, and fell into the sea. (Two other fringes of the glacier at present shall meet a similar fate, both trying to pull in the opposite direction of Ayer and company. One is mysticism taken to the extreme of being anti-rational, the other is the rear guard counteroffensive being conducted against evolution. Both will pull on the glacier, will fail to drag us along in spite of the noise they make, and will end up as icebergs, impressive but of nuisance value only.)

Meanwhile the glacial wisdom of our common sense has reasserted itself, having freed itself of an extreme, obstreperous, largely academic faction by shedding it into the sea. Does this modern common sense, viewing the world as a closed causal continuum and explaining physical effects—with some notable exceptions—with physical causes, allow for talk about God? Yes. Perhaps not the God of the Old Testament—the glacier has moved a good way since then—but yes, talk of God. Yes, because the strict dichotomies of matter vs. energy, body vs. mind, physical vs. spiritual, simply do not work. The two interact and are at times indistinguishable. Yes, because we recognize that there are mental and spiritual phenomena which cannot be explained in terms of the physical but which are nonetheless a real part of our world. Yes, because we recognize the power of the psyche to affect the body. Yes, because our common sense allows for something more beyond visible reality.

Our common sense does not allow for talk of a God that goes "zap" from "out there" somewhere, for a God who is a specific interventionist. But it does allow for a God who is in the context, who is somehow in and through the processes of our world, physical and spiritual, in processes that are much more varied and complex and wonderful than we have yet been able to comprehend.

II. Language, Truth and Logic
A. The Logic of God-Talk

Alright: our common sense allows us to talk about God. But talking about God is still different from talking about anyone else. This much is obvious. The question here is: is talking about God so different from talking about your best friend or your dog or Millard Fillmore that a different set of rules applies?

This is not a frivolous question. It is not uncommon for people engaged in theology to hold that human language, when applied to God, must have a very different meaning, since God is so very different from us—different not just in degree but in kind. God is perfect and infinite, we are imperfect and finite. Finite words cannot be used of God without altering their meaning.

This sounds reasonable, but one has to be careful where it leads. For instance, I have had a very intelligent young man tell me that he believed that God foreordained all of our actions and also gave us complete freedom. I pointed out to him that as I understood these words, *either* we have our actions foreordained *or* we have freedom of choice. (After all, if someone's already decided what we're going to do it's not really left up to us, is it?) My friend agreed that this was indeed so for the human use of these words but insisted that when used in connection with God foreordination and freedom, predestination and our own responsibility for our end, were compatible.

In other words, he was saying that when we use words to speak about God we change their meanings—so much so that opposites are no longer opposites. This presents a couple of serious problems. First, it allows for cheap talk about God. You can say something about God without meaning what you say, without taking responsibility for it. For example, my friend admitted that his words were contradictory for humans, but not, somehow, when used of God. Or for example, if I were to say to you, "God is angry at you." You might respond, "Oh, you mean God has emotions like you and I, and a negative one is directed at me." But then I could simply come back with, "No, that's not what I mean at all. It means something different when we're talking about God."

The second problem with this approach is that we can't be sure just what is being said about God. If the meaning of a word is stretched beyond recognition, if all we're told is that it doesn't mean the same as usual and opposites are no longer opposites—then we no longer know what the meaning is. In which case it cannot *have* a meaning for us.

If this offends those who would play fast and loose with language, it delights our old friends the positivists. I can see them now: descending upon us from their iceberg, flags waving and bugles blaring, cries of "tally-ho!" filling the air. "There!" they proclaim triumphantly. "It's as we said. You *can't* talk about God. Of course our language means something different when applied to God. Therefore we don't know what we're saying, so it hasn't any meaning. As we said, it's impossible!"

Fortunately, this sort of hysterical linguistic nihilism is quite unnecessary. Language, while flexible, has a fairly simple logic. (I realize that many theologians seem intent on proving otherwise.) Whenever we use a word, there are three possibilities: (1) we use it in its usual sense, the meaning you would find in a dictionary; or (2) we use it in a way that is an analogy to its normal sense, an analogy that is clearly understood; or (3) we use it in a way that has no meaning at all, or—what is the same to everyone else—we use it in a sense that is known only to us.

So: language is flexible, but there are limits to this flexibility. As an example, we can speak of healthy people, healthy dogs, and healthy African violets. The word "healthy" means the same in each case, or close enough so that we know perfectly well what we're talking about, even though the specifics of good health are quite different. I don't check to see if your leaves are green, or if the plant has a cold nose. But I know in each case that the life systems are working well. (The "formal meaning" is the same in each case; the "material meaning" or content is different.)

We can take this example further. If I said that a balance sheet or a car was healthy, you would know that I meant that the one had a good ratio of assets to liabilities, and that the other was in good mechanical shape. But if I were to speak of a healthy book or a healthy rock, you wouldn't know what I meant. I have gone beyond any apparent analogy. Out of kindness you might try to guess what I meant or decide I was making a joke. Or you might conclude that I was talking nonsense—quite properly, I fear. For we can easily see an analogy between healthy people and healthy cars, but when we speak of rocks we have moved beyond any clearly understood analogy to the normal use of the word "healthy".

If we refer back to our three ways of using a word, to speak of healthy dogs and people is number one above, the normal use. To speak of healthy cars is number two, a clearly understood analogy. To speak of healthy rocks is number three; there is no clear analogy, so it is meaningless.

We can illustrate these same three possible uses in talk about God by saying that "God knows", "God sees", and "God reads". To say that God knows what we are doing is to use the word "know" in its usual sense: God is cognizant of what we are doing, through whatever processes God (as opposed to you and me) comes to know such things.

To say that "God sees what we are doing", however, is a bit different.

In its normal use, "see" refers to a finite physical process involving eyes, nerves and brain which has the end result of a visual image. Certainly God does not "see" in this manner. But just as certainly we know that what is meant here is that God perceives what we are doing, however it may be that God does this. The analogy to the normal use of "see" is obvious. We understand how the meaning is modified by the subject, and there is no confusion.

But suppose we were to say "God reads about what we are doing". Hopefully, whoever we were talking to would be charitable. They might say, "I assume you don't mean that God is paging through the New York Times, or otherwise visually taking in printed material?"

"Quite right," we respond. "God doesn't do that as we do."

So we sit there smiling, and they sit there puzzled. For unlike "seeing", in the case of "reading" the analogy from our particular finite physical processes to an infinite God is not clear.

If our listeners were persistent they might continue with, "You don't mean God reads our hearts or our minds, do you, for you said 'reads about'?"

"Quite right," we say again. "We don't mean that."

But then what *do* we mean? Nothing identifiable. "Reading about" something implies involvement with the physical printed word or something clearly analogous. But nothing is clearly analogous here. If God does not read as we do, which we are assuming that God does not, then we must have something else in mind. But if this something else is not apparent, if there is no clear analogy, then we do not know the meaning of this. In which case it doesn't have any meaning for us.

So, to repeat: the logical rules for talking about God are simple. Either we (and others) know what we are saying, or it is meaningless and we had better not bother to say it. And we know what we are saying if (1) we are using words in their usual meaning, or (2) we are using words in a way that is an apparent analogy to their usual meaning.

The only alternative to these two is the explicit redefining of words as we go—in effect, making up our own language and providing a dictionary as we proceed. It may get cumbersome, but there is nothing in the rules of logic to prohibit this. However, we must note sadly that theology contains many more unknown languages than it does lexicons.

IIB. The Real Verification Problem

The intrinsic problem with God-talk is *not* that we don't know what our words mean when we talk about God. This becomes a problem only when people are inexcusably sloppy with their language—which has been far too often. The *real* problem with God-talk is: how do you know whether what you say is right? How do you verify it? How do you judge between conflicting statements about God? How do you know what to say in the first place?

This is the problem that made the positivists so uncomfortable that they tried to avoid it by declaring the whole business meaningless. (As Joshua Reynolds put it in the eighteenth century, "There is no expedient to which a man will not resort to avoid the real labor of thinking.") However, we can keep this problem from getting out of hand if we remember that different kinds of statements are verified in different ways. You don't verify the truth of "two plus two equals four" in the same way that you verify "that bird is a cardinal", and neither of these is verified the same way as "Millard Fillmore was a good president". "Two plus two equals four" is true by definition ("analytic a priori", if you wish). To see if the bird in question is a cardinal, you take a good look at it and check your Peterson's field guide if you have any question.

Deciding whether Millard Fillmore was a good president is a little more involved. There are two steps here: first, to ascertain what Millard Fillmore did as president, which is not nearly so easy as ascertaining the size, shape and color of a bird; and second, to decide what it means to have been a good president in the early 1850s, which involves not only historical knowledge but also some interesting value judgments. So this statement about Fillmore rightly calls for a different kind of verification than the statement about the cardinal. The facts are not directly observable, but must be discovered—and often inferred—from the historical record. And there is no consensus as to which facts count for a good president, unlike the unanimity about how being red or blue, crested or uncrested, count for a bird being a cardinal.

Statements about God have the same verification problems as statements about Millard Fillmore, only more so. They cannot be confirmed by direct observation and there is a pronounced lack of consensus as to what observable phenomena count as evidence for which claims about God. But we need to remember what is appropriate. To demand that what we say about God be verifiable by direct observation or by an airtight process of logical deduction makes no more sense than to demand this of statements about Millard Fillmore. This means, however, that discussions about God must have a certain inherent tentativeness, a certain openness to question. We must accept this. But then, so do discussions about Millard Fillmore and any of our other presidents, and this has never stopped us from talking about *them*.

In fact, most of the interesting and important questions in life can only be answered with a certain degree of tentativeness. This is because they involve questions of meaning, value and purpose—things which cannot be neatly weighed, measured or calculated. To a fair extent, propositions dealing with these areas are subject to verification in life, to confirmation through living. That is, your values and your faith are confirmed as they fit with your life experiences, as they bring meaning to events and help you find purpose, as they explain and cohere with what you see and feel and learn. They must still be in line with your common sense, but they cannot be confirmed for you unless they ring true for you in your heart.

Talking about God *is* difficult. But it is not inappropriately difficult (unless we make it so). The rules of definition and verification are appropriate to the subject matter, and problems in these areas are no more than we should expect when addressing a subject of ultimate importance.

III. Talking in Concepts, Talking in Images

We have addressed in section II the problems involved in speaking about God in concepts. But this is only one of the two ways we use to convey our ideas about something. We can speak in concepts or we can use images; we can describe something or we can paint a picture of it. In the present case, we can either describe God directly, using words in their normal or analogous meanings, or we can talk about God analogously by using vivid concrete images (with their normal meaning) and saying, "God is like this."

In many cases for the sake of clarity and accuracy it is preferable to deal carefully in concepts, to explain and to define. But images and metaphors are also important vehicles of human understanding and sometimes do better at communicating meaning and getting to the heart of the matter. Jesus himself often chose images, painting powerful images in his parables: "the Kingdom of God is like . . ." And perhaps this was the right choice for someone more interested in faith than in doctrine.

Because theology does not adequately feed our imagination, and because our language is inadequate for encompassing the whole of spiritual reality, it is still helpful and perhaps necessary to use imagery as well as concepts to get across our understanding of God.

CHAPTER 12: GOD: CONCEPTS AND IMAGES

"Lo, my eye has seen all this,
  my ear has heard and understood it."
"I will show you, hear me;
  and what I have seen, I will declare."

(Job 13:11, 15:17)

It is finally time to talk about God. This chapter will certainly not be an exhaustive statement of all that can be said about God, however. For one thing, that can't be done in one chapter or even in one book. It can't be done by any one individual. Probably as a whole species we will never fully understand God, much less as individuals.

For another thing, it is not the purpose of this chapter to give a complete statement about God. The purpose of this chapter is to set out a general framework of what we can say. We will first look at those aspects of reality which can serve to point to God (Where do we see God?). We will then ask how God acts (What does God do?), and briefly address some questions about the nature of God (What is God like?). Finally, in the last section we will shift from concepts to images as I briefly suggest some metaphors that may help us to understand God.[1]

One further note of introduction: while it is appropriate to be cautious in making statements about God, we showed in the last chapter that it is *not* appropriate to limit ourselves to that which can be empirically or logically proven. So while we will not appeal to revelation, there are insights about God that have been developed through the ages, passed on by the great religions, and confirmed or maybe even originated in our

---

[1]While the approach taken in this chapter will speak of God being in the processes of this world, this is not "process theology" in a technical sense. Strictly speaking, "process thought" refers to philosophy or theology based on the ideas of Alfred North Whitehead. While process thought is congenial to my approach, I am not sure that I can subscribe to all of the claims it makes (such as those regarding purpose) and I see no advantage to exchanging Nicene jargon for Whiteheadian jargon (such as "concrescence" and "prehension" and "mental pole").

own lives. (As Christians, of course, we are guided first and foremost by the witness of the Christ.) We can put forth these insights as statements about God so long as we can show that they fit with reality and with our common sense.

I. Where Do We See God?

Q: If we are going to look for God—what does God look like?

A: God doesn't "look like". God doesn't look like anything, in the sense that God could be said to have shape and size and color like most things around us. We cannot see God just as we cannot see the wind and cannot see love. Yet we can usually tell by looking outside whether there is any wind. If we cannot see what the wind "looks like" we can still tell, by looking or feeling, its strength and direction. And if we know what to look for we can see the presence of love.

Q: How, then, do you see God? Where can you point to God even in the same way that you see the wind?

A: Someone of the "specific interventionist" line of thought might point to a particular incident and say, "There! *That* was God's doing!" Perhaps this is the kind of evidence you want. We can, after all, point to a blown-down tree and say, "There, that was the wind's doing." However—besides being a bit suspicious about which events get credited to God—I simply cannot believe in a specific interventionist God. Our common sense does not allow it, nor does our faith (see Chapter 3). So it is inappropriate to ask us for specific interventionist type of evidence. This means we *cannot* point to God by means of an incident here or there which somehow violates what we know of natural law.

Q: At what, then, do we look?

A: At the pattern. You could examine every single separate happening and phenomenon, human and natural, and in each separate case not see God. But this would be like someone who examined an exquisite fisherman's knit sweater and decided to find out what it is about the yarn that holds the sweater together and makes it so beautiful. They could then examine the yarn millimeter by millimeter, perhaps pulling the sweater apart in the process. They might learn much about the qualities of the yarn and wool. They might even conclude that they had learned all there was to learn about the sweater. But if all they looked at was the strand of wool in itself, they would never discover what holds the sweater together and what makes it beautiful. Unless you look at the pattern, at the way the yarn loops and ties and fastens, at the way the rows are related and at the intricate interconnections, you will never fathom the structure or the nature or the beauty of a sweater.

Q: That's fine for sweaters. But what pattern do we look at in the world?

A: There are four aspects of pattern.

The Pattern Part 1: The Fact of Pattern Itself

To begin with, look at the fact that there *is* pattern. Not just that there is something rather than nothing—although this is impressive in its own right—but that there is a whole range of particular somethings rather than just a great lot of nothing in particular. There is order rather than chaos, there are things—all sorts of things—rather than a big primordial blob.

"Nonsense," you may say. "That's just simple natural law in action, the unavoidable result of the laws of physics."

Perhaps it is. But was it unavoidable that the laws of physics should work just this way? Others have pointed out how an absurdly small change in any of a number of physical forces would yield a radically different universe. For instance, if the force that holds protons in an atomic nucleus were even slightly weaker or stronger, stars—and so also life as we know it—would be impossible.[2]

And is it so simple? The manner in which infinitesimal something-or-others—they are, after all, neither energy nor matter, or perhaps *both* energy *and* matter, whose behavior can be predicted only in probabilities—the manner in which they manage to join together in the proper sorts of atoms and molecules is, to me, a cause for wonder. A greater wonder yet is how these still infinitesimally small molecules make the great leap from aggregations of infinitesimals—however numerous—to solid, visible *things*. How do any number of atoms, which are mostly empty space, turn into tables and chairs and mountains and little green lizards? How do subatomic whatever-they-are acquire color and solidity and identity as a chair?

I am not suggesting that God turns subatomic particles into atoms and then into molecules and then into chairs, giving them color and hardness in the process. I believe I have at least a vague idea of how this works. But the point is this: there is an exceptionally useful and necessary set of patterns here which allows for infinitesimals to become "things" of a very different nature, bridging such an improbable gap that if we did not take it for granted we would not find it credible.

All I wish to say is this: I wonder if we ought to take this so cavalierly for granted.

---

[2] See Freeman Dyson's essay "The Argument from Design" in *Disturbing the Universe* (Harper and Row, 1979). To be fair, also see Stephen Jay Gould's argument about drawing too strong a conclusion from this in "Mind and Supermind" in *The Flamingo's Smile* (W. W. Norton, 1985). (As we said, we are not dealing here with "proofs".)

The Pattern Part 2: Life and Consciousness

Look at this thing called life. Is this not a wonder? Is not the fact of life itself (not to mention its diversity, its beauty, its interrelatedness) a thing to marvel at?

There are some who would not agree. I do not mean those who would say that life's diversity, for instance, is a natural result of the process of evolution. I tend to agree, but it does not lessen the marvel for me. I refer here to the small group of scientists who argue that in fact there is no qualitative difference between living organisms and other chemical processes. They argue this on the basis that one can posit a series of intermediary steps leading from basic chemical reactions to what we call living organisms, which could be viewed as a simple chemical progression leading to the strategy of the cell.

But this is not a persuasive argument. To say that living organisms cannot be classified as different from other locales of chemical reactions because there are intermediate steps is like saying that animals ought not to be distinguished from plants because there are organisms that possess the features of both. However, while I cannot tell you whether protista are animal or vegetable or something else altogether, I can still distinguish a mammal from a conifer without pondering over it for too very long. And so can you.

Linguistic philosophy has long recognized that the existence of "borderline cases" does not argue against the existence of two genuinely separate classes. I do hope that no one believes that the presence of protista means that there aren't perfectly valid criteria for distinguishing plants from animals, petunias from porcupines. Similarly—and our common sense, modern philosophy, and the vast bulk of scientists are in agreement on this—while life and non-life both involve chemical reactions, life is qualitatively different in some very important ways.

And whether life represents the inevitable result of several billion years of chemical interactions on a planet such as ours, or whether it represents a one-in-a-trillion fluke, it is a source of wonder.

And among the living things of our world there are conscious beings. Descartes' famous utterance of "cogito ergo sum"—"I think, therefore I am"—is not nearly as important as the comment we can then make: "Because he thinks this, here is a conscious being."

Indeed, Descartes was a conscious being. I am a conscious being. I suspect that you are a conscious being as well. I not only feel, physically and emotionally, but I also think. And I am aware that I feel and think, and think about my feeling and thinking.

Life is a marvel in itself—and here is consciousness as well! We are, wonder of wonders, conscious beings.

I am *not* arguing that God gave us this consciousness by a special act or that this is what separates human beings from all other animals. In fact it is apparent that some other animals share a certain degree of self-consciousness, most notably the great apes. (Might we notice this more in dolphins and whales if they were not so different from us that real communication is more difficult?)

Nor are we concerned here with the question of humanity's uniqueness in the universe. Whether or not there are other sentient creatures is an interesting question which—as of this writing—is unresolved. I expect it to remain that way for some time.[3] But this is irrelevant to our point here.

Our point here is that consciousness and the mind—something that is non-physical, that transcends the physical, that is wondrous in itself—somehow develops from physical processes. Please note: I am not saying that we don't know how the brain works. Though there is much yet to learn, we understand more and more each passing year. And I have no doubt that if you and I applied ourselves to the subject we could acquire at least a basic understanding of neurons and synapses and the like. And obviously the mind, and consciousness, depend upon the brain. But they are not reducible to the brain. Again, we see the bridging of an incomprehensible gap: electro-chemical impulses give rise to a mind and to consciousness. Physical occurrences somehow translate into a thinking, feeling, willing, acting being.

And again, we take this pattern for granted.

The Pattern Part 3: Ethics and Aesthetics

To talk about the leap from subatomic particles and probabilities to objects as we know them, and to talk about the leap from chemistry to consciousness, is in a very real sense to engage in metaphysics. Of a somewhat different nature are considerations of our ethical and aesthetic senses, of the fact that we can recognize right and wrong and perceive beauty.

Let us turn first to the ethical. There are voluminous studies on how we acquire moral reasoning. But about the only conclusions they can draw are that we acquire this by stages as we grow up and that development of our moral reasoning can be encouraged by the right sort of instruction and example.

What these studies have not answered—what cannot be answered by studies and perhaps cannot be answered at all—is why we have this

---

[3] I find it interesting that those most familiar with the course of evolution on this planet—the paleontologists—are divided as to the likelihood of intelligent being evolving on other worlds, but are apparently united in the conviction that if intelligent life were to evolve elsewhere it would not resemble us. This is because of the immense number of circumstantial "accidents" over billions of years that form our particular path to consciousness (including, perhaps, periodic cometary bombardment of the earth and resulting extinctions). If this is correct, the strange creatures of science fiction movies, with two arms and two legs and a head, are far more like us than anything we are really likely to meet "out there". (See Stephen Jay Gould, *The Flamingo's Smile* [W. W. Norton and Co., 1983] pp. 403–413)

capacity in the first place. Remember, now, we are talking about our moral sense, *not* just about our ability to understand and comply with the rules of our society. Certainly our capacity to absorb the standards of our culture can be explained by psychology and sociology.

But we are not referring here to our ability to mimic our elders or to toe the line. Rather, we are referring here to our moral or ethical sense: our ability to recognize right and wrong, justice and injustice, even when inequity is socially acceptable and injustice is inherent in the existing structures.

Please note that we *recognize* what is right. This implies that there is *more* than our own subjective sense of right and wrong. Actions and situations are right or wrong in an objective sense, whether or not we have the ability to discern this. There is a right and a wrong. I'm not saying that it is always easy to figure out, although sometimes it is appallingly obvious. I am saying that it is always there, whether we can see it or not.

The conviction and drive of the great prophets did not come from their having devised a scheme of morality. It came from a sense of having discovered a truth so great and so powerful that it had to be shared. Some people, of course, feel this same way about "truths" that the rest of us find blatantly false and morally repugnant. The existence of fool's gold and the propensity of some people to be taken in by it do not, however, cast doubt on the existence of real gold, but rather on some people's faculties of discrimination. The fact that many people have value systems that do not appear particularly moral only increases the value and the marvel of good moral judgment.

You see, the wonder is not that we so often misidentify our society's standards with what is just and right, especially when it comes to those rules which favor our particular class or group. After all, these standards are inculcated in us on a daily basis in innumerable ways and are often reinforced by the heavy weight of self-interest. What is remarkable is the human capacity—in spite of this intensive societal indoctrination—to perceive where justice demands change, to discover that one's society or one's peers are morally wanting. We can recognize right and wrong, and we recognize that it is altogether independent of whatever may happen to be majority opinion at any given time or place.

Whence comes this moral capacity? And at the very least does it not make us aware of another level, another depth, of reality?

Then there is our aesthetic sense. You can explain why the sky is blue with reference to absorption and refraction and the length of light waves. Or you can explain why this wave-length looks blue to us with details about our retinas and optical nerves and brain processes. But how do you explain why this blue sky looks beautiful to us?

This faculty of ours is generally taken for granted and consequently overlooked, and the importance of beauty in our lives is greatly underrated. Beauty introduces an ethereal, uplifting breath into our lives. It affects our goals, our choices, our happiness. We find beauty not only in sunsets and grand vistas, not only in Rembrandt and Bach, but also in children's laughter and grandmothers' smiles, in acts of courage and self-sacrifice, in personal relationships and kindness and integrity. Whenever we allow ourselves to see past our own busyness and our own anxieties to recognize the beauty around us we allow ourselves an uplift that is more spiritual than we generally admit. (This is why beauty is an important aspect of the worship experience.)

To repeat the maxim that beauty is in the eye (or ear) of the beholder does not really help to explain this. Further, if you mean by this that the recognition of beauty is capricious or privatistic, without pattern or consensus—well, that is just plain wrong. Similarly, explanations based on aesthetic principles such as patterns, color, balance, harmonies, etc., can be helpful in explaining why certain paintings or symphonies (for instance) are considered masterpieces, but this still doesn't explain why we are able to recognize beauty at all. And any discussion just of the attributes of those things we consider beautiful is bound to fall woefully short of the depth and the richness of the reality we experience.

Again, we need to ask ourselves: whence comes this capability? What evolutionary purpose could it serve? And does it not make us aware of the non-physical as well as the physical realities of our universe?

The Pattern Part 4: Love

I now want to direct your attention to that aspect of "the pattern" that is perhaps best described by Robert Frost in "Mending Wall":

Something there is that doesn't love a wall
That wants it down.

Frost was speaking of an old stone wall between apple trees and pines. My own experience is that this same observation would apply as well to other walls, to the walls of fear and hatred and misunderstanding that we humans build between one another.

As easily as these walls seem to grow, as consistently as they separate individuals, factions and nations, how can I suggest that there is a force that works against them? Must we not then posit an even stronger force working *for* them?

This is an important question. It deserves a careful answer. The difficulties it poses could be escaped with the easy but unchristian approach of crediting humans with all that is bad and God with all that is good. Certainly this has been done before. Or we could go one step further and credit the devil with all the evil, thus leaving humans responsible for nothing at all. Both of these approaches negate our responsibility for our own actions and ignore the reality of human will and our ability to do good or evil. We will not resort to either of these all-too-easy non-solutions.

What, then, do we say about our human propensities to selfishness and cruelty and plain mistakes? What do we say about these tendencies which, in combination with the fragility of the human psyche, seem to make walls necessary? It is true that the human spirit can be hard to break, but it is easily damaged. Survival often comes only at a high cost as we wall ourselves off from others in one way or another.

It is also true that at times we see wise and courageous souls bridge these barriers in ways that make walls seem weak and superfluous by comparison. But how can we say that the pattern, or even God, encourages one and discourages the other?

To begin with, we must accept the fact that we humans are capable of acting in an extremely wide variety of ways. Along with a large body of morally neutral acts, we are capable of behavior ranging from the inexpressibly wicked to the ineffably saintly. There is a very real difference between good and evil actions and this difference is not only in how these affect others. Our behavior and its effects interact with our *own* psyche as well. Just as we can expect certain types of behavior from people with certain types of personality, it is also true that certain actions help to develop certain types of character in us.

At this point I am going to make an unabashed value judgment. I claim with no misgivings whatsoever that some characters are better than others. And I most emphatically do not equate this with some people being happier than others. This needs to be said for two reasons. First, too many people equate happiness with pleasure or with other shallow emotions that come and go with the ups and downs of each day. Second, there is an absurd tendency to believe that our proper goal in life is this same happiness, and in fact some even equate it with "mental health"—as if the highest achievement of the human spirit were to enjoy itself!

I claim that it is better for a soul to have a certain character. It is better for a person to attain wholeness and maturity. This can be seen in some people: they are at ease in the world in a way that far transcends material ease. They are able to offer love and hope and good humor to others who need it. They lend security and strength and offer hospitality in its broadest sense in a world where most are strangers. This is not to say that they do not suffer hurt and anxiety and depression—of course they do. But their spirit has depth and breadth and is not defeated by external events.

This is the character which it is simply better for a soul to have. Something in us knows this, though we do not always acknowledge it. And for attaining this particular character, love works better than hate. For the all-important work of molding our most important possession, our own self—which is in fact the only thing that is truly our own—for molding this into something that has depth and breadth and substance, for nurturing it beyond the shallow and brittle and empty, acts of love and courage and self-sacrifice are needed. This simply cannot be accomplished by living and acting in pettiness or hatred or fear. We must approach life with those attitudes which lead to as well as proceed from this great breadth of soul, if we want to have this kind of spirit ourselves. Caring, giving and sharing, without cavil or self-serving, with love for others—this is the way to develop a depth of character.[4]

Something in us recognizes this wholeness, this greatness of soul, either in others or in incipient form in ourselves, and desires it—desires it and recognizes it as a higher, more important goal. When we strive for it we find that the pattern is such that we can only reach this goal through love.

Of course, we have other needs and other goals. To make the most of our potential, we need relationships that nurture our growth and development. We in turn can better nurture these needed relationships through love. The problem here, which may well be *the* problem for humanity, is that if we do not manage to meet our emotional needs through loving relationships we will try to meet them in other ways. Thus we may seek status or wealth or power to give ourselves a sense of worth. Or we may hide by being very busy in our work or house or hobbies, either afraid to reach out or unable to, avoiding the challenge and risk of life through uninvolvement, avoiding facing our own unhappiness through busyness. But this is not enough. Neither success nor busyness is enough.[5] Our spirits suffocate with no more than this. Our walls look solid, but a close inspection shows no foundation shoring them up.

Of course, we can go further astray than this and find our driving force in hatred and bitterness. Indeed, whole nations have sustained themselves on this for generations, finding their meaning and purpose and—if ever they triumphed—satisfaction. But the cost! The cost in stunted growth, in twisted lives, in narrow distorted spirits, is appalling.

---

[4]And is this not also the essence of faith? In traditional terms, we are saying that good works, rightly done, can lead to faith—just as faith, rightly lived, will overflow in good works.

[5]"Oh, captive, bound and double-ironed," cried the phantom. "Not to know that any Christian spirit working kindly in its little sphere, whatever it may be, will find its mortal life too short for its vast means of usefulness. Not to know that no space of regret can make amends for one life's opportunities misused! Yet such was I! Oh! Such was I!"

"But you were always a good man of business, Jacob," faltered Scrooge, who now began to apply this to himself.

"Business!" cried the ghost, wringing its hands again. "Mankind was my business. The common welfare was my business; charity, mercy, forbearance, and benevolence were all my business. The dealings of my trade were but a drop of water in the comprehensive ocean of my business!" (Scrooge and Marley in Stave I of Charles Dickens' *A Christmas Carol.*)

Those souls who would grow must either transplant themselves or overcome the poison in the very medium of their culture.

In summary: both in order to foster the relationships that nourish our own growth and in order to create in ourselves the broadest and best character, we do the best for ourselves when we act in that way which is also best for others—in love. This is the way the pattern is, the way it works.

Even in the midst of anger and fear, of hatred and violence, when a billion years worth of instinct gears us up for either fight or flight, something calls for us to break the vicious cycle and instead to reach out to the other with caring and understanding. I have seen the walls we humans have built of fear and prejudice and misunderstanding. These walls are buttressed by years of suffering or superstition and by what are supposed to be some of our deepest psychological needs. These walls are fearsome; they are depressing and discouraging; they are an inescapable fact of life.

But I have seen these walls breached. And I have felt it. Something there *is* that does not love a wall, that wants it down. We may have physical appetites for food and sex and rest and emotional appetites for status and power, but there is something in the pattern that encourages us in another direction, that encourages us to breach the walls, that pulls us to love.

Where Then Is God?

We began our discussion of patterns to answer the question of where to look for God. We have looked at various aspects of the pattern of the universe: at the way infinitesimal entities consisting mostly of empty space make up a solid world; at the existence of not only life itself but also conscious life; at the presence of ethical and aesthetic faculties in us; and at the soft but persistent pull toward love. Each of these, properly considered, is an occasion for great wonder.

But do these various parts of the pattern *prove* the existence of God? Of course not. God cannot be proved or disproved in this way. Of course, neither can the existence of the tree in my back yard be "proved". You have to experience it—you can see it by day or run into it in the dark. God cannot be seen as a tree is, but can be inferred or felt or run into.

One can respond to the marvelous realities that I have pointed out in one of two ways. One can say that these are all to be explained by natural law or by chance or by evolution, and *nothing else* lies behind them. Or one can say that another force or reality lies behind these. One can see confirmation here of a God whose presence or love one may have felt. These wonders *fit with* the idea of God. Those who see nothing but the immediately visible, those who do not see or infer God, must believe that the rest of us are hallucinating, have strong imaginations, or simply misinterpret reality. Those of us who do see or feel the presence of God, on the other hand, are forced to conclude that the others are either blind, or closed off to the spiritual realities of this world, or simply unlucky enough not to have experienced God.[6]

For those of us who are open to God these aspects of the pattern help to point to this reality, to the way in which God is in the pattern. God is the context within which we all live.

II. What Does God Do?

Q: If God is to be found in the context of our world, how then do we speak of God acting? What does God do?

A: If God is to be found in the context, if it is this context that makes all action possible, then in one sense God can be credited or blamed for every single thing that happens. But this is not true in any meaningful sense. It confuses "making things possible" with "making things happen". (Some readers—precious few, I warrant—will want to relate this to the difference between primary cause and sufficient cause.)

But then what do we mean by God acting, by God doing? If you want to look for God acting in a way outside of the natural processes of this world, for God going "zap!" so that you have an obvious and indisputable miracle—well, then we need to go back to Chapter 3 and begin to work this through all over again. However, I will make two assumptions here: first, that you have absolutely no inclination to read the last hundred or so pages over again; and second, that you understand by now why someone who shares my common sense cannot conceive of God as acting in this way.

But if God doesn't do anything in the traditional sense of supernatural acts, then what does God do? Here is one of the central questions of all theology: What does God do?

God encourages. I do not mean that God is sitting on the heavenly sidelines rooting for us, shouting such things as "Come on, Smith, love your neighbor!", or "Way to go, Jones!" I mean rather that God encourages all acts that are in keeping with the rule of love. I mean that through the processes of this world, including forces that transcend the physical (as we think of it), God is pulling/urging/coaxing each and every one of us in a certain direction. God does this as the context in which we live and through the processes of the world, not by going "zap".

---

[6]Those who are particularly interested in this question and who are patient and persistent readers may wish to consult Hans Küng's *Does God Exist?* (Vintage Books, 1981)Küng considers the challenges from Feuerbach, Marx, Nietzsche, and Freud—among others—in a comprehensive overview of the question of religion and God in recent history. He argues that God does exist, that this cannot be proved, but that it is a decision we must make whether, in the end, to trust in reality.

Other aspects of God's "immanence" or involvement in the world also fit in this category of God's encouragement through the processes. Such themes as God's grace and the activity of God's love and forgiveness are ways that God affects us through the context. The divine pull toward love is a real and pervasive aspect of the world in which we live.

III. What Is God Like?

So far we have addressed the immanence of God—God as present and active in the world. What can we say about the transcendence of God and the nature of God's being?

Q: Can we say that God is infinite?

A: We must first admit that infinity is a difficult concept for us humans to grasp in any adequate sense. (Knowing how to use it in a calculus formula is not the same as understanding what it means.) We must also realize that we should specify, infinite in what respect? Size, strength, weight, or what? But insofar as we recognize "infinite" to mean that God encompasses the totality of being, is not bound by spatial and temporal limits as we are, is beyond what we see and know and beyond our ability to comprehend, then it is appropriate to speak of God as infinite.

Q: Is God omnipotent?

A: The question of whether God is all-powerful usually refers to God's power to control events here on earth. And quite often people are asking, "Is God in charge?" If God *can* control events here but chooses not to, then this power is irrelevant to those who are asking *this* question.

So how do we answer this question about the power of God? Well, if neither our common sense nor our faith allows for an interventionist God, then we must respond by saying, "What do you mean? How is a question about power relevant to God?"

Indeed, we can no more talk about God's omnipotence than we can about God's gender or color. It doesn't apply. God doesn't work that way. After all, did not the Christ show us that worldly power, the power to control, is ultimately vain and empty? What has this kind of power to do with the divine?

Q: Is God omniscient?

A: In whatever way it is that God knows—and it is surely not the same way that you and I know things—I am sure that this knowledge extends to all of us. I am not sure that this knowledge extends to the future, but then I am not sure how the concept of time applies to God anyway.

Q: Is God a personal being? That is, is God an entity or unity that can be called a "person" in the broad sense?

A: Whole books have been written on what it means to be a person, but we all have a reasonably good idea of what it means. We might summarize it in this way: a person is a self-conscious being conscious of the world, of his or her self, and of the relationship between the two. A person is a unity that extends through time, a unity of mind and experience.

So the question is not whether God is some sort of giant human being. The question is whether God is a self-conscious unity.

To answer this question requires speculation in arenas unfamiliar to us. It is hard for us to envision the possibilities for conscious being outside the narrow confines of our own kind of existence. My own conclusion is that we can, and must, relate to God as personal being to personal being. This is the only appropriate way to do so. I am convinced that whatever sort of being God is, the nature of God's being *includes* consciousness and self-consciousness, and very likely transcends our understanding of these as well. God's attributes include self-awareness and the ability to relate to us as personal being to personal being.

This is a very important claim. On what do I base it? Neither on mystical revelation nor on theological necessity nor on human emotional needs. Rather, God's relating to us as person to person seems to fit with what I sense of the world and of God.

Again, I do not mean that we have God zapping in with personal communications like: "John Brown, this is God calling. Attack Harper's Ferry!" Rather, God relates to us as person in the context and through the processes of the world. The context in which we live is *not* impersonal.

It needs to be noted that two distinct claims have been made here: First, that God is a conscious and self-conscious being; and second, that there is an aspect of God that relates to us in our mode of existence as conscious personal beings, and that we can appropriately relate back to God only in this same way. The second is the more vital to our relationship to God, the one that makes it possible.

Q: One last question: does God care?

A: Now we are asked about God's feelings! But it is a necessary question. If God were omniscient and infinite and a whole range of other superlatives, but did not care about us, then God would not be the God we worship and might not even merit the name of God.

But God *does* care. This is a basic part of God's nature. Not only does God love us, it is even appropriate to say that, in pulling us to love through the context, God *is* love.

Obviously, the claim that God loves us is a statement of faith. It cannot be proven. But remember, neither can many other important parts of our lives be "proven". And how would you respond if your spouse or child or parent asked you to prove that you loved them?

Still, our faith claim that God loves us must be consistent with our understanding of the world. So we point to God's encouragement or pulling of us to love, and to the other wonders, as facts that fit well with our feeling of God's love.

A related claim which elaborates and strengthens our understanding that God loves us, is the claim that God suffers with us. What stronger form of caring could there be than this?

But how do we conceive of God suffering with us?[7] There are actually three possibilities in keeping with our theology. First, we could posit that God is omnisciently aware of all of our hurts and sorrows, and that God's desire for our well-being is such that this causes God to suffer the equivalent of emotional pain. This is certainly conceivable and understandable but it will leave some people uncomfortable with its anthropomorphism.

A second alternative is to envision the gentle pull towards love as not merely an action of God, but as a part of God, an aspect of God's being. Our resistance to this pull, our moving in the other direction, would then be a pulling or even a tearing of the fabric of God. God is then conceived of as suffering directly instead of vicariously.

A third alternative is to posit that if God is in the context, then God must be in each and every one of us as well. We all share in the being of God; God's being includes each of us. In this conception God experiences our suffering even more directly, for our suffering is God's as well through our being a part of God's being.

Each of these three is a suitable conception. And any one of them strengthens our understanding of how God cares for us.

IV. Images of God

So far in this chapter we have looked at some of the wonders of our reality that fit with a belief in God, we have briefly answered the question of how God acts in this world (in keeping with our common sense), and we have addressed a few questions about what God is like. In all of these we were dealing with concepts, with the realm of ideas that must be logical and consistent. We have already spoken of the necessity of speaking clearly and carefully about God.

But concepts are not the only way in which we convey our understanding and our truths. As we noted in the last chapter, images or metaphors are also important and sometimes do better at communicating than do concepts. So in this section I will put forth some images of God which fit

---

[7]Our success or failure in conceiving how this works does not, of course, determine whether or not it is a fact. But we ought not to postulate things like this without showing how they are compatible with the rest of our beliefs and with our common sense.

with our understanding. These images are only partially developed. You are encouraged to further develop these yourself and also to think of different images which you find helpful to your understanding of God.

In talking about God with images we do not say that God *is* such and such, we say that God is *like* such and such (the same way that Jesus spoke about the Kingdom of God in his parables).

1. God Is Like the Sun

This is an analogy that has been used often and in a variety of ways over the centuries. And of course the sun has been worshipped as divine itself. Nevertheless, a helpful image can be found here.

We do not mean that God is like the sun in that it is distant and "up there", or in that if you come too close you will be consumed or if you look at it directly you will be blinded. Rather, God is like the sun in this way: it may seem far away, but its rays are all around us. Its effects are diffuse, pervasive. It made possible the world in which we exist and continues to make it possible. It creates the context in which we live.

It not only sustains life, it also provides light to see and warmth for comfort. And (as an analogy to us) many plants are drawn toward the sun. They succeed only by growing sunward.

In these ways God is like the sun.

2. God Is Like Gravity

Before the tools of modern science, gravity could not be measured. We could only infer its existence. It cannot be seen. And yet there it most definitely is.

Gravity serves to hold things together. It is the attractive force which pulls bodies towards one another. It balances centrifugal forces to hold planets in orbit. It pulls things together, acting against the forces that pull things apart. Gravity *is* the pull, acting unseen through all creation. In these ways God is like gravity.

3. God Is Like the Magnetic Field

The magnetic field is invisible but surrounds us everywhere, encompassing the whole earth. But though it is all around us, it can only be detected by the right kind of sensitivity. Iron that is not magnetized will not respond to it.

And though it is all around us, it leads in a certain direction. Someone who is aware of it, who has a proper compass and who pays attention to this compass, can find their way.

In these ways God is like the magnetic field.

4. God Is Like the Water Cycle

We see water in our world in many different individual rivers and streams, oceans and ponds, puddles and raindrops. Yet it is all water. It all derives from and is a part of the water cycle. Thus do we derive from God, and thus does God participate in everything.

And God participates in us as the water cycle does. We may think of it as being "out there". But water is an integral part of us, a constituent part of every cell in our body.

In these ways God is like the water cycle.

These are but outlines of images, but perhaps they will help some to understand how we are conceiving of God. Certainly these and other images need to be developed.

And now, having considered how God acts, we can continue our consideration of Jesus of Nazareth as the functional Christ with the basic question of "Why Jesus?"

CHAPTER 13: WHY JESUS OF NAZARETH?

"Wisdom is justified by all her children."

(Jesus, Luke 7:35)

"Take him yourself and judge him."

(Pilate, John 18:31)

If God is in the processes, if God is the context, if God is not a specific interventionist . . . then how can this Jesus of Nazareth be related to God any differently than anyone else? How can we justify looking to the Christ for meaning any more than looking to Nietzsche or the Buddha or your next-door neighbor? Or your own selfish desires?

In previous chapters we have shown why we cannot identify Jesus either as God incarnate or as a person specially sent or chosen by God. God just doesn't work that way. Instead, we identify Jesus as "the Christ", meaning by this that it is he whose life and teachings function as the focus for our understanding of reality. It is he through whom we find meaning in our lives, and in whom we find the key to our understanding of God.

The interpretations of Jesus which we can no longer use—as God incarnate or as specially chosen—did have the advantage of making a clear claim about his authority to speak of God and moral truths. But how do we justify now our claim of Jesus' role as key to our understanding of God, as focus to the whole complex of meaning in our lives?

In traditional language this is the question of authority: the question of the authority of Jesus Christ. But why do we speak of "authority" here? What does it mean in the realm of value and meaning and common sense theology to speak of authority?

The Question of Authority

Usually when we speak of authority we are referring either to the state, that is, the authority of the government vested in certain positions

139

and so in the people who hold those positions, or to the legal authority that derives from ownership or contract. Obviously, this is not the kind of authority that we mean here.

We also commonly speak of someone being an authority on a certain subject, meaning that he or she is recognized as an accepted source of expert opinion in that area.

Or we might recognize the moral authority of an individual, either because of their relationship to us (e.g. parent) or because of something about their life or wisdom.

These three types of authority—legal, expert, and moral—were combined in first century Palestine in a way that is foreign to us today. Scripture was the highest authority, of course (within the limits set by Roman law). Legal decisions, whether by local lawyers or the high council in Jerusalem, were in fact interpretations of God's will as found in the Scriptures. And interpretations were generally made by citing recognized (authoritative) rabbis.

Jesus of Nazareth, however, was neither a member of the high council nor a local official nor a recognized rabbi. Naturally, then, the people who heard him "were astonished at his teaching, for he taught them as one who had authority, and not as the scribes." (Mark 1:22) Two questions must be answered: first, what was the source of this authority? That is, how was he able to speak this way and be recognized this way in first century Palestine? And second, does this translate into authority for us today? If so, how? And with what meaning of authority?

Jesus' Authority in First Century Palestine

He spoke as one who had authority. He did not just repeat the traditions of the elders or justify what he said by the teachings of Rabbi somebody-or-other. "You have heard that it was said of old," he said, "but I say to you . . ."

How was he able to do this? Because he was sure of himself. He knew he could sense the pull of the God that spoke through the law and the prophets, and knew that he had to point the way to others. So he did.

He saw that some were perverting justice and that others were trapped in their own greed. He saw that some tried to be faithful but couldn't get past their lists of rules and that others stood in the need of the freeing word of God's love. So he acted accordingly, and he did so with self-assurance.

This sort of moral certainty is much out of favor today, being identified in our minds with fascists and Ayatollahs and other out-of-touch-with-reality fanatics. Too often we have heard the narrow-minded offer simplistic solutions to complex problems. We have, rightly, rejected these so-called "solutions". We have recognized that there are no easy answers.

But it seems that we have often gone one step further: we justify our own confusion by being suspicious of *any* certainty, and we interpret the lack of easy answers to mean that any answer is as good as another, that we cannot be sure about right and wrong.

This last step is a tragic and inexcusable surrender of human moral responsibility. Even if we cannot know the answer to all of society's ills, even if we cannot pretend to know how to solve the problems of crime and drugs and inflation and poverty, we can still proclaim that it is obviously and unquestionably a moral wrong to maintain a penal system based on vengeance instead of rehabilitation; to allow human rights violations to go unchallenged (on either side of the iron curtain); to waste vast quantities of food and resources while others are malnourished and sick and poor; or to allow so many children in our own midst to go through childhood unwanted and unloved and even abused. The lack of easy solutions cannot be used as an excuse to cease recognizing and proclaiming right and wrong.

Jesus of Nazareth did not surrender this responsibility. He proclaimed right and wrong. He spoke with the authority of someone who saw clearly, someone who was not distracted or blinded by self-interest, someone who was not a prisoner to societal conventions. But most simply, he spoke with authority because he spoke from his own deep convictions.

So he preached his call to God, his call to love and repentance and reconciliation, with courage and conviction and charisma. And he preached it in such a way that his listeners were presented with a choice. They felt compelled to either accept or reject his message. Indeed, this is not an unusual reaction to someone who is secure in who they are and sure of their vision.

Those who responded positively to his message recognized him as having authority as their leader and teacher. Those who responded negatively also recognized the claim of authority in the way he taught and acted, but they rejected this claim.

So we can explain a claim to authority in first century Palestine in terms of convictions and charisma and a demand for decision. But how do we address the question of the authority of Jesus of Nazareth today?

The Question of Jesus' Authority Today

The question of Jesus' authority today cannot be answered by an appeal to his compelling presence or to ancient Near Eastern understandings. Rather we must look at our own response to his life and teachings. And we need to address three different questions here: (1) What is involved in recognizing in Jesus, or attributing to Jesus, authority? (2) How do we justify this in terms of our common sense theology?

(3) Why recognize authority in this person rather than in someone else or in no one at all?

1. What Does It Mean to Recognize Jesus' Authority?

There are three steps involved in an individual recognizing the authority of Jesus of Nazareth. The first step is a real awareness of who he is. This does *not* mean the vague and comfortable awareness that we get from our culture—and all too often from our churches and church schools—that Jesus was a good guy who talked about love. Neither does this mean an awareness of creeds, or an ability to say that Jesus Christ is Lord or Savior or Son of God or whatever. To begin with we need to seriously confront the life and teachings of Jesus himself. If this is done earnestly and sincerely we will be forced to ask ourselves whether indeed he may have been right, whether he knew what he was about, whether he did in fact correctly perceive God and truth, value and meaning.

The second step in an individual's recognition of Jesus' authority is an affirmative answer to this, a recognition on our part that, yes indeed, this guy *was* right in his central message. He had the key: service of others and of God is our greatest purpose; love in return for hate is the greatest triumph; there is something in life more important than our own selfish fears and desires. Step two is thus the recognition that Jesus of Nazareth points to the truth, that here we have an accurate compass.

This in itself would be to recognize a certain authority in this person. But this remains only an abstract authority, an authority that we recognize for others but not ourselves, unless we move on to step three. This third step is the decision that since Jesus was right, we will try to live by his teachings. Since he illustrated the way to live in accordance with truth and meaning, we will follow his lead in orienting our own lives. Or, to put it another way, after deciding that here we have an accurate compass (step two), we now decide to follow where it points (step three). In the terminology we used earlier, this is what makes us Christians; this is what it means to confess Jesus as the Christ.

This is what is involved today in an individual recognizing the authority of Jesus of Nazareth. Now we move on to question (2): How does this fit without common sense?

2. How Do We Justify This Authority?

How can we justify this authority for Jesus of Nazareth in a way consistent with our common sense theology? It fits with our understanding of the Christ, with our conception of God, and with our modern common sense to claim that Jesus of Nazareth was particularly sensitive to the presence of God as the context for our lives and to the possibilities and demands that this creates for us. If we use the image of God as magnetic field, then we can similarly picture Jesus as a compass. A compass is not made of the same substance as a magnetic field, nor is it sent or chosen by the north pole, but it is accurately sensitive to the pull and direction of the magnetic field within which we live.

It is well known that some other animals can sense color and smell and sound beyond our range. Bees home in on brilliant ultraviolet patterns that we see as plain white daisies; pigeons can literally align themselves to magnetic north because of magnetite in their brains. Similarly, we recognize that some people are more sensitive than others to the spiritual dimensions of human existence and that some are particularly sensitive. And this is the claim that we make of Jesus of Nazareth. We claim that he was particularly aware of and in tune with God, that he was aware of and in tune with the ultimate truths and values and meaning.

We do not have to claim that he is the only person who was ever this sensitive to God, that he was in tune with God in an absolutely unique way. Rather, our claim is that Jesus was particularly sensitive to God. We claim that he was right, that he is an accurate compass. This is sufficient for our faith—that we have a trustworthy guide—and this fits with our common sense in a way that other kinds of claims about Jesus do not.

3. Why Jesus of Nazareth?

If we do not claim an absolutely unique relationship between Jesus and God, then how do we justify recognizing Jesus' authority? Even if it fits with our common sense, how can we justify choosing this person as our compass when there may be others just as accurate?

This is a legitimate and important question. But we need to remember that we do not need to claim that Jesus is the *only* trustworthy guide to God. I hope we are not so insecure that we need to claim that everyone else in all other religious traditions is hopelessly misguided. As we pointed out in Chapter 8, we can consider each other to be wrong without necessarily impugning the validity of the other's religious beliefs, *if* their beliefs lead to right relation with God and people. And indeed, should we not rejoice if others find themselves directed to truth and to God, even if it is by other paths than our own?

Well, if we don't claim (and so don't need to try to prove) uniqueness for Jesus of Nazareth, how then do we justify giving him the role and authority of compass? There are four parts to our answer: (A) we are not aware of any equally good alternatives; (B) Jesus has been confirmed in this role by many faithful lives; (C) our interpretation of Jesus' role is subject to the correction of tradition and ongoing public discussion; and (D) in the end, it depends on the response of our hearts. You will note that these are mostly reasons of historical accident, dependent on our own historical situation. We are historical creatures, influenced greatly by our circumstances. Our claim is that—partly because of these circumstances—Jesus can function as the Christ for us, and does function this way for those who choose him.

(A) Why choose Jesus of Nazareth when there may be others who were as sensitive to God? The plain fact is that we don't *know* of any others who would fill the bill for us. The other people of whom I am aware who show in their lives this same sensitivity and devotion to the cause of God and rightness are themselves acknowledged followers of Jesus. If we were to choose one of them as a guide we would find ourselves directed right back to Jesus as compass. The one exception to this with which we in the West are familiar is Mahatma Gandhi. However, it is unlikely that we could bridge the cultural gap and choose as compass someone who was an ascetic and a vegetarian and who promoted celibacy even in marriage for the sake of spiritual growth.

Now I freely admit that my not being aware of good alternatives to Jesus of Nazareth may be due to simple ignorance on my part and is no doubt culturally conditioned. Nevertheless, it makes no sense to withhold our allegiance from Jesus merely because it is possible that there may be other options, if in fact there are no actual viable alternatives in sight. (And I must say, even with the honey-wagon load of self-proclaimed saviors now in evidence, there has never been a greater and more obvious dearth of good candidates.)

(B) If we were to become aware of another individual, or even several people, who seem to point to God and to the deepest truths as consistently and accurately as Jesus of Nazareth, we would still have another question. What kind of confirmation is there for the ability of these individuals to serve as accurate guides in aligning our lives with God?

The fact is that the teachings and example of Jesus have been tested out in many lives over many years. It is painfully true that his principles have been tested out by only a small fraction of those who have called themselves Christians through the centuries. But we do have numerous examples of people who, orienting their lives by the Christ, have lived in right relation with their neighbors and God, displaying unselfish caring for the hurts and needs of others.

This is very mundane historical fact. But the fact of the matter is that Jesus' ability to function as a compass has been tested and confirmed over many generations. It is unlikely that we will find an alternative with this kind of confirmation, in whom we can have the same level of confidence.

(C) We need also to consider the fact that the content and implications of Jesus' message are the subject of ongoing public discussion and debate. The importance of this must not be underestimated. When someone chooses to follow this particular compass they have as a resource an existing institution—the Church—to provide support and encouragement as well as the challenge and reminder of what it means to live in this direction. Who among us does not need this encouragement from time to time?

Furthermore, the existence of an established group with an established tradition tends to restrain personal extremes and idiosyncracies. Within this context our beliefs and actions are subject to the correction of public scrutiny. The mass suicide of Jonesville, for instance, was only possible in the isolation of the Guyanese jungle. And while it is also true that tradition can petrify into inflexibility, and can even at times inhibit the correct understanding of the original message, it contains within it the kernel of its own renewal. Given a free exchange of ideas, untraditional points of view are free to test themselves against accepted beliefs and a new and stronger synthesis may emerge.

(D) Points A, B, and C address the intellect. However, we cannot answer the question "Why Jesus of Nazareth?" by appealing to reason alone. It is a question of value and meaning, and as such is a question that addresses the heart. The first three points show that the choice of Jesus of Nazareth as compass makes sense and has certain arguments on its side. But the choice itself must be made with our hearts. In the final analysis, the question "Why Jesus of Nazareth?" must be answered by each of us individually, and the only adequate answer is a strong conviction in our deepest being that Jesus' message is indeed the wonderful and powerful Truth. Why Jesus? Because the message that he preached and lived grabs us, permeates our values and gives our lives meaning. People other than Jesus, for reasons both circumstantial and substantial, do not grab us as profoundly.

What is this? Does it all boil down to a subjective response? Has Jesus of Nazareth no more of an objective claim on our loyalty than Sun Myung Moon or the Dalai Lama or the latest self-proclaimed messiah?

In one sense, he has not. Jesus has no claim of authority apart from our own subjective choice of him as compass. Democratic symbolism is appropriate here: he has authority only as we "elect" him or choose him. His message is authoritative for us only as we recognize its truth.

In another sense, as we pointed out in A, B, and C, there are some objective reasons which support this subjective choice. It can further be pointed out that there are some very real and important differences between Jesus and the others who have been put forth as authoritative guides, both in their messages and in the fruit that is born in the lives of their disciples.

Those who fully appropriate the central message of Jesus into their lives, whatever portion of "Christians" this may be, evidence a combination of freedom, moral concern, inner peace and good works of love that often bear fruit in the lives of others. In contrast, the brainwashed disciples of a guru may have inner peace, but they have attained this through the loss of their freedom and their ability to think, and their goal seems to be not to help others but to entrap more disciples. The pleasure-seekers in our society may seem free in comparison, but they lack inner meaning and bear no good fruit. Seeking to be free from responsibility, they all too often lack a responsible self to *be* free, and end up in bondage to the frenetic activity in which they hide from their own emptiness. Our solid burghers seem responsible: good parents and good citizens, active in civic endeavors, enjoying the peace and the satisfaction of respect and status and social conformity. Too often, though, these solid citizens cannot break through the walls of prejudice and habit, economic security and "what will the neighbors think", to reach the possibilities of love and freedom and justice to which God calls us.

I have claimed, and I claim again, that the life lived in love and right relation, and the character of one who lives in such a way, are in the most important sense *better*. If someone were to produce as gripping an example of this and as sure a guide to this as Jesus of Nazareth, then there might not be grounds for choosing one over the other. (And certainly this poor world of ours can make use of more good compasses!) However, for whatever reasons, I do not see this other someone.

So why Jesus of Nazareth? Because we find in him a key that yields meaning, a guide to value and truth that is confirmed as we live out our lives. Because his example and his teachings first grab us and then prove themselves over time. Because we find that the attitude, the faith, embodied in him leads to right relationship. And because we know, in our deepest heart of hearts, that his call to love and service is the call to that which is right and true in a way that transcends all other rights and all other truths. This is why we confess Jesus as the Christ.

CHAPTER 14: RECONSTRUCTION: SIN AND SALVATION

"What does the Lord require of you but to do justice, and to love kindness, and to walk humbly with your God?" (Micah 6:8)

"The Lord is good; his steadfast love endures forever, and his faithfulness to all generations." (Psalm 100:5)

Now that we have laid out our common sense theology and Christology it is time to consider the effects of these on traditional Christian themes. In this chapter we will look at those which can be grouped under the general heading of "sin and salvation".

I: Sin

Sin has generally been thought of in two different ways: as an action or as a condition. We will consider sin as a condition under the heading of "original sin" below. At this point we are concerned with sin in the sense of bad deeds.

What does it mean to call a human action a sin? To begin with we are saying that the action is morally wrong. And traditionally, it was to say that this action violated the will of God. This is what makes it a sin. To sin, then, meant betrayal of the God who loves you, the God who had "given his only son" on your behalf. Obviously, this added a degree of perniciousness: You not only have injured a fellow human being with your sin, but you have also transgressed against God Almighty. Furthermore, besides having an additional connotation of moral wrong, to sin was dangerous: it could wind you up in hell.

Nowadays, however, we are reluctant to take the step from calling an action morally wrong to calling it a sin.[1] Why is this? There are several factors involved:

---

[1] Thus Karl Menninger's *Whatever Became of Sin?* (Hawthorn Books, 1973).

1. First, to call an act on the part of someone else a "sin" may be felt to imply an unattractive self-righteousness on our part. And a lot of us would rather be considered wishy-washy or even sinful rather than self-righteous. Self-righteousness, while sinful itself, is less socially acceptable than most other sins.

2. Second, to call a wrong action a "sin" is to bring in the religious dimension. Heaven forbid that we should cause our friends to think we're religious, of all things! They would surely consider us to be some sort of fanatic.

3. Third, to call something a "sin" is to imply that we do in fact know what is right and what is wrong, and for some people this further implies that we know the will of God in a particular situation. Both of these claims are very out of fashion in this day of no absolutes. Our resistance to such claims is further increased by the fact that those who are most likely to make them are equipped with nice, neat lists of what God disapproves of—lists that generally reflect the bias of a certain class and culture and that show a special interest in sexual mores, lists that all too often cannot distinguish between minor personal failings and major injustices. We are justifiably suspicious of such lists.

4. Finally, the traditional connotations of "sin" cause it to be perceived as language that is simply too strong. "Sin" brings with it connotations of the sacred, of dealing with a superior moral law, of having transgressed against the Absolute, of having offended the one eternal God and put oneself at risk. This is heavy stuff for people who have gotten unused to dealing with the sacred as a part of their lives. It has become a foreign element to many, and (as with much that is alien and unfamiliar to us) it is feared.

Now the question is: given our present aversion to the use of the word "sin" for all these reasons, and given our common sense view of God which does not encompass the divine giving of specific commandments on stone tablets or otherwise—what do we do with "sin"? What should we, what can we, mean by it? Or should we abandon it altogether? (The concept, I mean. I doubt we shall ever abandon the practice.)

No, we do not need to abandon the concept of sin. In fact, we *must* not abandon it. It makes the crucial point that our choices between right and wrong are not made in a vacuum. How we act, how we treat people, how we live, affects our relationship with the ultimate. We must not forget this.

But if we must keep (or resurrect) the concept of sin, how do we define it and how do we use it? To begin with, we state again that there is a right and a wrong. Even in complex situations there are generally some actions which clearly grow out of fear and hatred, and which lead to a continuation of the sad and vicious cycle of human unkindness. These are wrong. Likewise there are generally some actions which demonstrate a true concern for all involved, for love and justice, and which may lead to reconciliation and improvement. These are right.

And God, we have said, calls us into right relationship, calls us to do what is right. A sin, then, is an action that goes against this call. To give it a proper definition: a sin is an action by a mentally competent person that goes against or avoids the call of God to right relation.[2]

With this as the definition of sin, how do we use it? In fact, we find there are three important uses for the Christian concept of sin:

First, it gives us a way to say that morally wrong acts are just that: they are wrong. They are bad. They ought not to be done. The idea of "sin" carries with it this connotation and helps us to make a point which we are sometimes obligated to make. We do not need to make this point in those cases where a wrong has been acknowledged and repented of. Rather, it is when sins are socially acceptable, unrecognized, or a part of our cultural fabric that we need most to pronounce them as such.

Second, since sin carries with it the connotation of danger to the sinner, to identify certain actions as sins is to call attention in a strong way to the need for repentance and change for the good of the sinner. In order to do this we do not need to postulate a God standing in judgment and threatening damnation in response to particular acts. It fits better with our common sense to adopt a view not unlike that found in parts of the Old Testament: sin will have its harmful consequences for the person doing as well as for the person done to, not as a result of a special interventionist act of God but as a natural result of the sin itself. And a natural result of sin is a warping of our character.

What is at stake here in deciding between right and wrong is nothing less than the shape and the depth of our selves. We can carve our selves shallow and narrow and crooked by opting for the selfish and the vengeful and the wrong, by selling out our human integrity. Or we can hew a broad and solid foundation for our selves by making hard choices for the loving and the right. In deciding between right and wrong we are not only choosing what actions to take. We are choosing as well the shape and the nature of our only true possession, our self.

Third, when we say that a wrong act is a sin, even if we do not conceive of God as standing in judgment we are still pointing out that there is another dimension involved in our choices between right and wrong. When we make a moral decision we are also determining the nature of our relationship with God. It is not that God rewards or damns us in response: rather, it is we ourselves turning towards or turning away from God.

Because it is so vitally important to point out that doing the wrong thing is bad in the first place, is damaging to our selves, and harms our relationship with God, we can and must continue to speak about sin.

---

[2]To satisfy the ethical philosopher, we can add the usual stipulations: that one acted according to reasonably expected consequences consistent with the available information, and that one made efforts to assure adequate information proportionate to the importance of the potential effects.

II: Original Sin

Now we must consider sin as a condition, the human tendency toward sinning that is traditionally called "original sin". This two-word phrase has more unchristian implications to it than any other I can think of—a remarkable achievement for a concept that is such an integral part of Christian tradition. For theologians from Augustine to Luther (and all too many since) the concept of "original sin" has included the following tenets:

(1) That we are born in a state of sinfulness. That is, because of our human nature it is inevitable that we will in the course of our lives commit sins. Some theologians put it more strongly than this and say that we are born with a human nature such that, without the action of God's grace, we are bound to be dominated by the motivations that lead to sinning.

(2) That this state of sin or tendency to commit sins is somehow or other our own fault. Even though we are born with it without anyone so much as asking our preference in the matter, it is our fault. It is certainly *not* God's fault. After all, we were created by God in a state of perfection. And we blew it, thanks to Adam and Eve and the serpent. And the responsibility for our sinfulness is passed down to us along with the condition itself.

(3) That, being guilty of sinfulness in this way, we are therefore unworthy of God's love, to the point that God could forgive us for this sinfulness—and thereby save us from the damnation that would otherwise be its natural and deserved consequence—only if someone free from this sinfulness were to offer himself or herself as a sacrifice in our stead and thus atone for our guilt.

(4)That in order for our forgiveness to be effected by this atonement we must "believe in" Jesus Christ, which allows God to pretend that we are not sinful after all. This is justification by faith, or by grace through faith.

The unchristian implications of these are:

(1) That we humans are in and of ourselves unworthy of God's love.

(2) That a newborn infant is guilty of sinfulness and would presumably not qualify for salvation without a special act of grace.

(3) That however much good a person may do with their life, however much faith they may have, they still need God's forgiveness in order to receive salvation, which God either could not or would not grant until innocent blood was shed in the crucifixion.

(4) That God still cannot or will not grant this forgiveness unless a person believes in Jesus Christ; and therefore that it is a belief or doctrine that is necessary for salvation, not a life lived in love and faith.

These implications of the traditional idea of "original sin" stand in direct opposition to the whole of Jesus' life and teaching. The God of Jesus Christ loved the world, sought out sinners, and forgave those who repented. Anyone who shares the Christian understanding of God cannot help but find these ideas—humans as unworthy of God's love, babies as evil, and God not forgiving anyone until innocent blood has been shed—to be repugnant and blasphemous.

If the implications of the idea of "original sin" are absolutely unacceptable, what can we do with the concept itself? I fear that these traditional ramifications are so identified with the phrase "original sin" that there is no alternative but to heave it into the theological garbage dump.

However, connected with this concept is a pair of important Christian insights that need to be retained. They are much too important to lose sight of. The first of these is a well-developed appreciation for the finitude of each human being, for our imperfection and our separation from the eternal and the perfect. The second is the realization that humans are as a matter of fact capable of immense evil, not to mention an incredible number of entirely unnecessary petty cruelties.

These two insights certainly have the depth and the importance to stand on their own. There is no need to merge them with the rest of the complex that is associated with "original sin".

Furthermore, while we need to recognize the gravity of our human propensity to sin, we need to balance this with the recognition (demonstrated so vividly by Jesus of Nazareth) that each and every human being has the ability to turn to God and to do good, that each and every human being is intrinsically worthy of love. To speak of "original sin" without at the same time speaking of "original virtue" is to ignore precisely that potential that Jesus saw and reached for, precisely that aspect of humanity that is most relevant to the Christian message.[3] If we ignore either the pull toward evil or the pull toward good we are holding a view that is unrealistic and will hamper our effectiveness in dealing with the real world.

To arrive at a balanced view we have to discard the traditional concept of "original sin". We need to replace it with a different concept, with a theme which is in keeping with the Christian message and which recognizes all our potential. We might say that humans have "bidirectional capabilities" or an "open orientation". However, I would prefer simply to say that human beings have within themselves the potential both for great evil and for great good. This observation, as simple as it is, constitutes one of the great basic understandings of Christianity, but is nonetheless disregarded in one way or another by great numbers of us.

III: Salvation

Is this not the central tenet of the Christian faith, that Jesus came and suffered "for us men and for our salvation"? Nevertheless, the traditional

---

[3] Matthew Fox addresses this in *Original Blessing* (Santa Fe: Bear and Company, 1983), in

concept of salvation has serious problems. It is very closely associated with the unchristian ideas just noted under "original sin". We must ask whether it has a useful meaning independent of the ideas of human unworthiness and blood sacrifice.

First of all: what do we mean by "salvation"? In general, of course, it means being saved from something, from some danger or evil. Additionally, as a part of being saved *from* something, one must be saved *to* something else, to a different place or state of affairs. In Christian theology in particular salvation is from sin or from the penalties of sin. There is a double aspect: one is saved by being brought into a state of grace (or forgiveness or justification or even sanctification) instead of bondage to sin in this life, and by being brought into heaven instead of hell in the next life.

For both of these aspects we can and must find a better term than "salvation". We must use concepts and phrases that are not so identified with "blood of the lamb" theology, concepts that emphasize the positive instead of the negative. We will approach this task by looking at each of these two aspects of salvation in turn, in this life and in the afterlife, to see just what it is we wish to be saying.

IIIA: Salvation In This Life

In the case of salvation from bondage to sin in this life, what we want to stress is the good news—the gospel—that we do not *have* to be enslaved by our fear and hatred and selfishness, that we *are* in fact free to love, free to be kind and generous and even great of soul. We can best communicate this message not by emphasizing our need to be rescued from negative possibilities, but rather by emphasizing our potential for living in a loving and faithful way. So instead of speaking of "salvation" we ought rather to speak of living in right relationship, of faithfulness and commitment and love. It's not so much that we need to be saved from sin as it is that we need to commit ourselves to a life of faith. (And truly we *cannot* do the first except by doing the second.) This is especially true in a society where the greatest temptation is not to murder or steal but is rather to orient your life toward your own self-satisfaction measured in terms of worldly success or possessions or pleasure.

"But," challenges the traditionalist, "as weak and imperfect human beings we are incapable of doing the right thing and living the right way until we have been saved from the power of sin, whether you view this power emanating from within us or from Satan."

which he criticizes "fall/redemption spirituality" and proposes "creation spirituality", a fascinating blend of panentheism, feminism, ecology-awareness, and Medieval mystics such as Meister Eckhart and Hildegarde of Bingen. Unfortunately, he undergirds this positive approach to creation and spirituality with the ancient "Logos" Christology, thus basing it all on a divine and cosmic Christ.

To which I say, "Horsefeathers!" I am weary of this calumny against humanity and against God. At the risk of being repetitious, however, I will respond in more detail.

First, as we said under "original sin", we are no more inhabited and owned by evil that we are by righteousness. Certainly we make mistakes, and sometimes do horrible things, but we do have the ability to choose between right and wrong. Otherwise there would not be as much good in the world as there is.

Second, we cannot be saved from "bondage to sin", we cannot avoid the habits and choices that lead to sin, except by opting for the good and striving to live faithfully. We cannot be saved from sin as a separate step *before* choosing to orient our lives towards the good.

Third, to treat humans as base prisoners of our own vice who need saving before we can try to live faithfully is to exaggerate the darkness, and is to encourage us simply to try to avoid evil instead of trying to live rightly and do good. This will not work! There are too many people on the moral sidelines who think they are living well just because they avoid specific acts of evil. Enough of this telling us to hide from the dark. On to light and life!

Our conclusion stands: we must replace the concept of salvation from sin in this life, and its negative and inadequate emphasis on avoidance, with the idea of living a faithful life. We must stress that this life of faith is a real possibility for us, is in fact the only possibility that yields meaning and wholeness and depth of character and right relation to God.

IIIB: Salvation In The Next Life

The other aspect of salvation is salvation from the "wages of sin", being saved from hell and admitted into heaven. The traditional understanding of this is that all humans need to be saved. Without divine intervention we would all as a matter of course end up in hell. But we could not be saved, except that Jesus Christ died for us, sacrificing his sinless and perfect self in our place. So now if we attach ourselves to this Jesus through faith, God will forgive us our sins and will attribute to us the sinlessness of this our Savior. Only thus is God able to welcome us into heaven.

Salvation, then, is a gift given graciously to the undeserving. No one deserves it since no one is perfect.

There are several real problems with this idea of salvation:

First, this reeks of the same repugnant attitudes as "original sin": that we are essentially evil and unworthy of love, and that God could only forgive us after being satisfied by innocent blood. These attitudes are incompatible with the message of the Christ.

Second, this idea of salvation depends on the double premise that (a) human beings who are without sin are deserving of heaven; and (b) there are no human beings without sin. Which is to say that heaven—whether you think of it as a place or as a state of union with God—was set up with rules that exclude all human beings to begin with. This certainly does not fit with the Christian view of God as one who is seeking out sinners in love, calling them to turn and come.

At this point the concept of "salvation" cannot be separated from these negative connotations which are so much a part of its tradition. These connotations are not only undesirable, they are untenable in the Christian faith. Therefore we must retire the term "salvation" from current use.

But if we do not use "salvation" to speak of the goal of Christians, of our eternal destiny, then what do we say instead? We need to ask, what is it that we wish to emphasize?

Again, instead of stressing the negative aspect ought we not rather to stress the positive? Instead of emphasizing "salvation from" that which we wish to avoid, ought we not rather to emphasize the reality that we are seeking?

So: what is our goal, and how do we attain it? Our goal is the same as we said above: to live faithfully and to orient our selves towards God. And if we are truly oriented towards God then it makes sense for our ultimate destiny to be the oneness with God which the death of our physical bodies makes possible. I do not pretend to know the nature of this oneness with God, nor the extent to which our individual identities are preserved, nor the quality of eternity. But if faith consists of the orienting of our lives towards God in this life, then it would seem natural for our selves to continue in this direction once they are released into the next life.

This brings us to the topics of judgment and grace.

IV: Judgment And Grace

The classical picture of judgment is that of an individual, his or her life finished, standing before God as their life is weighed in the balance, then receiving the fair judgment that determines his or her eternal fate. Of course only those who are forgiven, who are saved by their faith and by God's grace, go on to heaven.

Surely, though, our tradition offers a much better image than that of God sitting in judgment on our earthly lives and then imposing a final destination as a separate interventionist act. Instead of this, we should emphasize our belief in the God who has accepted us, who loves us, who seeks us, who waits for us to turn and accept this love. This gives us the image of God holding open the door of reconciliation, waiting for us to respond and walk through. It is we who reject God, not the other way around.

This image better represents the gospel's central motif of a reconciling God, and it also fits better with our common sense understanding of God being the context within which we live. There is no necessity for human perfection or for blood atonement. God's forgiveness is extended at all times along with God's love, available to us if we only repent and turn and accept this love. It is *our* choice as to whether we will live toward God or away from God. And if we truly set the direction of our souls toward God then we continue in this direction and are united with God after death.

Do we then (to use traditional language) "save ourselves"? Do we achieve heaven through our own good works? Certainly this would be contrary to the basic Christian understanding that it is God who gets us into heaven, not we ourselves.

But tradition also recognizes that it takes both parties, God and humans, to get us to heaven. It takes our faith as well as God's grace. And this is what we are saying here. God's grace is the constant pull on us. It is the encouragement to live in right relationship, a part of the world in which we live. God's grace, God's love, and God's welcome for us all are already a feature of reality. When we respond to this by living in faith, by living towards God, this is not "saving ourselves" but is rather to provide our share of the necessary ingredients. God provides the call; we must provide the answer. God's grace holds open the door; we must walk through it.

To conclude then: a life of faith, oriented towards loving God and loving neighbor, is what constitutes an affirmative response to God's call. To set our selves on this course will naturally result in continuing on this path to God in the afterlife. We need not think of this as "salvation" from anything, and in fact because of the negative connotations of this word we should *not* use it. We need rather to stress the positive aspects of saying yes to God's call: living in right relation, forming a noble self in a life of faith, learning truly to love our neighbors, experiencing this love in our hearts. This, not escape or salvation from anything, is the greatest purpose available to us.

CHAPTER 15: RECONSTRUCTION: CHRISTIAN MYTH

"For you bring some strange things to our ears; we wish to know therefore what these things mean." (Acts 17:20)

In Chapter 14 we looked at the "sin and salvation" complex of traditional concepts. In this chapter we will look at the themes that deal with Jesus of Nazareth himself. Our primary question, however, will not be whether these themes fit with our common sense. We have already asked this of many of these, and it is clear that major portions of the Jesus story and its interpretations are simply incompatible with modern common sense. But in the story of Jesus we are dealing with more than just doctrine. We have here ideas and images that are central to the Christian faith itself. So the question for this chapter is, since some of the Jesus stories and concepts are so eminently incompatible with common sense—what do we do with them?

The usual alternative to defending their literal truth is to ignore those particular stories we find incredible, shoving them like unwanted family skeletons into hidden closets and bolting the door with a fervent prayer that the lock will hold. We badly need to discover a way to disavow neither our common sense nor this large portion of the Jesus tradition. We need a way to use them *both* constructively in our faith.

There is a way to do this, but only if we dare to be bold, only if we can be different and creative in our approach. We need to take the most honest and most constructive option available to us: creation of the category of "Christian Myth". We do not mean this in the technical sense of any story referring to the supernatural (see Chapter 4, p. 44). This has already been done by scholars. What we mean here is myth in its everyday, nontechnical sense as understood by you and me: a story that is told as if it were literally true, but which is no longer accepted as factual, and which explains or symbolizes a belief or insight.

"Myth" in this sense has been applied before to the story of Jesus, but almost always by people who were trying to dismiss Jesus of Nazareth and undermine the Christian faith. These people saw it as a weapon against Christianity. What we are doing is to wrest this from the grasp of those who know not its proper use. We are claiming it for our own, using the concept of "Christian Myth" to mean something valuable and meaningful to us.

To classify a story or theme as Christian Myth is therefore not at all to dismiss it but rather to elevate it to a special status. In fact, the question of its historic accuracy is rendered irrelevant at the same time as we affirm the story's meaning and value.

To qualify as Christian Myth a story must meet four criteria:

(1) It has a place in Christian tradition and was originally understood as factual;

(2) We no longer claim that it represents factual truth;

(3) It serves to exemplify or reinforce proper Christian belief, attitude, or action; and

(4) It can do this without being taken as literally true.

The majority of the elements that make up the Christian Mythology can be grouped in three broad clusters corresponding to the birth, the life, and the death of Jesus of Nazareth.[1] The *nativity cluster* includes not only the supernatural and pseudohistorical events preceding and attending his birth (the annunciation, the virgin birth, the angels and shepherds and wisemen, the location in Bethlehem, etc.), but also the claims as to the nature of Jesus' being and identity that are not in keeping with our common sense theology. The *life and ministry cluster* includes many of the miracle accounts, those prophecies and messianic claims which were quite apparently inserted by the early Church, and any claims as to the perfection or total sinlessness of Jesus as an individual. The *death and resurrection cluster* includes the theme of the atonement and various elements of the resurrection and of the post-resurrection appearances. After considering these three clusters, we will then look at a couple of other concepts that are ideal candidates for inclusion as Christian Myth.

It is important to note the obvious: major aspects of the story of Jesus cannot be included as Christian Myth for the simple reason that they are very probably true. These would be such things as the fact that Jesus was baptized by John, kept company with sinners, called disciples and chose twelve as a special group, performed some "faith healings", reached out to outcasts, entered Jerusalem in triumph, defied the authorities, was arrested and crucified, and was experienced afterwards by his disciples. Also not classifiable as myth is the most important thing about Jesus of Nazareth: his message. In fact, his message of God's call and God's love is the norm to which Christian Myth must conform.

---

[1]There are also other stories and themes from the Old and New Testaments that meet the criteria of Christian Myth and can be constructively used in this way. We are limiting ourselves here primarily to the Jesus myths due to space limitations and due to the centrality of Jesus to our faith.

But how do we relate the mythical to the non-mythical? How do we relate what we claim as Christian Myth to what we claim as historical fact?

To repeat: we are not setting up this category so that we can then ignore those stories that fit in it. But neither can we pretend that they don't require to be treated any differently than anything else we say about Jesus. Neither of these is appropriate or helpful. Christian Myth must be treated differently precisely in order that we neither ignore nor dismiss it, precisely in order that we can claim its positive significance for us.

What then do we do? Do we need to create a different kind of "red letter edition" in which we print in red not the words of Jesus but instead all those passages that qualify as Christian Myth? Or do we need to do with the New Testament as is sometimes done with the Book of Daniel— parts of it included in the text as canonical, parts of it relegated to an appendix of Apocrypha? No, this sort of thing is hardly necessary. And while something like this might be helpful in specialized teaching circumstances, in general such an approach would be unwarranted and unhealthy. We don't need to go to such extremes. What we need to do is recognize that:

(1) The stories and themes about Jesus of Nazareth fall into two different categories, those which we claim as factual and those which we do not.

(2) Our beliefs about who Jesus was, his relationship to God and his role for us, must be based on the factual, as indeed our theology in general must be consistent with the factual.

(3) Once our theology and faith themes are established, those stories and themes about Jesus which we do not claim as factual, but which are consistent with our faith themes, can be used as Christian Myth to illustrate, illuminate, and emphasize these themes.

This is all neither terribly difficult nor very mysterious, as we shall see as we now proceed to look at some important parts of Christian Myth.

I. The Nativity Cluster

The nativity cluster of Christian Myth can be subdivided into the circumstances of the birth itself, the events announcing the birth, and the claims made about the nature and identity of this child.

IA. The Birth: Born of a Virgin in Bethlehem

Matthew and Luke agree that Jesus was born in Bethlehem of a virgin and was descended from David through a man who was not his father. Mark and John are either unaware of this or do not think it worthy of mention. Matthew and Luke do *not* agree on how it happened that

Mary and Joseph were in Bethlehem for Jesus' birth but later resided in Nazareth,[2] or on how Joseph was descended from David.

How do we explain this? We must consider the circumstances of the followers of Jesus after his death. We can reasonably assume that they searched their Scriptures for any explanations that would help them understand this man who had had such an impact on their lives. Since they had come to believe him to be the Messiah they naturally gave great importance to those Old Testament passages traditionally identified as messianic prophecies. We need also to remember that these early Christians were human just as we are. Besides the established fact that legends have a way of springing up about great public figures, there must also have been an almost irresistible urge on the part of some to bolster the claim that Jesus was indeed the Messiah, especially since his behavior was in some ways most unmessianic (see p. 99).

Among the passages which were widely interpreted at the time as referring to the Messiah were II Samuel 8:12f and Isaiah 11:1, both of which say he will be a descendent of David; Isaiah 7:14, which in its Greek mistranslation says that a virgin shall bear a son (the original Hebrew says "young woman"); and Micah 5:2, which indicates that a ruler would be born in Bethlehem. Matthew and Luke—written later than Mark's Gospel and Paul's letters—tell us that Jesus fulfilled these prophecies (but as we said, have different explanations of *how* he fulfilled two of the three). Does it not seem likely that the conviction that Jesus was the Messiah gave rise to the belief that he fulfilled these prophecies, and not the other way around? Does it not seem likely that the prophecies occasioned these birth stories? If so, then what do we do with this part of the Jesus story?

What we do is affirm these aspects of the Jesus story as Christian Myth. This means we do not claim that Jesus of Nazareth was actually born in Bethlehem of a virgin (which is not the least bit important to his message). As myth, however, these elements of the story that claim this specialness for him serve to symbolize the Christian theme that Jesus of Nazareth is indeed "he who was to come"—not in the sense that he fulfilled human expectations nor in the sense that this particular person was foreseen by any of the prophets, but rather in the sense that it is in *this* individual that we find the key to understanding God and God's call, the key to meaning in our lives.

The virgin birth in Bethlehem as well as the descent from David, even if not taken as factual, serve to connect Jesus with the hundreds of years of seeking God in the Old Testament. They also serve to highlight the importance we give to Jesus and so draw attention to his message. If

---

[2]In Matthew the wisemen find Jesus and his family living in a house in Bethlehem, from where they flee to Egypt, later to return to a different part of the country—Nazareth. In Luke, Joseph and Mary already live in Nazareth and come to Bethlehem for the census.

these parts of the story are not viewed as Christian Myth, however, but are claimed as true, then they distract from the message and in fact impede access to it for many people.

IB. Angels and Shepherds and Stars and Wisemen

We have here a combination of (1) events that are incompatible with our common sense, and (2) events that just don't seem historically very likely. The former include an appearance by the heavenly host and a star that served as a trail guide. The latter, the merely improbable, include the resulting visits by the shepherds and the wisemen. We might also include in this category the trip to Bethlehem to be enrolled, the too-full inn and the birth in a stable.

Both of these kinds of events are peripheral to the message of Jesus but both can be appropriated as Christian Myth. I expect that the Sunday School Christmas play will continue to include angels and shepherds and crusty innkeepers and three wisemen who travel by camel and whose names are Melchior, Caspar, and Balthazar. And rightfully so, for the purpose of these stories is not to tell us about angels and wisemen but to say something about Jesus of Nazareth. We can use these stories, as myth, to help us celebrate the good news of Christmas and to emphasize the point, "Hey! This is the Christ! Here is the message, the key!" Their use is analogous to the flourish of trumpets that introduces the protagonist in an old melodrama. And if adding some detail to the stories helps them to do this, so much the better—as has happened with the wisemen, about whom Matthew tells us neither their number, nor their mode of travel, nor their names.

There are some additional points made by these stories as well. The wisemen's recognition of kingship in a powerless infant, the angels' choice of humble shepherds to whom to announce the news, Jesus' birth as an outcast in a stable—all these point to a very different kind of king, to a power and truth that transcend worldly power and the socially acceptable status quo. Here is a new and freeing message!

IC. Implications: What Child Is This?

We also include in the nativity cluster the ideas about Jesus' special nature and origin. Such ideas range from the full-blown doctrine of the Incarnation to the pre-existent semi-deity in the prologue to John to the idea of Jesus being "sent".

What do we say about the Incarnation, the orthodox consensus about Jesus' nature for all these centuries? We have discussed in Chapter 7 why we can no longer support this belief. Can we not, however, appropriate this as Christian Myth? We can, and the Incarnation then becomes a symbol that emphasizes in a beautiful way several important Christian themes: (1) that God is here with us, not in some far off dimension;

(2) that God loves us so much as to come seeking us out; and (3) that God does not merely sympathize with us but rather shares in an important way in the human condition. We do not have to claim that the Incarnation is literally true in order for it to have meaning for us. As Christian Myth, without affronting our common sense, it can signify and help us to grasp these important truths.

II. The Life and Ministry Cluster

The life and ministry cluster of Christian Myth includes the miracle stories, prophecies and messianic claims erroneously attributed to Jesus, and claims of his perfection or sinlessness.

IIA. Miracles

The miracle stories are among the very first to come to mind when we speak of Christian Myth. But do they qualify? This is not an idle question, especially when Jesus himself rebuked those who sought a sign from him. We must see if miracle stories meet the four criteria we have established for Christian Myth.

The first two criteria are clearly met: miracle accounts are a part of Christian tradition, and we do not now claim that they are literally true. (The exception, again, is those faith healings which fit with the genre as we understand it today, and which we need not understand as miraculous).

The third criterion is that these stories serve "to reinforce or exemplify proper Christian belief, attitude, or action". This is not so clearly met. The miracles can signify different things to different people, not all of them appropriate. For instance, Jesus' stilling of the storm or coming to his disciples across the water or multiplication of the loaves and fishes could all be taken to symbolize Jesus' love and concern for the human fears and bodily needs of people. This would certainly meet this criterion. But these miracles might more readily be understood to symbolize things inconsistent with our common sense theology such as Jesus' divinity or God's willingness to interfere with natural law. Likewise they might be understood to symbolize things inconsistent with our Christian faith such as Jesus' worldly kingship or material power and, therefore, to mean that the Christian message is about what we control instead of about whom and how we serve. The symbolism of magic and power is strong in the miracle accounts. Before they could meet the third criterion for Christian Myth they would have to be clearly reinterpreted so that they did in fact come to symbolize appropriate Christian themes. This could be done, but it would entail a lot of work.

The fourth criterion, that these accounts could symbolize these themes without being taken as literally true, is the key to helping us work on proper interpretation. When we make it clear that we do *not* in fact understand the miracle stories to be true (per criterion #2), that Jesus did not actually still the storm or walk on water, then the implications of magic or worldly power or divine intervention fade away. We can also understand that to Jesus' contemporaries these stories would have entailed claims about his authority. But these miracles no longer have religious significance for us, and could not carry these claims if not seen as true. So again some real work is needed on reinterpretation of the miracles for them to have appropriate Christian symbolism.

Do the miracle stories, then, qualify as Christian Myth? I'm not sure that they presently do. But they *can,* if enough creative Christians do the necessary interpretive work on them.

IIB. Jesus' Prophecies

Some of the sayings attributed to Jesus are thought by scholars to have very probably originated with the early Church and not with Jesus himself. In the next section we will consider his messianic claims, in this section his predictions of his crucifixion and resurrection.

There are three "predictions of the Passion", as they are called, in each of the first three Gospels ("passion" in the ancient sense of "martyrdom", meaning here the suffering and crucifixion of Jesus—as in the medieval "Passion plays"). There is also Matthew's version of the "sign of Jonah" saying (see Chapter 4, p. 49), as well as various references in John.

The first prediction follows "Peter's confession" that Jesus is the Christ. Jesus responded with an admonition to tell no one and then told the disciples "that he must go to Jerusalem and suffer many things from the elders and chief priests and scribes, and be killed, and on the third day be raised." (Matthew 16:21; cf Mark 8:27f, Luke 9:18f.) This is echoed by the second prediction: "The son of man [that is, himself] is to be delivered into the hands of men, and they will kill him, and he will be raised on the third day." (Matthew 17:22–23; cf Mark 9:31, Luke 9:44.) This is expanded in the third prediction: "Behold, we are going up to Jerusalem; and the son of man will be delivered to the chief priests and scribes, and they will condemn him to death, and deliver him to the Gentiles to be mocked and scourged and crucified, and will be raised on the third day." (Matthew 20:18–19; cf Mark 10:32–34, Luke 18:31–33.)

The attribution of these predictions to Jesus himself is extremely dubious. They are simply too specific and too detailed. They are *too* good to be true. No one has ever made such precisely accurate predictions before the fact.[3] If Jesus *had* made these very specific predictions, how could the

---

[3]The other best example in the Bible of very precise predictions is in Daniel. Supposedly writing in the 6th century B.C., he reports an astoundingly accurate vision of the rise and

disciples possibly have remained unaware of what was to happen? Yet unaware they were, as is obvious both from the story of events and from remarks such as Luke 18:34: "But they understood none of these things; this saying was hid from them, and they did not grasp what was said." (cf Luke 9:45, Mark 9:32.)

So the only reasonable conclusion is that Jesus did not in fact make these specific predictions. This is not to say that he might not have spoken in more general terms of danger and suffering. It seems quite likely that he did and that these general sayings were later given a more specific content by people who knew what actually transpired. (We can easily imagine the process: "Why, I bet he knew all along what would happen. He must have tried to tell us, and we just didn't understand him. Don't you think that's what he meant, that day on the way to Jericho? Remember?")

But if these and the other notably accurate predictions of Jesus were the product not of his foresight but of somebody else's hindsight, what then do we do with them? Can we use them constructively as Christian Myth? As with the miracle accounts, these prophecies obviously meet the first two criteria. So the question is: do they reinforce Christian themes, and can they do so without being taken as literally true?

The original function of these passages was twofold: to support the claim of Jesus' special nature and authority, and to show that he knew what lay ahead and nevertheless stuck to his course. If these predictions were not actually his, however, they can no longer reinforce claims as to his special nature or his status as a seer. But they could not do this in any case, for this kind of prediction is irrelevant to our concerns about God and morality. They are not religiously significant.

But the predictions of the Passion *can* serve to reinforce Christian themes nonetheless. First, because they doubtless represent Jesus' general awareness that he would be going into great danger. And he went anyway, in faith and in love. So the predictions illustrate how our values are more important than our fears; our faith is more important than preserving our own lives, which are limited anyway.

Second, even if these predictions were not uttered by Jesus they exemplify quite vividly a basic understanding of his: greatness does not mean comfort and ease and earthly power. They stand as statements that the Messiah, God's chosen one, is chosen not for worldly glory but for suffering, not to rule but to serve. Along with Jesus' actions, they reinforce the teaching that he or she who would be greatest must be the servant of all. Interpreted in this way they are a valuable part of the Christian Myth.

---

fall of Middle Eastern kingdoms part way through the 2nd century B.C. However, the book appears to have been written around 165 B.C., on linguistic and other evidence— and prophecies for events after this date were not fulfilled.

IIC. Messianic Consciousness

By "messianic consciousness" we mean Jesus of Nazareth's own awareness of being the Messiah. Did he in fact claim this title for himself?

This strikes most people as a preposterous question. How could Jesus not know he was the Messiah? How could he not have acknowledged and claimed this? Yet as inconceivable as it may seem, the question of his messianic consciousness is a very live one in scholarly circles.

The question is not whether Jesus considered himself to be a prophet conveying God's message. This is apparent. The question is whether he considered himself to be that person whose coming was foretold as the Messiah. Since the Messiah was expected to re-establish the kingdom of David in keeping with the prophecies (see p. 99), and since Jesus was evidently not interested in worldly kingship or in driving out the Romans, this is a very good question.

Certainly Jesus did not claim to fill the messianic prophecies that speak of establishing a government or defeating Israel's enemies (see Isaiah 9 and 11). And many scholars have concluded that he never claimed to be the Messiah at all, that all such statements were put into his mouth by the early Church. As Hans Küng puts it:

> According to the Synoptic Gospels then . . . Jesus never himself assumed the designation of Messiah or any other messianic title.

> Probably Jesus did not describe himself as Son of David, Messiah (Christ) or Son of God (Son). It is also possible that he did not use the term "Son of Man" of himself, at least not in an unequivocally messianic sense for his own time.[4]

I am not quite as convinced as Küng and others that Jesus made *no* claims with messianic implications, in part because of the nature of his entry into Jerusalem (see Zechariah 9:9). But apparently his outright claims of being the Messiah are of dubious authenticity.

But this, then, qualifies these statements to be part of the Christian Myth, as long as they can promote Christian themes. They would *not* do this if we understood the claims to mean that Jesus was the messianic warrior-king. But neither we nor Jesus understand him to be this. We have, in fact, given a new meaning to the title of Messiah. Christians have understood it to mean the one sent from God—the Son of God, or maybe God the Son—the Savior. While we have not been able to buy into any of these titles in our common sense reconstruction, we do use the messianic title of "the Christ", redefined to mean the one through whose life and teachings we interpret God, the one through whom we find focus and meaning for our lives.

The important question regarding Jesus' self-identity is not whether he identified himself with any particular title. None of the titles or expecta-

---

[4]Hans Küng, *On Being A Christian*, (Doubleday and Company, 1976), p. 288, 290.

tions were adequate. The important question is what he understood himself to be doing and how he understood his relationship to God. Our position is that he did not understand himself to be fulfilling the role of Messiah as understood either by his contemporaries *or* by Christian tradition. But he certainly did claim to be the one who carried God's message, the one through whom to interpret God.

Therefore, if we can view the messianic claims not as claims to be the heir of David or claims to be a divine Savior, but rather as symbols that point to the fact that we confess Jesus of Nazareth to be the Christ, then they can take their place as part of the Christian Myth.

IID. Jesus' Perfection

The claims made of Jesus' perfection or sinlessness constitute a fourth part of the life and ministry cluster of Christian Myth. In the New Testament we find Jesus referred to as "holy, blameless, unstained, separated from sinners, exalted above the heavens," (Hebrews 7:26) and as he "who knew no sin" (II Corinthians 5:21). Similar claims have been made about him ever since.

To people who saw Jesus as God incarnate and/or as the required unblemished sacrifice to atone for our sins, it may have been both necessary and believable that he was perfect. But for us it is neither. Whether by "perfect" we mean simply sinless, or whether we mean perfect in knowledge and love and judgment and other aspects as well, it is simply impossible for anyone who is human to be this. Being human means precisely that we are limited in our knowledge, that emotions affect our judgment, that we get tired and frustrated and depressed, and that we will not always overcome these imperfections to choose rightly.

Jesus of Nazareth was human. Therefore he was neither sinless nor perfect. We can ascribe claims of his perfection to a desire to make the point that he was "the one", whether "the one" was identified as the Son of God or God the Son, as Savior or the Lamb. But do claims of this sort have a place in Christian Myth? It comes down to the same two questions as before: do they reinforce Christian themes? Can they do so if not literally true?

These claims do *not* reinforce Christian values if they serve to emphasize the difference between ourselves and Jesus. If he was able to act with love and forgiveness because he was perfect and sinless, then why should we who are imperfect sinners think that we might be capable of the same sort of life? Why should we even try?

Only by recognizing that the claims of Jesus' perfection are untrue can they serve to encourage Christian values. Perfection is not even an appropriate moral category, because it does not exist and certainly does not apply to human beings. But by using these claims to point to Jesus' extreme goodness and love, a goodness and love which as his followers and fellow humans we can strive to attain, we can use them in a way that makes them appropriate for Christian Myth.

III. Death and Resurrection

The principal elements in the death and resurrection cluster of the Christian Myth are (A) his death as sacrifice and atonement, and (B) the "magical" elements of the resurrection stories.

IIIA. The Atonement

We have already made the point that the idea that God required the blood sacrifice of an innocent individual before forgiving our sins is awesomely unchristian. Atonement conceived of in this way has no place in Christian Myth or Christian anything else.

But there is an alternative understanding of atonement. The archaic and original meaning (which is refreshingly alive in some theological circles) is "at-one-ment", reconciliation. And instead of viewing the crucifixion as reconciling God to humanity—for the Christian view is that God is always seeking us, reaching out to us—we need to view it as reconciling humanity to God. So instead of the repugnant idea of the crucifixion as satisfaction of a divine blood thirst, we have instead a paradigm of self-sacrificing love for others, calling people to God and to right relation.

In this view Jesus' ultimate act of love is *not* that of taking upon himself the sins of the world. As loving as that would be, it entails an unchristian view of God. Instead, his act of love is his doing that which was required to make known to us the true meaning of faith and of victory, of love and of life.

One might ask why Jesus' death was necessary to accomplish this. After all, he had been preaching this message all along.

We must say that it was *not* necessary in any metaphysical or theological sense. It was not necessary to God's plan or to our "salvation". It probably was inevitable that the forces of the status quo and oppression would see his liberating message as a threat and so act to silence him. And it was necessary for him then to take the only course of action that was faithful to his message, and this was the path to the cross.

The crucifixion stands as a triumph of faith and integrity and a triumph of the love for others that Jesus preached. This faith and integrity and love were not vanquished by worldly powers or diminished by death. Instead they rose in the face of death to their greatest heights.

The crucifixion, then, can serve as at-one-ment by showing people the nature of the love of God's messenger and—by inference—the nature of the love of God. The crucifixion shows the real possibility of love, and so calls us to turn and accept God's love. In this way it can reconcile us to

God, and in this interpretation the atonement could qualify as Christian Myth.

I remain unsure whether "atonement" can sufficiently shed its classic unchristian connotations. I am also unsure—if we are able to give it the proposed reinterpretation—whether it would qualify as myth, for the atonement in the sense of reconciling us to God is certainly true. But if we do use the concept of atonement in our common sense Christianity it must be in this latter sense.

IIIB. The "Magical" Elements of the Resurrection Stories

The central element of the resurrection—Jesus of Nazareth's triumph over death—does not qualify as Christian Myth for the simple reason that we claim it is true. We maintain that this person was in fact not brought to an end by his physical death on the cross. However, when it comes to the various resurrection stories it becomes difficult to make any claims about the specific nature of what actually happened.[5] What is important, of course, is the reality to which these accounts bear witness. Having said this, certain elements of the story become candidates for Christian Myth: the appearance of angels, the miraculous rolling away of the stone, Jesus' ability to pass through shut doors and also to ingest solid food, etc.

The question here is whether we need to claim the literal truth of any of these details in order to maintain the truth of the resurrection itself. If we do not claim the specifics of the angel or the stone or a post-resurrection Jesus that ate fish or showed nail holes or walked to Emmaus, then what is left to claim as the resurrection event?

What we claim is that the person of Jesus of Nazareth survived the death of his body on the cross and made himself known to some of his disciples. We do not claim to understand exactly what happened or how the disciples experienced it. As we pointed out in Chapter 6, we cannot claim great theological significance for this event, but we do claim that it occurred. This claim is not dependent on any of the details or supernatural manifestations. So we can use these aspects of the resurrection story as Christian Myth as long as we use them to point to and symbolize the Christian understanding that Jesus was victorious on the cross and survived death.

IV. Other

There are two other concepts in particular that do not fit neatly into one of the foregoing three clusters but which we need to consider as possibilities for Christian Myth. They are the devil and the Trinity.

---

[5]See Appendix B for a consideration of the scholarly arguments.

IVA. The Devil

In the Bible we see a transition from "the accuser" in the Old Testament (which we too often render as the proper name "Satan") to the devil as tempter and personification of evil in the New Testament. (What we know as the traditional story about the devil, by the way, is best found in Milton's *Paradise Lost.*) Today, however, we have no need to claim that evil is a personal being. While we do not claim that human beings are enslaved by sin, we are aware of the great capacity that humans have for evil as well as for good. We do not need the assistance of a devil to commit great sins; we do well enough at it on our own.

Can the devil be a part of the Christian Myth? Not if the story of the devil has the result that we blame someone else for our sins or that we view the world as a place where there is an ultimate force of evil. We believe in one God, not two—not one good and one evil.

However, by making it clear that we do not mean these stories as literal truth we should minimize the likelihood of these results. If we can instead use the idea of the devil to symbolize that human beings are capable of evil, that we each have within us motives and impulses and temptations that can lead to evil and so must be held in check, then (but only then) the devil can be a part of Christian Myth.

IVB. The Trinity

Here is the centerpiece of orthodoxy: God the Father, God the Son and God the Holy Spirit. We explored in some detail in Chapter Seven why we cannot accept the Incarnation, Jesus as God the Son. For similar reasons we cannot accept the broader concept of the triune God in the sense of three "persons" with one "substance". This idea is neither logical nor Biblical nor necessary nor particularly helpful. We do not claim the Trinity to be literally true in our common sense theology.

There are two possible ways that the Trinity might function as Christian Myth to symbolize Christian themes for us.

First, the Trinity has represented for many people the mystery of God, the fact that God is ultimately beyond our comprehension. (This is a virtue of the otherwise lamentable fact that the idea of the Trinity itself does not make sense.) Certainly we have to admit that a total understanding of God is beyond the grasp of our limited minds. The idea of the unknowability of God is a traditional one, and is especially strong in the Eastern Orthodox spiritual tradition.

But if we use the Trinity as myth to point to this unknowability of God, we must make clear that we are *not* claiming that God is in fact tripartite. In fact, we might do better to point to the unknowability of God by using concepts that do not affront our common sense—and there are certainly enough unknowables (not just unknowns, but unknowables) in the universe to do this. Or we could simply state that God is unknowable instead of using incomprehensible language of God to prove our point. Otherwise someone might think we are trying to say something about God instead of just pointing to God's unknowability.

Second, the Trinity can symbolize for us the different aspects of God and the way we relate to God. God the Father represents the transcendent aspect of God: creator of the universe, beyond all that we know. The Holy Spirit represents the presence of God with us, God's pulling and encouraging, the fact that God is the context within which we live. The Son, of course, represents Jesus the Christ, but we cannot call him "God the Son". He is not divine. So "the Son" does not represent an aspect of God, but is the one through whom we best understand God. "The Son", in fact, shows us what our relationship to God can be and should be. This understanding of the Trinity might be acceptable.

But a further problem here is the masculine imagery. Obviously, Jesus happened to be male, so in his case this is legitimate. But I can see no reason for enshrining the maleness of God as part of our orthodoxy, and to the extent that the Trinity supports a patriarchal society or sexism it is not in keeping with the Christian message and cannot be used.

It should be noted that throughout this book we have assiduously pursued the use of gender-free language in speaking of God. This is important, for certainly God is neither male nor female. If this avoidance of personal pronouns is found to be clumsy or fails to give a proper sense of God as a being who is related to us in a personal way, then certainly one is free to speak of God both as male and as female so long as these usages are understood to be metaphorical and not to be claiming gender for God, and so long as the male and female references are relatively balanced. (I recognize that there may be legitimate pastoral concerns about breaking with our traditional patriarchal images, but there are also legitimate pastoral concerns that join with a correct theology and proper symbolism to impel us to gender-neutral language.)

It is time now to move beyond theology to the Christian life.

PART FOUR

THE CHRISTIAN LIFE

Having removed some of the lesser stumbling blocks of archaic doctrine, and having seen that to be Christian means to try to live faithfully with Jesus of Nazareth as our compass, we now confront the greater stumbling block of living this way. In Chapter Sixteen we describe briefly some of the themes of a Christian life: self-acceptance; right relationship with God, self and others; and a balance between passion and perspective.

In Chapter Seventeen we consider what it means to live faithfully specifically with reference to possessions and the use of money. We explore the two alternative ways of living faithfully: the radical response and the uncomfortable middle, and we conclude that above all we need to take this question seriously.

In Chapter Eighteen we pursue the question of wealth to a consideration of economic systems. We point out the differences among capitalist systems and among socialist systems, conclude that neither is in itself the problem or the solution, and then look at the challenges confronting our own system of democratic capitalism.

In Chapter Nineteen we conclude with a brief consideration of the new spirituality which we need to encompass the whole of life, and we look at the sacred, worship, prayer, work, and the Church.

171

And then it is time for us to get to work following the lead of Jesus of Nazareth, the Christ.

CHAPTER 16: THE STUMBLING BLOCK: LIVING THE FAITH

"We preach Christ crucified, a stumbling block to Jews and folly to Gentiles." (I Corinthians 1:23)

I preach a common sense approach to doctrine. I deny the need to believe in the traditional concepts of original sin, salvation, miracles and the Incarnation. Have I simply thrown out all the difficult parts of Christianity? Does this make Christian faith "reasonable" to our modern society?

No, it does not. In fact, all we have done is to remove a lesser stumbling block precisely *in order that* people can confront the greater one: living the faith.

The lesser stumbling block has been thrust aside by our modern common sense. The greater stumbling block stands intact and confronts our understanding of what is important in life. The distinction between these two is the same as the distinction made between doctrine and faith in Chapter 8. It is the distinction between logic and meaning, between reasoning and values, between head and heart.

The head is concerned with understanding, with making sense of things. Doctrine is the way in which the head explains the heart to other heads. Since we have a modern world-view our doctrine must be consistent with this view. Our theology must be coherent and understandable and reasonable to other heads that share our common sense. Otherwise our explanation becomes a stumbling block in itself.

It is the head's job to understand and explain, but the head must be given direction by the heart. It is this heart-given direction—or faith—that the head must render understandable. If it doesn't, then the values and meaning that we live by will not be able to get through the other person's head to their heart. And what we want is for these values to be confronted by the other person's heart. We want others to be able to make the all-important choice to live *for* love or *against* love, *towards* God or *away from* God.

But if the challenge to make this choice is put in concepts that cause the other person's head to balk, their heart will never even face this choice. So it is precisely to allow people to confront this greater stumbling block, precisely to enable the heart to confront this all-important choice, that our doctrine must make sense. It would be tragic if the lesser stumbling block to the head prevented the heart's confrontation of the great stumbling block.

So our doctrine must be reasonable. But the great stumbling block *cannot* be made reasonable. The choice for or against Christian faith, the choice of how to live our lives, is not a matter of reasonableness.

This is true for two reasons: first, because this choice is not based on reason, but is based instead on value. And basic value is felt, not reasoned.

Second, because the choice to live towards God and (therefore) away from material success and security, away from selfishness, away from what is easy and popular, will never seem reasonable or even possible to anyone who finds their value in success and security and popularity. Christian faith cannot be made "reasonable" to those who accept the dominant view of our culture. Those who define success in material terms, those who see the goal of life as attaining possessions or status or even happiness, will find the teachings of the Christ to be both folly and a stumbling block. Living for others is clearly *un*reasonable to these people.

But this is the call. This is the great choice we must make with our lives. And this is why it is such a stumbling block: we are not called to think Christianity or to talk it or to believe it, all of which we could do while serving other gods in our daily lives. We are called to *live* it. We are called to live Christianity, for living towards God with Jesus of Nazareth as our guide is what it means to be Christian.

In the next chapter we will look at some specific questions about what it means to live as Christians with regard to possessions and the use of money. In this chapter we will take a broad look at what it means to live this choice by considering the themes of the Christian life.

Themes of the Christian Life

I will not pretend that I can exhaustively define the Christian life or that a satisfactory description of it can be given in one chapter. Nevertheless, we can usefully point out some characteristics or "themes" which mark the Christian life. I am not going to use "love" as a separate theme, for two reasons. First, because this word is so misused and misunderstood and has such different meanings for different people. And second, because these other themes can be understood as an elaboration of what Christian love and faith entail.

We will be looking at three clusters of themes: (I) acceptance; (II) right relationship; and (III) perspective and passion.

I. Acceptance

The message of God's acceptance of us—yes, even you, and yes, even me, imperfect creatures though we are—is central to the Christian message. We in turn need to accept this acceptance, which means also accepting ourselves so that we are then able to accept others. This self-acceptance and other-acceptance find expression as inner strength, gentleness, tolerance, hospitality and other similar attributes.

Self-Acceptance: Source of Compassion and Strength

So much of what is desirable in a person's character depends on self-acceptance and a sense of worth. This generally grows from a sense of being loved and valued, a feeling that ought to be imparted by every parent to every child. But (may God forgive us!) it isn't, and so it often has to originate from elsewhere. But whether or not it originates early in the family, it needs to be reinforced later from elsewhere. Certainly we will continue to value other people's opinions, but if we are to be mature and responsible adults we must arrive at that point where our own feeling of self-worth is not determined by the opinions of those around us.

I will not claim that there is only one way to arrive at this point. It is possible that different people may travel different routes to becoming comfortable with themselves. But there is one way that is at the very heart of the message of Jesus Christ: the good news that God loves us, just as we are, and that this love is available to us if we only turn to God and accept it.

This doesn't mean that we are perfect the way we are or that we're always right. It doesn't mean that we don't have to change or grow or struggle. What it means is that God loves us in spite of all our imperfections, that we are valued by God as the individuals we are. This is what gives us the strength and the courage so that we *can* struggle and grow. If the God of all creation finds us worthy of love then we can accept ourselves and discover that we are worth improving.[1]

---

[1]We have pointed out that much traditional theology maintains that we are not *worthy* of God's love, but receive it in grace (if we believe) only because of Jesus' sacrifice on our behalf. This is a perversion of Jesus' message of God's unconditional love that is there for us to turn to and accept.

There are, no doubt, many Christians with a sense of self-worth who do not attribute this to the knowledge that God loves them. We don't go around saying to ourselves, "God loves me, so therefore I'm OK." When I examine my own feelings of self-worth and self-acceptance I attribute them to a variety of factors: family and friends, times of success, times of suffering (which have probably been more important than times of success in this regard), introspection, and simply living through a certain number of years and experiences.

Nevertheless, there is an important element that remains over and apart from all of these that is not dependent on any particular person or event. This is the feeling that I am on good terms with the universe, that I am accepted by and am at peace with that which is, that I belong here and am grounded here in such a way that I can offer hospitality to others.

How do I explain this? I am embarrassed to admit that prior to this I hadn't tried to. But now, as I examine it, I cannot separate this feeling from my faith. To do so would be dishonest. For as near as I can fathom it out, it is based on the knowledge deep inside that I am accepted and valued and loved by that which is in all and through all reality: God.

The self-acceptance which results from this sense of being accepted is what makes it possible for us to be accepting of others in turn. Once our own self-worth is not dependent upon being better than others or on being admired by others or on winning over others in one way or another, then we are able to accept other persons and accept them for who they really are. We are able to offer what Henri Nouwen calls "hospitality": a space in our lives where other people can feel at home, where they are given room to be themselves.[2]

This self-acceptance also provides the inner security and strength that make possible two traits which are often thought of as opposites: gentleness towards others, and strength or steadfastness in conflict.

By "gentleness" I do not mean just refraining from physical violence. There is much more to gentleness than this. It also means a strict avoidance of mental/emotional violence, a healing of wounded psyches, a nurturing of the dreams and abilities and feelings of worth of others. Gentleness is a positive way of showing our love to those all around us. The insecure person is too concerned with justifying their own worth to be able to nurture others in this way.

The secure person can also be gentle in the sense of turning the other cheek, of admitting that the other person might be right, of giving in when only pride (and not principle) is at stake. It takes a strong person to be gentle in this way, a person who depends for their sense of self-worth not on other people but on God. The bully mistakes this gentle-

---

[2]Henri Nouwen, *Reaching Out* (Doubleday and Co., 1975).

ness for weakness, for he or she is a weak person who feels a need to prove precisely what they are so unsure of, and never can prove: their own personal worth. A weak person such as this can't afford to compromise or give in because their personal worth is felt to be at stake. A strong person, secure in their acceptance so that their self-worth is not at stake in the ups and downs of daily life, can afford to yield, compromise, give in.

On the reverse side of this same coin from gentleness is steadfastness and what is sometimes called courage. The person who is secure in their acceptance is much more able to hold to their principles (as opposed to their pride) in the face of the opposition and displeasure of others. Now, this must not be confused with the desperate, irrational clinging to a position by the insecure person who always *has* to be right. It should also be noted that in many (but not all) cases, once a majority decision has been reached it ought to be supported as such. It should further be said that steadfastness is not always easy or painless. But the ability to stand by our principles in conflict and public debate—even when difficult and painful—is an important one, and is more likely if you are comfortable with your acceptance, if your self-worth depends on a power far greater than the squabbling mortals around you.

Recognizing that God loves us and accepting this love, which is to respond affirmatively to the good news of Jesus the Christ, is a central mark or theme of the Christian life. And while on the one hand this self-acceptance is one of the rewards of the Christian life, on the other hand it is the prerequisite for many of the characteristics which we as Christians ought to have in our personal lives: tolerance, gentleness, hospitality, the nurturing of others and inner strength. These traits should be in evidence as we deal with our families, our friends, our colleagues, employees and employers, and our brothers and sisters the other children of God wheresoever we come into contact with them.

II. Right Relationship:
with Self, with God, with Others

Regardless of how secure or insecure we may feel, we are called to be in "right relationship", the term which encompasses our second family of themes. This used to be called "righteousness", but this word has been ill-treated in its usage so that it now conjures up images of self-righteousness or indignation or someone striving for saintliness by avoiding the real world.

However, we are called to be "right" not by ourselves, but in relationship to the world. We are called by God to put ourselves in right relationship with ourselves, with God, and with others. This is not a chronological sequence. In fact the three are interdependent and we cannot do any one of them without the other two.

IIA. Right Relationship with Self: Integrity

If we are not in right relationship with our self we cannot put ourself in right relationship with anyone else. Right relationship with our self is best described as integrity.

Integrity means a consistency of principles and a wholeness of self. This works out best if we—like Jesus—have a moral code that is not a rigid set of rules but rather one that consists of a few basic principles that allow us to work out the best expression of love in each situation.

Integrity means that the principles and values that are a part of our self are not for sale. Humans are tempted to sell out for monetary gain, for employment opportunities or other personal advancement, for popularity, in order to avoid conflict, in awe of authority, or out of ambition or insecurity or greed or lust or fear, and so on through the whole range of selfish human desires and motivations. Integrity means being true to ourselves and our commitments in the face of all of these, which in turn requires that we be honest with ourselves about what we are doing and why.

All too often, of course, our choices are not this simple. Sometimes we have to choose between commitments. For instance, we may have to choose between a commitment not to work for an employer who produces products which we consider to be unsafe, and a commitment to provide for our family. And on the one hand we find it hard to condemn someone who refuses to place their personal purity above the well-being of their loved ones, but on the other hand we must ask whether there are not more important things to give our families than material well-being, things such as spiritual values and integrity.

But the fact remains that many times our choices are not between two commitments or principles but between a principle and a desire. Desires are normal, of course. It is only human to have them. And desires can be noble and altruistic, but they can also be selfish and base. And they can be very strong.

If we are able to be honest with ourselves—a very helpful if not exceedingly popular habit—then we should be able to discern which of our desires are selfish, which are contrary to our own principles. Integrity means being true to these principles that we have made our own and not denying our own self for some other thing that we want. It means not acting or speaking in a way we don't believe is right, not for popularity with peers or for success on the job or for acceptance by a church.

Integrity does not require being loud or pretentious or obnoxious about this. It doesn't mean being proud or hard to get along with. It just means being true to yourself, which you can do as gently as possible and as quietly as appropriate, but as steadfastly as necessary. The reason why it is worth bothering with all of this is that integrity is the only way you can be sure that you relate honestly to yourself, the only way to be sure that you have your self—which is the only thing we really have in this life. And there will be times in your life and mine when this is more obvious than usual, when if we do not have integrity we will be lost even to ourselves.

IIB: Right Relationship with God: Faithfulness

God is reaching out to us with accepting love. Our response—that which puts us in right relationship with God—is faithfulness.

What does it mean to live faithfully? It certainly doesn't mean we're sinless or perfect. It doesn't mean we have all the right answers and never make mistakes. To live faithfully means to live our lives above all and through all towards God, means that the dominant direction in our lives comes from our decision to take Jesus as our compass.

We can only succeed at living faithfully if this takes precedence over all of our other goals. Our other pursuits and objectives must be in line with—and subordinate to—this primary direction. It just doesn't work any other way. If other goals lead us in a different direction then we have in fact made these goals more important than living towards God. Indeed, we are then worshipping other gods—these other goals—before the one God. Obviously this is not to live faithfully. We can only live faithfully if our lives are imbued with a thorough-going monotheism. As Jesus said, you cannot serve two masters. We must make sure that the master we serve, the God we live towards, is the one eternal God.

This doesn't mean that there is no place in the faithful life for fun or recreation or simply goofing off, or for careful financial planning, or for working hard to attain personal goals. All of these are fine—in fact they are commendable—as long as they fit into the context of a life lived towards God, as long as they do not become direction-giving gods themselves.

It is difficult to keep these other pursuits and goals in proper perspective. After all, for most of us employment is exceedingly necessary and occupies most of our waking hours five or six days a week. Time with our family takes up most of the rest, and we may have difficulty squeezing in a couple of hours of recreation as the highlight of the week. And then besides these pressures of time there are also other enticements: who among us is immune to the thrill of achievement and recognition or to that of working for and buying that new possession?

So we find it difficult to keep these in proper perspective. But it is very important that we do. When the direction of our lives—not our geographical location, but our inner direction—is dictated by the compensation or prestige levels of employment, or by our dreams of a bigger house or new car or nice vacation trip or comfortable retirement, then we have chosen to place these first and God second, and the god we worship is not God. Not that a better job isn't worth working for or a new house worth saving for. They can be. But these must take a back seat, must not be the driver, must fit in with our over-all goal of living faithfully.

Certainly we should strive to be successful—but successful at what? This is the key question. It seems as if we are all working hard to be successful in our business or in some avocation. But is it not more important to be successful at *life?*

For the Christian, a successful life must mean a life lived faithfully. It is very possible for us to be great successes in our profession or our hobby but to fail at life. Why else are there so many "successful" people with broken marriages and alienated children, who depend on drugs or alcohol or workahol because they can't face their empty inner selves?

There is no greater failure than succeeding at the wrong thing. And it is this failure which most tempts us today: the failure of succeeding in worldly terms, a "success" that takes precedence over faithfulness, precedence over love, precedence over God, and so fails at the only endeavor that really counts—life.

Right relationship with God means putting this relationship first among our goals, serving no other gods before God. This relationship informs and transforms all our other pursuits, ensuring that in all we do we are living towards God. By doing this we live faithfully and thus succeed at the one undertaking that matters.

IIC: Right Relationship with Others: Caring and Sharing

Putting ourselves in right relationship with God entails both right relationship with our selves—integrity—and right relationship with others, which is where we give concrete expression to our right relationship with God. This right relationship with others includes hospitality, compassion, nurturing and other similar qualities which I include under the heading of caring and sharing.

The first step in right relationship with other people is to care about them: to admit and to feel that it does matter what happens to them. Part of this is simple consideration, a recognition that other people have feelings, too, and desires and needs and dreams. For reasons beyond my ken—if there *is* a reason for it—some people either can't or won't break out of their own self-centeredness. All that matters to them is their own feelings, their own goals, their own efforts. Maybe this is all they can see!

I am told we all begin this way as infants, so seeing that other people matter involves a certain amount of growing up. But only enough to see that we are not after all the center of the universe, that our desires and ambitions have no more right to fulfillment than those of several billion other individual dreamers and workers.

This recognition that other people have hopes and hurts just as we ourselves do, and that these do matter, is only a first step. If this remains just an intellectual understanding on our part then we haven't yet really gotten to caring about others For us to care about others, what happens to them must matter to us.

Now, obviously we cannot be intimately acquainted with the ups and downs of thousands of people. And obviously what happens to those closest to us is going to affect us the most. But we cannot put on blinders to keep us from knowing what goes on in the rest of the world. On the contrary, we have an obligation to keep ourselves informed. And even if we are not personally acquainted with people on the other side of the county or the other side of the globe, it must still matter to us if these our fellow human beings are suffering from hunger or disease or persecution or strife. If we care about them then to some extent we hurt at their hurt. Through empathy we share, although in a different way, in their suffering.

Once we care *about* others, the next step in right relationship is to care *for* them. This caring is done by sharing of ourselves with them. Sharing of our material wealth with those less fortunate is perhaps the way of sharing that we think of first. This is certainly an important way, one which we will address in the next chapter. But it is not the only way, and in some situations it is quite irrelevant. Sometimes what is important is just to be there, to share your time with your neighbor who is hurting or ill or lonely. Sometimes we need to share our "space", to allow people into our lives while still allowing them to be themselves, not forcing them into our mold. (This is "hospitality" in the sense we spoke of it earlier in the chapter.) And sometimes we need to get to work to change the conditions that cause their suffering.

We need also to care enough to try to discover who these "others" really are. This means sharing in another way: an openness to the ideas and insights and contributions that these people can bring to *our* lives, a willingness to receive and try to understand their experience and their wisdom.

Right relationship with other people, which is part of right relationship with God, means caring. And caring means sharing: a sharing of others' burdens, a sharing of our own blessings, a sharing of our time and space, a sharing of our love and of our self.

III: Perspective and Passion

Right relationship has to do with the direction and content of our lives while perspective and passion have to do with the level-headedness and the intensity of our lives. Perspective and passion are more generally thought of as inhabiting opposite ends of the spectrum than as walking hand in hand, but both are marks of the Christian life.

By "perspective" I mean the realization that things will never be perfect in this world, that the ultimate good is unobtainable, that there is no such thing as a human cause or human institution without error and sinfulness, that only God deserves our ultimate loyalty. This perspective helps us not to see the world in the stark contrast of black and white, good and evil, but to see instead the many shades of gray. It enables us not to invest ultimate importance in any human endeavor, and so not to get discouraged when our efforts fail to bring in the kingdom of God.

Furthermore, if we don't see everything in absolute terms of black and white we are then able to appreciate the very important differences between shades of gray, between different levels of imperfection. Rather than giving up when our hard work fails to result in perfection or to accomplish our goals, we are able to see that *improvement* in justice or compassion or social conditions can make a difference in the lives of our fellow human beings that really matters.

Our sense of perspective must include this understanding that the difference between degrees of imperfection can be crucially important. Otherwise it would be too easy to decide that since no human cause is without sin or deserving of our ultimate loyalty, since none will result in the perfect good, we may as well just sit back and sagely observe from an uninvolved distance the vain and foolish strivings of humanity. This is where Christian perspective joins hands with passion.

By "passion" I mean intense devotion to the cause of justice and righteousness. It is a zeal to bring about the conditions which *ought* to exist in the world, to strive to approach as closely as possible the unobtainable perfection, to argue and struggle for the right—on behalf of others and on behalf of God as a natural outgrowth of being in right relation with them. We feel the hurts of our neighbors suffering from persecution or injustice or hunger. And we feel how contrary this is to what is called for by God and know we must do what we can to confront and to change the causes of these hurts.

Passion fuels our drive to reform the world. It is a necessary ingredient. But without perspective, passion is too likely to see the world in black and white, too likely to result in missing the achievable good by aiming without compromise at the unachievable perfect, too likely to produce unnecessary division and acrimony that can make progress more difficult.

So we need both passion and perspective in the Christian life. Our right relationship with others gives us the passion to bring about a better world. Out right relationship with God and our acceptance of God's love give us the perspective that saves us from giving ultimate loyalty to any human cause, that perspective that keeps us going in an imperfect world.

These are the themes of a Christian life: acceptance of God's acceptance of us; right-relationship with self, God and neighbor; and the balance of passion and perspective. It is important to note that these themes not only mark a life that succeeds in being faithful—which is what it is all about—but these are also the ingredients we need in our lives in order to achieve a deep sense of satisfaction and meaning, to experience joy in the wonders of the world, and—dare I say it?—to be happy.

Happiness is not something we can pursue in itself; it is not to be equated with entertainment or passing pleasures. Happiness is the result of a life that has purpose, goals and meaning. A deep, abiding peace and happiness can be ours if we succeed at life by living faithfully, by living towards God.

We will now proceed to explore what faithful living means with regard to possessions and the use of money.

CHAPTER 17: POSSESSIONS AND THE USE OF MONEY

"No one can serve two masters; for either he will hate the one and love the other, or he will be devoted to the one and despise the other. You cannot serve God and mammon."

(Matthew 6:24)

In Chapter 16 we looked at the themes of a Christian life and at how such a life is oriented towards God and neighbor. There is, however, one god in particular that competes for our loyalty with a great deal of success. This god named Mammon—money or wealth—commands the devotion of so many in our society that we need to ask how we as Christians can deal with a pagan god whose worship seems institutionalized in our very economic system. If we are to live faithfully and in right relationship, what does this mean for our participation in the middle class of a capitalist society? In this chapter we will look at our approach as individuals to possessions and the use of money, and then in Chapter 18 we will consider the economic system itself.

But first this note: I am not saying that how we use our money is more important than how we use our time and our talents. Certainly how we use these is crucial. But our time and talents often follow our treasure. (I have often heard it said that it's easier for people to give money to a project than time, but I have never seen the resulting flood of funds that this would lead one to expect.)

We do need to be as careful in how we use our time and talents as in how we use our money. This understanding is implicit in the discussion that follows.

But it is with regard to money and property that the apparent values of our society most obviously conflict with the values of Christianity. This difference in values must be seriously confronted by anyone who has decided to try to live as a Christian. An individual is considered a success by our society if they earn a lot of money, gain power and influence, and/or accumulate valuable possessions. On the other hand, an individual is successful at living as a Christian if they live for others; if they are oriented towards sharing (not gaining for themselves), towards people (not things), towards values (not status or public opinion); if they are concerned first and foremost about living in right relationship.

Since this faith orientation is incompatible with the direction and the singleness of purpose usually necessary to acquire significant wealth, it is uncommon for serious Christians to be rich (by American standards— are we not all rich in comparison to most of the world?). But this problem confronts all of us, not just the wealthy. The serious Christian cannot wholeheartedly buy into the "American Dream".

And is there any such thing as an "unserious" Christian, a Christian who is not serious about his or her faith? How could there be? Only if we acknowledged as Christian all those people who say they "believe" but do not live accordingly. But to call these people Christians is to make a mockery of the word, a mockery of faith and commitment and Jesus Christ.

This is not necessarily to condemn those who do not live as Christians (except—if they claim to be Christians—as hypocrites). Going against the accepted values of society, especially when it means turning away from material rewards, is a difficult thing to do. We should not expect that a large percentage of people will do this, and those who do not, need not be thought of as immoral or inferior in any way. There are many fine human beings among them. But if they place pursuit of the American dream above living faithfully then they simply aren't Christians.

This being the case, how then does a middle class American live as a Christian?

I do not ask this as a trivial question. I am myself a child of the great American middle class, and I love it dearly. It is, as a whole, the best-educated, most civic-minded, most tolerant and charitable majority of any society anywhere. Yet I have struggled long and hard with the question of whether it is possible to be a member of this class and at the same time to be a Christian.

It comes down to the age-old challenge of being in the world but not of it. We can live as Christians in this world and therefore as members of a particular socio-economic class as long as we do not automatically accept its values and standards. We must judge these by a higher standard, accepting what is good and loving and rejecting what is not.

This may sound difficult. At least at first, it is even harder than that.

The values of the middle class by which we must beware being seduced include the presumption that we have a right to aspire to a certain level of material prosperity, and that this prosperity will (and ought to be) our primary goal, and will (and ought to) show itself in a certain level of material possessions. For example, we must recognize and challenge the all-too-common presumption that the higher paying job is necessarily better. (This presumption is in fact being challenged by many people who are placing more emphasis on job satisfaction and lifestyle, but this is all too often merely a reorientation of our selfishness from one kind of satisfaction to another.) We must also challenge the presumption *in ourselves* that if we earn enough money we have the right—some probably feel it a middle class duty—to provide ourselves with a large house, new car, nice furniture, more new clothes, vacations trips, TV, appliances, the newest electronic gadgets, and so on *ad clutterum*.

Where is it written that it is our duty to provide ourselves and our families with the best homes and all the possessions we can afford—or maybe can't afford? It is written in the advertisements that confront us constantly in newspapers and magazines, on radio and television. It is spoken in the actions of so many around us. It is shouted out in the lives of those who cannot find security or acceptance within themselves and so seek it in status and possessions.

Don't we have the right to spend our own hard-earned money as we please? When the price of a new suit will immunize a thousand children, when the money we would spend on a new television or a fancier vacation would feed a starving village for a week, when the down payment on a new car would dig a new well and provide new life and hope—*do* we have this right?

What do we have the right to provide for ourselves? Certainly food, clothing, shelter and other basic necessities. Enough and nutritious food, good clothing and a decent place to live. And certainly we ought to be able to enjoy the world, to partake of the pleasures of recreation and hobbies, of sports and culture. But how much is necessity and how much is luxury? How much is helpful? To how much do we have a right?

In answering these questions there is a temptation to go to one of two extremes: asceticism on the one hand or self-indulgence on the other. While both of these are dangerous in their one-sided approach to the material world, the former will hardly strike the disinterested observer as much of a threat to the American middle class. As for the latter, however—what could be a more natural excess for a class of people which defines itself primarily by reference to monetary earnings and material possessions?

How do we find the responsible middle ground? For that matter, does the responsible answer lie in the middle?

Thoughtful Christians (as well as others) will agree that there is a limit to the luxuries which we can in good faith bestow upon ourselves while others less fortunate than ourselves are in serious want. But where, and how, do you draw the line?

There are three questions that will help us to address this: (1) What is necessary and what is luxury? (2) What do we owe our own families? (3) What, then, would constitute a faithful approach to the use of our hard-earned money?

1. What Is Necessary?

In order to appreciate the huge amount of money that we spend on luxuries for ourselves, either on "things" or on enjoyment, we need to take a hard look at just how much—or rather how little—is truly necessary.

We need enough food to keep us going, clothes to cover us, shelter from the elements. A strict constructionist might point out that we would have what is strictly necessary if we had a room (or a small apartment in the case of a family), a change of clothes (and a warm coat up north), and if we ate 1500 to 2000 calories per day (the American average is 3200). How miserable such an existence would seem to most of us! Yet how much better off than a large percentage of the world's population we would be!

I am not suggesting that we limit our lifestyles to this level, although many of us would be better off spiritually and emotionally if we did, and many others of us may need to do something like this to free ourselves from captivity to the gods of consumerism. I *am* suggesting that we keep in mind how little is actually physically necessary as we establish in our own minds our own level of "necessities". Surely we do not need to consider everything above this physical minimum to be a luxury. But just as surely we had better not buy into what our society tries to tell us is necessary, and keeping in mind the low level of strictly physical necessity should help us in this regard.

2. What Do We Owe Our Families?

What do we owe our families, our spouses and children? We owe them a decent and safe home, a healthy environment, a good education and an atmosphere of love and discipline. The most important thing that we can do as parents is to prepare our children to live meaningful, productive lives. But by "productive" I do not mean producing material goods or wealth, but rather productive in the sense of being effective, of pursuing and reaching goals in keeping with our deepest values. What our children need in order to be able to lead this kind of life is a feeling of self-worth, the ability to think for themselves and make decisions, and the underlying values to guide these decisions and give meaning to their lives.

Too often we think that what we should do for our children is to make them happy. And too often we think that the way to do this is to buy them *things:* things that are pretty, things that are fun, things that snap and pop and whir and race and entertain—until we have taught our children that the purpose of life is to be happy and that being happy means having pleasure or being entertained. Someone who is oriented this way will go through life always lacking the deeper inner contentment

which "entertainment" cannot give, seeking value in things and in pleasure, and never finding true happiness.

Happiness itself is not the goal. Happiness is a by-product of having
meaning in our lives. For children, this requires a loving and secure
home. For adults—which our children will become—this requires values
that transcend pleasure and possessions, values that give meaning to our
actions and our relationships and our whole way of life.

If, then, our most important task as parents is to impart these values—
Christian values if we are Christians—we must ask ourselves whether it's
more important to buy that new car or sofa or refrigerator or suit or toy
or thing-a-ma-jig (for us or for our children), or whether it is not more
important to make do without this and share out of our resources with
the poor and the hungry, the persecuted and the refugees and the homeless. Which course of action is more likely to teach the values we want to
pass on?

The same reasoning applies to spouses. We need to encourage each
other not to seek shallow pleasures, but to grow and to mature and to
live up to our highest values and greatest potentials. Too often in marriages there is the real temptation of settling on the lowest common
denominator or of going along with our mate instead of our conscience
in order to keep the peace. We should not sacrifice our integrity this way.
Neither should we try to buy each other's favor or please each other with
an excess of "things", which is another great temptation. Instead, it is
much more important that we help our spouse to be the person he or she
should be—by helping each other become mature, loving Christians,
realizing our fullest human potential, becoming what we can and ought
to be.

3. What Constitutes the Faithful Use of Money?

In light of all this, what is the faithful Christian approach to the use of
money? There are two general approaches open to us, each with its
advantages and disadvantages, but each representing a legitimate Christian option. We can call these two responses: (A) the radical response,
and (B) the uncomfortable middle.

(A) The Radical Response

By calling this the "radical response" I don't mean that it is better or
worse, nor do I mean that those who follow it are more radically Christian. I simply mean that this approach seems more radical, more extreme, in its departure from the normal pattern of life in our society.

This approach to money and possessions (and life in general) has the
advantage that it seriously confronts some important facts about our

world: (1) that there is a great inequity in the distribution of wealth in the world, with a relative few enjoying great wealth while a great many remain trapped in abject poverty; (2) that many people in our own affluent society are psychologically trapped by material things to the point that these things come between them and God; (3) that many of those who are suffering from severe want could be helped with the money that we would otherwise use on non-essential things for ourselves; and (4) that we are called by God to be in community with each other, across divisions of race and nation and class.

The radical response to these facts is to restrict our own consumption of goods and services, our own material standard of living, either in order to share more of our wealth with those in need, or in order to serve God better by using our time to work for justice and peace or by sharing the lot of the poor. (The more we share their lot of poverty, of course, the less we are able to help in material ways.) This decision to restrict or reduce our standard of living means a conscious decision to forego many of the common aspirations of our middle class, whether in terms of possessions, travel, social status, or security.

This may sound either scary or appealing, or both. It certainly takes God's call seriously. But we need to be aware of several drawbacks or dangers to the radical response.

The first danger is that, with its strong appeal to the sense of the dramatic and the romantic, the radical response may attract individuals who see the world in black and white, who may then see themselves as "holier than thou" because they make do without new furniture or red meat or homogenized peanut butter. It may be that these people are in fact hiding from complexity. On the other hand, maybe they recognize that they need to do this in their own lives in order to be faithful. But there remains a danger of self-righteousness. Certainly it must be tempting to look at all you're doing without, especially in comparison to much of our affluent society, and to feel that you are better, that you have demonstrated your faith and devotion—maybe even to feel you have done your part. Besides leading to a sinful pride, this can also lead you to miss the point entirely. The point is right relationship. So the question is not, "What are you doing without?" The question is, "What are you doing for the rest of the world?"[1]

A second danger is inherent in one of the strategies commonly used in the radical response: living in community in the sense of shared or communal living. This involves the sharing of living space and resources in order to reduce one's personal living expenses and/or to free up more

---

[1]There are those who strongly disagree with this position, who maintain that God sides with the poor and therefore if we are to side with God we must be among the poor, or who maintain that what matters for our own soul is how much we sacrifice. Along these lines, for example, see Jim Wallis, *The Call to Conversion* (Harper and Row, 1981).

individual time and energy for mission of one kind or another and/or to provide mutual support in living a more person-centered and God-centered life. Often the avowed purpose includes all three of these, and there is much about living in community in this way that is very attractive. But there is an inherent danger in this approach which derives from the fact that human nature makes it difficult for a group of people to share money and meals and chores and living space equitably and harmoniously, particularly if they try to do this in a democratic way. (Perhaps this is one reason why monasteries are so strong on structure and obedience.) So it is not unusual for an immense amount of time and effort to be needed just to keep the cooperative venture going. Quite often a great investment of energy must be made just to decide who is responsible for what—who does the dishes and takes out the trash—and to deal with all the human interrelationship problems that can sometimes just be endured from 9 to 5 but which must be resolved if we are to be in community together. And a natural result of this is that no one in the community has any energy to deal with anything else, so instead of having a ministry to anybody else the venture becomes so inward-looking that it has no impact on the rest of the world.

A third problem with the radical approach is that it is essentially an option only for the relatively affluent. You can't give up something you never had, or make a virtue of doing without something that was never a possibility for you. There are many people in our society who are struggling hard just to remain at a very moderate standard of living. The danger is that some advocates might promote voluntary poverty or near-poverty as *the* Christian option while in reality we need to be working as a society to help people work themselves *out* of poverty. In fact voluntary poverty remains a luxury available only to the well-to-do, who always seem to have the personal resources and abilities to get back out of it if they should change their minds.

Finally, since one of the purposes of the radical response is to share more of our material resources with others, we run into a fourth drawback. Christianity has always recognized that self-interest is a strong motivator for us human beings, that selfishness is hard to overcome. The fact is that there are very few human beings who will work as hard to earn money for someone else as they will to earn it for themselves, or who will work as hard to earn $10,000 for themselves and $10,000 for others as they will to earn $20,000 for themselves. Therefore, if we simplify our lifestyle and reduce our needs as part of the radical response, it seems likely that this reduction in needs will be followed by a reduction in income. The result, and the fourth drawback, is that those opting for a simpler lifestyle or a "Christian community" may very well end up with *less* disposable income to share with those in need.

Of course, our gifts to the cause of God cannot be measured only in terms of money. If we change our job and earn less and so have less to give others, we may more than make up for this by devoting our time and energy to the poor and the hungry, by campaigning for peace and justice. That is, if we don't succumb to the second danger above and get so absorbed in the internal workings and personal relationships that we have no time or energy left for the rest of the world.

These four drawbacks represent a real danger involved in the radical response. Those who choose this approach must beware lest they end up as self-centered and self-righteous communities of upper middle class people playing at being poor, preoccupied with their own problems and contributing little or nothing to helping others or to resolving the world's problems.

In spite of this danger, however, this radical response must be recognized as a viable and important Christian alternative. It is viable because these temptations and drawbacks *can* be overcome with wisdom and persistence and hard work. And it is important because the people who choose this option are at least confronting the important issues, are at least asking the right questions.

It is also important, even if it appeals to only a few, because it serves as a valuable and maybe necessary reminder to the rest of us. Those of us who are struggling not to be owned by our possessions at the same time we are struggling to be able to buy more or newer or better *things* for ourselves need the example of people who simply do *without* these things—by choice!—as a reminder of how unimportant they really are. We need to see people around us who are free of the slavery to worldly goods, who find meaning and satisfaction without them, who challenge our middle class stereotypes and assumptions and values.

The drawbacks and dangers of the radical response can be overcome, if with difficulty, and those who respond to the gospel in this way have the great advantage that they are taking their faith seriously. Is this true of the rest of us? This is the great challenge to those of us who remain members of the affluent society, those of us who are unable or unwilling to make the sacrifices or the great change in lifestyle of the radical response: are we able to be serious about our faith? Is there a way in which we can be faithful? This is an important question, because if the answer is "no" then the radical response is in fact the only viable option for Christians.

(B) The Uncomfortable Middle

For this to be a Christian alternative we must make several assumptions: (1) that the world is good and is to be enjoyed, and that there is nothing intrinsically wrong with enjoying travel or fine food or nice furnishings or an attractive home; (2) that the important question is not what we are doing without but what we are doing to help others; that is, the goal is not in itself to lower our own standard of living but to live for others (which we may or may not be able to do without a reduction in our own material standard of living); (3) that many people can be challenged and inspired to follow this alternative who would never adopt the radical response; and (4) that individuals following this response can accomplish a lot of concrete good in the world.

But all this is nothing more than a fatuous rationalization for a selfish way of life if we do not have a commitment above all to live faithfully, to deal with the challenge of right relationship with God and neighbor. All this is empty if we do not take seriously the call of Christ and the needs of our fellow human beings.

How do we do this? How do we live comfortably—by which I mean no more than enjoying a lifestyle typical of the American middle class, which compared to most of the world is very comfortable indeed—and also take seriously the needs of our neighbors?

Probably the most important element here is seriousness of intent. There are various strategies that can be adopted regarding the use of money, but first you must be willing to accept the fact that all that you have is ultimately God's, that there are alternative uses for your money, that your decision on how to spend $100 can literally be a life or death decision for a starving child half a world away. Without this seriousness of intent, without this willingness to struggle with the question of what discipleship means, we cannot hope to discover what our faith means to our way of life—which means we cannot hope to be faithful.

Once you have this seriousness you may not absolutely need a system for the use of your money. On the other hand, to avoid a constant succession of agonizing decisions, for the sake of consistency, and to keep ourselves honest and faithful in the face of constant temptation, a standard or system seems called for. No one standard is right for everyone, for our circumstances vary a great deal. But there are several ways of developing an appropriate standard which would apply to any one of us.

One way of doing this is simply to set a dollar figure, a certain amount per week or per month, that you give to church and charities. This amount should be more than you think you can easily do. There are too many people who put their dollar in the collection plate every week (or whenever they go to church every month or so) and think that takes care of that. I cannot recommend this particular method of setting a standard for anyone above the poverty level because it is too easy for us to be satisfied with doing too little.

A second method, long advocated and practiced by many Christians, is to give a certain percentage of your gross income. The traditional norm for this is "tithing", or giving 10% of your income to the church, but nowadays this needs to be treated more flexibly in two regards: first, the percentage that you give can be shared with more than just the local church, and perhaps should be. There are many individuals in need of help and many organizations doing God's work and it is not inappropriate for some of our giving to go directly to these other ministries.[2] Second, ten percent is often not a realistic figure. For individuals earning the minimum wage, who have to feed and clothe and house themselves just like the rest of us, ten percent is often unrealistically high. For many Americans, whose earnings are several times the minimum wage, ten percent may be unrealistically low. The responsible and faithful level for our own situation is something that we must each prayerfully decide.

A third method for determining how much you ought to be sharing with the rest of the world is based not on a percentage of income nor on how many (or few) dollars you feel you can spare each week, but instead on your own needs and your own use of money. The idea here is to keep track of what you need to provide yourself with necessities, the assumption being that what you have left over to spend on luxuries for yourself ought to be shared in some meaningful way with those who lack even basic necessities. (This can be combined with either of the first two methods to give a balanced approach.)

This method requires a good measure of real honesty with yourself as to what constitutes a necessity. In fact, judging from all the luxuries that people seem to feel they *need,* it must require an uncommon amount of honesty. A house in good repair and large enough for your family, with furniture in good condition, would qualify as a necessity (or as a necessary decency) for almost all of us. A house with extra rooms for everybody's hobbies or with furnishings that look like a *Good Housekeeping* centerfold is a luxury. A motor vehicle in good working order and a stove and refrigerator are necessities for most of us. A new car, new appliances and many household gadgets are luxuries. Time off from work and time to be with your family is a necessity; vacation trips and nice meals in restaurants are luxuries. We must keep in mind that wanting something very badly or feeling a great need for it does not make it a necessity.

Once we have exercised the necessary discipline to thoughtfully challenge ourselves and establish a fair and faithful standard of what is truly necessary for us, the next steps are to follow this to its logical conclusion and then to take this conclusion to heart: once we have what is necessary, anything else is unnecessary, is a luxury. Yet while we spend money on luxuries for ourselves so many others lack even basic physical necessities. Can we do this? How do we deal faithfully with this situation?

Some of those who follow the radical response would say that we cannot indulge in *any* luxuries for ourselves while our neighbors (wher-

---

[2] I should like to point out that denominational and inter-church agencies have by far the best track record on keeping overhead costs down and can often deliver one hundred percent of your donations to the cause for which they are given.

ever they may be) are suffering. While such intense commitment and self-sacrifice as this may be admirable and in many ways appealing, it also smacks of asceticism and supererogation. It is also unlikely to attract adherents. And furthermore, we do have a right to enjoy life, to taste and see the uplifting pleasures of God's world. A standard of morality that recognizes this while it calls us to be faithful just might succeed.

So, once we have provided ourselves with the basic necessities, we need to balance our spending on luxuries for ourselves with spending on necessities for others. Once we have what we truly *need* we should use our money to buy what we don't need only if this is accompanied or preceded by using some of our money on behalf of others who need so much. This is a clear implication of our Christian faith.

But how do we set the proportion? This is a difficult and important decision. How do we set the proportion between what we spend on luxuries for ourselves and what we spend on necessities for the rest of the world? Is it unreasonable to expect that we spend as much on food and medical care and justice for the whole rest of the world as we do on luxuries for ourselves? I think not. For some, because of unusual circumstances, this may be too high a proportion. For those who can afford whatever they want this may be too low. For many it would make sense to give a certain percentage each week and then match what we spend on luxuries with additional giving.

What about money that is put into savings and investments instead of into luxuries? Money put aside for purchases in the not-too-far-distant future can appropriately be shared either when it is saved or when it is spent. But what about people who prefer to add to their own wealth instead of spending? Surely this, too, must be shared to the extent it surpasses our own needs. But what about all those of us who are trying to save up enough to be secure in our old age? Are there not also limits to how much we can in good conscience lay up for ourselves?

There are two separate but related questions here, one about security and one about wealth: (1) To what extent does living faithfully allow for storing up treasures on earth for our own future security? And (2) is it possible to accumulate or keep great wealth and also to live a faithful life?

The answer to both is, only in so far as this security or wealth is a means and not an end, only in so far as it is a means to living faithfully. We will look at what this means in each case.

(1) *Security:* "Therefore do not be anxious about tomorrow." But we *are* anxious about tomorrow! Is this sinful? Perhaps this anxiety is the wages of sin, the result of an unhealthy attachment to things and to our own comfort and to our own selfish desires for the future.

But there is also something else at work here. Our society is not the same as that of first century Palestine, where families were close-knit and stable and elders were respected and those few who lived to a ripe old age could count on living out their years as an honored member of an extended family. A good majority of us now live past the Biblical goal of three-score and ten. Our children live in their own homes, often far away, and we don't want to have to live with them or they with us ("What? Give up my home?") even if we could get along for more than a short visit. Nor do they have the resources to support us.

In this different kind of society it is irresponsible for us not to plan ahead, not to figure out how we are going to make ends meet, not to plan for retirement. The cyclical ravages of inflation, the doubts about the future of Social Security and the continuing escalation of health care costs must cause at least occasional anxiety for any prudent person. To dismiss this by saying that God will take care of you is really to say that someone else will provide for your needs, that you are planning on luck or on being a burden to society (or to some group or individual), and that you are planning not only on not being able to help the poor but on taking resources yourself that otherwise could have gone to help others.

Nevertheless, if it is responsible and faithful to arrange it so we can take care of ourselves, there are definite limits to the extent we can faithfully go in this effort. Again, the question is: Who are we serving? Ourselves? Mammon? Or God? Even as we plan for our future security this must not be an end in itself but a means to allow us to continue living a life that is active, helpful and caring for others. And again, a certain balance is required. We cannot just pile up assets for ourselves while others are in need.

The more secure our own future is, the greater the proportion of our wealth in excess of our necessities we need to share. If we own our own home (and will have it paid for), if we have vested rights in a good pension plan or have significant investments, then we need to give much more to others than if this were not the case. But even if our future is uncertain we cannot invest all of our resources in our own security, for that would be to build our own well-being on sins of omission, on the suffering of others that we could have alleviated and didn't.

(2) *Wealth:* "It is easier for a camel to go through the eye of a needle than for a rich man to enter the kingdom of God." (Mark. 10:25) While Jesus does then allow that "all things are possible with God", it is evident that he considered a rich man or woman's entry into the kingdom to be rather unlikely and very difficult. This is not so much a judgment upon the rich as it is a recognition of human nature. We humans are always tempted to serve ourselves instead of others, to put our trust in ourselves and our possessions instead of in God. Those who are wealthy simply have that much more temptation: privileges to protect, comfort to be seduced by, power to put faith in, wealth to serve and worship. How strong must be the soul who would be faithful in the face of this!

Can you be wealthy and also faithful? Yes, if you serve God first. But this may mean that you can't stay wealthy. And certainly faithfulness is more difficult when you have so many glittering gods clamoring for your devotion.

You can be wealthy and faithful the same way you can be talented and faithful or intelligent and faithful or famous or beautiful or popular and faithful. To be faithful you must serve God with your talent or your intelligence or your fame or beauty or popularity. To be faithful, the wealthy must serve God with their wealth.

How do you do this? How do you serve God with your wealth? This should be obvious: by using it to help others in need. You can do this by giving to the poor and the hungry (or other worthwhile causes) all that you have in excess of what you need for a moderate middle class lifestyle. In principle, you can also do this by holding on to your wealth and using it to help the poor and powerless or to accomplish other good. We must ask under what circumstances this could be justified.

Hanging on to great wealth is justified only when it is done *in order to* help others. That is *not* the same thing as doing some good in order to justify to yourself your holding on to your wealth. It does not mean giving a few thousand to charity when you are worth a million. Nor does it mean retaining ownership of a business and justifying it by the fact that you provide jobs for people if your successor would do the same.

Hanging on to substantial wealth can be justified only if you can accomplish at least as much good by hanging on to it as by giving the whole lot to a relief agency that would use it to fight hunger or to a scholarship fund for the underprivileged or to similar good causes. But it seems quite unlikely that an individual could in fact do as much good as this for the world by keeping his or her wealth to themselves. So the argument usually comes down to this: we just don't want to let go. "It's mine, dammit! It's my money, my property, and I earned it or inherited it fair and square. It belongs to *me,* and I'm going to *keep* it, because it's mine and I want it!"

Whatever our stated rationale, this is almost always the real reason we hang on to our wealth: we're selfish. And surely it is our *legal* right to keep it all to ourselves. But just as surely it is not faithful. When we just won't let go or can't let go, we are being sinful, grasping and hoarding. We are worshipping Mammon.

We need to say that it is *possible* for an individual to have faithful reasons for hanging on to substantial wealth: if, for instance, that person uses ownership in a business to pursue policies with important benefits to society, or is able to provide jobs for people that no one else would hire, or is able because of keeping their wealth to accomplish some unique and valuable good that at least equals the good that could be realized if this wealth were wisely given away. Another possibility is that an individual could give away the income produced by their wealth on an annual basis as wisely as anyone else. However, while there is something to be said for avoiding the bureaucracy of agencies and foundations, there is also something to be said for making use of their expertise. Furthermore, income taxes may mean that a significantly smaller amount is available for giving if the income is an individual's than if it is a tax-exempt organization's.

The biggest problem, though, is that it is just so extremely difficult for a human being to hold on to wealth with one hand and give away most of the proceeds with the other. With rare exceptions the temptation to indulge ourselves and the drive to amass more for ourselves is just too great. In fact it is almost never the case that we can accomplish as much good by hanging on to wealth in excess of our needs as we can by giving it away. We would like to think that we can because we don't want to give up the power and prestige and prerogatives of being wealthy. It's simply too nice being rich to want to give it up. So we buy fancy cars and travel first class and build mansions for ourselves and furnish them with luxuries to satisfy our whims while our neighbors on this planet live in shacks and struggle against oppression and watch their children die young from lack of food and medical care. It is not enough to say, "Ah well, the world is an imperfect place." We who would be faithful must do what we can in the name of the Christ. If we have the resources to help others but do not, if instead we keep our fists tightly closed on what is "ours," then we have turned our backs not only on the least of these our brethren but also on God.

We have now considered several methodologies for arriving at a standard of what we must share of our own with the rest of the world if we are to remain a part of the middle class of an affluent society and still be faithful. Which particular approach we follow is not nearly as important as the need for us to faithfully confront the fact of our own good fortune and others' misfortune, and to share of what we have in a significant way.

In some ways this is more difficult than following the radical response which we considered earlier. It is more difficult because the temptation is stronger to follow the gods of gold and silver, to keep up with the Joneses, and to buy into society's definition of success. It is more difficult because those who follow the radical response are at least asking the right questions, and sometimes the rest of us don't even question. It is more difficult because living faithfully in the middle class requires constant attention and will power. This is to be expected, though, when you dwell in enemy territory, or at best in no man's land. This is why I call this option the uncomfortable middle.

Of course, living in gray is always more difficult than living in black and white. But most of the regions inhabited by human beings are gray, and if we are to reach them we must have a gospel and an ethic that can withstand the lack of easy answers. So even though trying to live faithfully as part of an affluent society, with all the temptations this entails, is in some ways more difficult and more uncomfortable than living the radical response, it does have several important advantages:

(1) First, it is possible. It is possible not only in a theoretical sense and not only for a few, but it presents itself as a real chooseable possibility to many people who could never see the radical response as a live option. It confronts people with the challenge of living faithfully right where they are.

(2) Second, it can accomplish a lot of good in the world. Those who are well off have more resources to share with those who are suffering from poverty or disease, hunger or injustice. God *expects* more from the affluent middle class: "To whom much has been given, of him will much be required." (Luke 22:48) It is all well and good to identify with the poor by joining them, but the poor need more than to have their ranks swollen by children of the middle class who, being poor by choice, will never know the real ravages of poverty. This is not to say that people following the radical response cannot play an important and valuable role. Indeed they can. But the hungry need food and the sick need medical care and the homeless need shelter, and all of these cost money—money that a faithful and sharing middle class could provide a good measure of, certainly enough to do a lot of concrete good.

(3) Third, if our society is to change for the better, this will come from a change in the people who influence our political policies and make our economic decisions. This change will *not* happen if every Christian who decides to take their faith seriously thereupon drops out of "the system." It will only happen if the men and women inhabiting the great gray area of every day life, in our homes and shops and factories, in boardrooms and legislative halls, work at living faithfully in all aspects of their lives right where they are. The uncomfortable middle course is the way in which they can do this.

This chapter has dealt specifically with the use of money. But, we need to remember the truth of Jesus' saying in Matthew 6:21: "Where your treasure is, there will your heart be also." If we are giving significantly of our own money to combat hunger or poverty or injustice we are very likely to become interested enough in these efforts to invest some time and energy in them, to work with individuals and to become involved in policy debates and to confront the economic system.

And—since policy and structure do matter—it is time for us to proceed from our own personal use of money to an examination of economic systems.

CHAPTER 18: THE ECONOMIC SYSTEM

"Thus says the Lord: for three transgressions of Israel, and for four, I will not revoke the punishment; because they sell the righteous for silver, . . . (and) trample the head of the poor into the dust of the earth."
(Amos 2:6–7)

In addressing the question of how we as Christians relate to wealth we must also consider the economic system itself. A lot has been written about the morality of economic systems, much of it pure bunk. There has long been a conviction in certain political and theological circles that capitalism itself as a system is to blame for much of the injustice, oppression and poverty in the world. This point of view periodically gains strength before undergoing a counterattack from those who claim that capitalism is ordained by our faith and blessed by God. Both of these views on capitalism, of course, are matched by complementary positive and negative attitudes about socialism. And all of these convictions about a particular economic system being the bane or blessing of the world involve immense oversimplification and misunderstanding. I will argue that we need to re-think and refine the distinctions we make between economic systems and also that systems do not absolve individuals of moral responsibility.

The role of any economic system is to meet the two challenges of production and distribution. The strength of capitalism is unquestionably in the production of goods and services; the attractiveness of socialism lies in its approach to their distribution. But what do we mean by these two terms, capitalism and socialism? Broadly speaking, capitalism is the economic system in which the means of production and distribution are owned by individuals and/or by non-governmental corporations, and in which production and marketing decisions are made by these individuals and corporations. Socialism is the economic system in which the means of production and distribution are owned by the state, which decides through central planning what is to be produced and how it is to be distributed. (In theory it is to be the workers who own the means of production, but so far it has always turned out to be the state.) However, there are vast differences within each of these two categories between economic systems that are nominally grouped together, greater differences than there are between some systems that we place on opposite sides of the capitalism/socialism dividing line. We will take a look at these differences below. But first we well begin by examining the case against capitalism.

The Case Against Capitalism

We have discussed the difficult challenge of living faithfully in an affluent capitalist system, and we cannot ignore the charge that this system itself is sinful. The case against capitalism rests on (1) the motivation upon which capitalism is based, and (2) the observable results of capitalism.

First, the motivation: capitalism is based on each individual earning what they can for themselves through their own efforts. It cannot be denied that this is essentially selfish. It is the profit motive that fuels the system, and this system depends on competition for its efficiencies. Compared to this, does not the socialist premise of cooperation, of working together for the common good and seeing that everyone is taken care of, seem preferable? Second, the results: in a number of capitalist countries there is a vast disparity between the wealthy elite and the poverty-stricken masses. Even in the United States of America there are notable differences between owners and workers. Can we justify this?

Let us look at each of these in turn.

(1) "Capitalism is based on selfishness."
Some defenders of capitalism try to deny this. This is silly. It is obvious to all of us that capitalism is indeed based on each of us looking out for our own self-interest. We must admit that this is true. But is this wrong? Does pointing this out constitute a criticism of the system? Only if it is a practical or moral weakness for a human economic system to be based on selfishness. I am not at all convinced that it is, *provided* that steps are taken to alleviate any unjust hardships brought about by this.

Let me spell out my assumptions here: first, that an economic system is not an end in itself but a tool for reaching certain ends; second, that the first purpose of an economic system is to encourage adequate and efficient production, without which there is nothing to distribute; and third, that this system should also promote (or at least be conducive to) certain socio-political goals, among which are freedom, equality of opportunity, and the provision of basic necessities for those unable to provide for themselves. Therefore, if a capitalist economic system meets these goals—and I will argue that some do and some don't—then it meets our goals for an economic system, in which case it makes no sense to complain because it is based on selfishness.

Furthermore, if we grant that people are concerned first and foremost with their own well-being—for which there is ample evidence in the world and ample precedent in Christian theology—then capitalism is only being practical in appealing to this. People are motivated by self-interest. We work harder and produce more when we realize some benefit from this ourselves. There is nothing demonic about this. And even if we wish we were different, we aren't—this is human nature. Is there anything wrong with an economic system being realistic and practical? Might it not function better if it is?

But, say the critics, capitalism encourages our selfishness and promotes competition over cooperation. This is a serious accusation that deserves careful consideration.

To begin with, it must be stated again that so far as I can determine, selfishness is indeed a predisposition of the species. It is not *caused* by capitalism. Capitalism does allow more freedom for selfishness and more opportunity for the acquisitive, but some capitalistic systems also allow more freedom and opportunity for everything else as well. But does capitalism *encourage* this selfishness?

If we are honest we must say that what encourages this selfishness and acquisitiveness is *us*. You and me. It is our "American Dream", the pursuit of materialistic possessions as our goal in life. It is our turning our backs on God and on faith and depending instead on worldly well-being for our meaning in life. For us to blame "the system" is a cop-out. For us to blame capitalism while we live for ourselves alone is to compound our sin of selfishness with the hypocrisy of denying responsibility. Pogo was right: "We have met the enemy and he is us."

Having said that, however, we must also admit that capitalism has produced the affluence that results in more and more temptations to us. But this is because capitalism has succeeded in its primary purpose as an economic system, that of production. Certainly a successful consumer-oriented economy encourages us to want things for ourselves. But do we blame it for its success? Ought not the question to be: "Can we as a society establish a way to complement capitalism's success in production with a just distribution? And are we as a society up to the moral challenge of the temptations of materialism?" Indeed, these are the questions. They remain to be answered.

As for competition, capitalism—or at least "free enterprise" capitalism (see below)—certainly encourages this. But is this bad? Yes and no. Competition for business should and does encourage efficiency, innovation, improvement in products and services, and lower prices. These are certainly results to be desired. But competition also encourages an array of unethical practices to gain business and to make profits. Again, the question is whether we can sufficiently discourage the bad results while we benefit from the good results.

(2)"Capitalism is responsible for the vast disparity between the rich elite and the poor masses, and so is responsible for much injustice and suffering in the world."

It is true that such disparities exist, in some places to a shocking and indefensible degree. It is also true that some of these places have economic systems which are called capitalist. Before we blame capitalism as such, however, we need to look at the differences between various types of capitalism and to see whether there is a particular variant of it that may be involved.

A Typology of Capitalism

We need a way to categorize capitalist systems that takes into account those differences which are relevant to our discussion. We can do this by setting up three pairs, or "dichotomies", to consider three different aspects of any given system. Each dichotomy contains two opposing types, and while there are intergrades in the real world, this method will allow us to point out the most important distinctions. The three dichotomies are: (i) elite vs. free enterprise capitalism; (ii) democratic vs. despotic capitalism; and (iii) responsible vs. irresponsible capitalism.

(i) Elite vs. free enterprise capitalism: this first dichotomy has to do with whether the system actually functions as an open competitive marketplace. On the one side is elite capitalism, in which a few families or individuals own a large percentage of the wealth, there is a consequent absence of a large middle class, and control of the economic system is by the elite. (Not surprisingly, such systems are often also "despotic" as defined below.)

The second type in this first dichotomy is free enterprise capitalism. This is characterized by competition for the marketplace which is open to anyone who can produce the goods and services, unhindered by government subsidy, monopoly, or other interference with competition.[1] For a system actually to function as free enterprise capitalism there must be opportunity for individuals in the general populace to obtain education and also to obtain access to capital and resources for new ventures. Without these there is no real access to the marketplace. Free enterprise capitalism depends on actual competition or at least the real potential for it. In elite capitalism, where a small group of families may control the vast majority of land, capital, or other resources, this openness to competition is seen as a threat and is not present.

Thus the competition and the "efficiencies of the marketplace" that are often thought of as intrinsic to capitalism are in fact present only in free enterprise capitalism and not in elite capitalism. There are many who would define capitalism as necessarily involving free enterprise and competition. If we accept this argument then we have to say that elite capitalism is in fact not capitalism at all. Instead it must be categorized with feudalism, a system to which it is in fact much closer than it is to other variants of capitalism. (This distinction should be helpful in foreign policy decisions. It is not enough to know we are supporting a nonsocialist economy. Is it free enterprise? Or feudalism?)

(ii) Democratic vs. despotic capitalism: this second dichotomy is not

---

[1]Regulations establishing such things as a minimum wage, safety standards and pollution controls apply equally to all parties and thus do not interfere with competition.

concerned with the economic system per se but with the political system with which it cohabitates. The question here is, to whom does the government answer? Who's in charge? Who determines what rules shall govern the society and its economic system?

Democratic capitalism is characterized by a functioning, representative government—that is, it is governed by individuals who are chosen by the populace in free and fair elections and who are then able to freely legislate and enforce such laws and rules as they deem proper. Despotic capitalism, on the other hand, is characterized by control of the government by an individual or a relatively small group such as military junta, an aristocracy or elite class, or a minority political party. It is important to note the political basis of an economic system as one of our basic dichotomies because there is a very real difference in the foundation of a capitalism in which the rules governing the system are determined by a few—rules concerning wages, monopolies, taxation, use of natural resources, government benefits, etc.—and one in which these rules are determined by representatives who are chosen by the general populace.

(iii) Responsible vs. irresponsible capitalism: any economic system is going to have drawbacks and negative effects. They all have social costs. This third dichotomy is concerned with whether a society takes steps to offset these negative effects. To the extent that it does we can call it responsible. To the extent that it does not address the known social costs of its economic system, it is irresponsible.

A capitalist economic system can encourage initiative, efficiency, production, freedom, self-sufficiency and the accumulation of wealth. A society may choose capitalism for these reasons. But when it does, it is also choosing a system which leaves some people unable to provide for themselves, whether for reasons of disability, age, industrial dislocation, lack of marketable skills, etc. For a system to be responsible capitalism, it must include mechanisms that either enable these individuals to provide for themselves or else provide basic necessities and decencies for them. These mechanisms may include such methods as unemployment insurance, retirement and disability benefits, and anti-poverty health and welfare programs. What these various programs do is redistribute the wealth created by a capitalistic system in order to compensate those in the society who are unable to gain an adequate measure of this wealth on their own.

For an economic system to be responsible it is also necessary that it include adequate public health and safety regulations to ensure that industrial practices do not endanger employees or the present or future public welfare, and also that it provide adequate protection of the natural environment. To the extent that a society has adopted capitalism but has not put into place these measures to protect its public and to provide for those in need, this is an economic system that can only be called irresponsible capitalism.

By now it is obvious that there can be vast differences among economic systems that are all categorized as "capitalist." The difference between one that is elite, despotic, and irresponsible and one that is free enterprise, democratic and responsible is so great as to make one wonder how they can be lumped together in any meaningful way.

We began this section with the question of whether capitalism is to blame for the unjustifiable disparity that is found in some societies between the wealth of a few and the poverty of the masses. It cannot be denied that the particular economic system in these societies at least made this disparity possible. It is much more problematic as to whether these economic systems ought rightly to be considered capitalist. But even if they were, given the great differences between capitalist systems, it does not seem reasonable to blame capitalism in general if a particular type of capitalist system encourages gross inequities.

But are not poverty and injustice present even in the best of capitalist systems? And are there not in all cases large disparities between the wealth of the owners and that of the workers?

We must admit that there are. But there are problems with every economic system devised by human beings. What we need to do is to compare the benefits and problems of actual, feasible economic systems. It serves no purpose to compare a real system—whether capitalist or socialist—with the imaginary perfection of a system which has never existed (and which never will in any manner resembling perfection).

So: yes, we must admit that capitalism does indeed permit some individuals to get very rich and others to be poor, and that even in a responsible capitalist system that ameliorates the effects of poverty this disparity exists. But we also need to remember that we said the goal of an economic system is to provide equality of opportunity, not equality itself. There will always be differences in wealth and lifestyle. The question is, does responsible, free enterprise capitalism provide sufficient equality of opportunity? And how does it compare with the alternatives?

The Case Against Socialism

We have examined a couple of the popular arguments against capitalism. Now we must take a look at socialism. I have said that we must compare real and imperfect economic systems with each other, not with imaginary perfect systems. What is the reality of socialism, and what are its advantages and disadvantages?

In theory, socialism is the ownership of the means of production and distribution by "the workers" or the people. In practice, however, socialism means ownership by the state, which may or may not represent the people. The attractiveness of socialism lies in its approach to distribution, as opposed to its effectiveness at production, and in its stated underlying principles—that is, socialism is not supposed to be based on our self-interest but on the principles of providing for everyone, of distributing the wealth in an equitable manner.

There are two principal types of socialism: "full socialism" in which the state owns all (or the vast majority) of business and industry and controls production and marketing decisions through central planning; and "partial socialism", in which the state owns major businesses deemed to be essential to the national good, and/or subsidizes certain industries to save them from the impact of competition, and provides certain goods and services deemed to be essential at reduced or no cost, but still allows major sectors of the economy to operate as free enterprise capitalism. Both types of socialism can point to accomplishments which include (1) a vast improvement in education and health care for the general populace, to the point where the education and medical care of the poor is in some cases better than that available to them even in advanced capitalist countries; and (2) a reduction in the disparity between the poor and the rich, through supplying goods and services to the poor and also through elimination or heavy taxation of the rich.

While their accomplishments may be similar, however, the negative aspects of these two types of socialism are drastically different. Full socialist economies, without exception, involve governments that are undemocratic—"despotic", according to our earlier definition. They are all Marxist and outside of Africa they are all communist. The social cost of their party-dominated political tyranny is immense: control of information, censorship, suppression of dissent and debate, and prison and exile for those who speak out in unapproved ways. Full socialist countries match the despotic feudalisms in tyranny while surpassing them in social services but also in the thoroughness of their suppression.

As an economic system the weakness of full socialism is merely that it doesn't work very well at what it is supposed to do. Central planning and the lack of incentive have produced agricultural shortfalls, industrial mismanagement, shoddy products, permanent shortages in housing and consumer goods, economic collapse staved off only by Western credit, and a shockingly low standard of living in what are supposed to be modern industrial nations. These results have become so evident that even the leaders of China and the Soviet Union have acknowledged them and are currently involved in efforts to institute some of the efficiencies of partial socialism or even of capitalism. Since they are attempting to do this without renouncing their Marxist principles and without giving up the political tyranny of the party it will be interesting to see what develops here, for it seems likely they will get either less economic reform than they want or more political reform than they want.

Partial socialism is a very different matter. In the first place, economic systems which are partial socialist can and do exist in functioning democracies. And they do permit many of the efficiencies of free enterprise in large sectors of the economy and so tend to have a better standard of living than comparable countries which are full socialist. Their primary weaknesses as economic systems are (1) that subsidization of major sectors of the economy (either through ownership or subsidy) encourages inefficiency and discourages the moving of resources into new areas that may be more productive, and (2) that the high tax rate necessary to provide substantial governmental services and subsidies reduces incentive. Together these two create a real danger of inefficiency and stagnation. We need to be aware that this is not just a nuisance: if it is unchecked it can result in economic collapse.

Capitalism vs. Socialism?

When considering economic systems the question has too often been put in terms of capitalism vs. socialism. But as we have seen, the differences *within* each of these broad categories are such as to make the distinction *between* the two well-nigh useless except for propagandist arguments intended to produce heat rather than light. The similarities between democratic/free enterprise/responsible capitalism and democratic/partial socialism are so strong that it is hard to say where socialistic capitalism ends and capitalistic socialism begins. If one looks at the world it is clear that the big differences are not between these two, but between these as a group on the one hand and despotic elite capitalism grouped with despotic full socialism on the other hand. Thus the big difference is not between the United States and Great Britain, for instance, but between the U.S.A. and the U.K. on one hand and countries such as certain feudalistic Latin American ones grouped with communist eastern European ones on the other hand.

It is a sad fact that too often when we have been called upon to "defend democracy" we have in fact been defending one kind of despotism against another. The only reason a despotic capitalism should be preferred over a despotic socialism is that the former usually isn't as good at despotism and is somewhat less difficult to change. An elite/despotic/irresponsible capitalism (which might better be called feudalism) needs to be changed not only because of the evil it causes in itself, but also because of the even more intransigent evil it will lead to if it is *not* reformed. The unfortunate aspect of socialist revolutions is not that they destroy a "capitalist" system. This particular kind of capitalism or feudalism—one that allows so much human suffering as to engender rebellion, one that refuses to reform itself—deserves and needs to be destroyed. The unfortunate aspect is that all too often people exchange despotic capitalist poverty for despotic socialist poverty.

My personal belief is that democratic, free enterprise capitalism can provide a higher standard of living and more freedom than the socialist alternatives and can still be responsible in providing for those who are unable to provide for themselves. The problem is that it is extremely difficult to move from feudalism to democratic responsible capitalism. The reason for this should come as no surprise: it is plain old-fashioned selfishness. Those who have the power and wealth generally want to keep it, even if it is more than they could possibly need. So those who have the power to change the system all too often choose not to, trying to hang on to everything instead of promoting peaceful reform that would still leave them well-off and comfortable, all too often forestalling peaceful reform altogether. If the evolution to a decent capitalism is thus prevented we need to keep in mind that at least some variants of socialism would be considerably preferable to the status quo. (One has to wonder why there has not been more encouragement of democratic capitalist rebellions against feudalism. Have we so forgotten our own rebellious origins that *any* such enterprise is now seen as Marxist?)

To repeat: a cursory look at the nations of the world makes it clear that the important differences in social responsibility and freedom are between the democratic types (of both capitalist and socialist economic system) and the despotic types, not between capitalism and socialism as such. Therefore, if we as Christians are going to work to improve the systems in which people live—as indeed we must—then we need to avoid promoting or condemning capitalism or socialism as such. We need rather to oppose and to try to change those systems of *both* kinds which oppress and dehumanize, to recognize the strengths of the best systems of both kinds, and to help find ways to eliminate the inequities and ameliorate the injustices that exist in even the best of socialist and capitalist systems.

The Challenge to Capitalism

I have said that free enterprise/democratic/responsible capitalism can provide more freedom and a better standard of living—even for those who are unable to provide for themselves—than can socialism. The big question, however, is not one of ability. It is one of will. The question is whether we *will* be responsible, whether we can be capitalists without losing our moral fiber and our very souls.

This is the challenge to those of us who profess to follow the Christ while living in and enjoying the fruits of a capitalist system. This challenge presents itself in the form of three dangers: (1) the danger of a growing disparity between economic classes; (2) the danger of materialism, of the rewards of the economic system becoming the goals and values of society; and (3) the danger of a selfish pseudo-individualism that evades individual moral responsibility.

Danger Number One: Class Division

We must be concerned about the possibility of serious and permanent class divisions developing in our society. This could happen along the traditional lines between owners and workers, and could also develop between what we might call the comfortable and the marginal. We will take a look at both of these.

Several very important changes have taken place since socialism developed in response to the inequities of a capitalist system that allowed owners of industries to get rich while their employees worked long hours in often unsafe conditions for low pay with no health or retirement benefits. First of all, the government has responded to justifiable public concern over the years with the enactment of legislation governing child labor, minimum wage, health and safety conditions, overtime pay, and other labor practices. Second, the right to collective bargaining has been enshrined in law, and the results of these contract negotiations worked in combination with the supremacy and prosperity of American heavy industry in the mid-twentieth century to produce a previously undreamt of affluence for skilled laborers.

Third, it is no longer clear in many cases just who the owners are, with millions of shares of stock being held by the public, many by individuals but also many by pension funds, insurance companies and other investment concerns.

So, for these and other reasons, we do not now often see our society as one divided into wealthy exploiting owners and poor exploited workers.

We have also had a chance to see the reality of socialism. It does not, after all, offer an alternative to working for someone else. The difference is that in socialism the "someone else" is the state, which has the ability to be as enlightened or as despotic as any private owner, although if you don't get along with your employer it's harder to find a new one. It might also be noted that there are a whole set of special conditions involved when one tries to do collective bargaining with a prime minister or a general.

Nevertheless, in spite of the great advances made by workers and in spite of having seen that socialism cannot offer them a worker's utopia or even an alternative to working for someone else, we must take note that there are still a couple of very troubling aspects to the division between owners and workers. The first problem is one of attitude: even though owners are dependent on workers' labor, and the workers are dependent on the owners' capital and initiative, too often both sides view their relationship as adversarial. Those companies in which their interdependence is recognized and in which people are treated with respect tend to do better for both owners and workers in the long run. The fact that this mutual respect is not as common in the United States as it ought to be remains an important underlying cause of our problems with productivity and foreign competition.

The second problem is not one of attitude but is rather a glaring and dangerous disparity that we act as if we are blind to.[2] When our nation began there existed an economic democracy and equal opportunity because of the high value of labor and the availability of land for those willing to work it. This was a unique historical combination, both elements of which have long since disappeared. The industrial revolution devalued the real worth of labor and increased the productive capacity of capital. Capital is now much more important to producing wealth than is labor. A 1985 study reported that according to the Federal Reserve Board only two percent of all U.S. families own "20 percent of all residential property, 30 percent of all liquid assets, 33 percent of all business property, 39 percent of all bonds, 50 percent of all stocks, and 71 percent of all tax-free financial holdings".[3] It can be argued that the ownership of such vast portions of our capital by so few threatens our democratic system. It certainly makes for very *un*equal opportunity.

But what can be done? Would I advocate a socialist approach to redistribution of capital? On the contrary, I recommend a very capitalist approach to addressing this problem. Worker ownership of whole companies or of significant amounts of stock is a real and proven possibility, with established financing vehicles and enabling federal legislation. The details involved are beyond the scope of this book, but suffice it to say that the mechanisms are in place.

Some observers of the American scene would go so far as to say that we do not now have a democratic/capitalist economy but rather a plutocratic/capitalist economy. This claim is well presented by Louis and Patricia Kelso in *Democracy and Economic Power*,[4] in which the Kelsos argue that because of the disparities in capital ownership we do not now have the equality of opportunity necessary for free enterprise capitalism, or economic (in addition to political) democracy. They argue cogently that worker ownership plans would tremendously increase our productivity and prosperity and can be brought about through methods that have already proven successful in a number of corporations.[5] Additionally, they propose a number of other ways to distribute our wealth

[2]I am indebted for the background to these three paragraphs to Louis O. Kelso and Patricia Hetter Kelso, *Democracy and Economic Power: Extending the ESOP Revolution* (Ballinger Publishing Company, 1986).

[3]*Grey Matter*, "Auditing American Affluence: Are We Really Getting Richer?" (New York: Grey Advertising, 1985), pp. 5–6. (Quoted by Kelso and Kelso).

[4]Kelso and Kelso, *Op. Cit.*

[5]We refer to true worker ownership with advise and consent powers, not the pseudo-ownership plans sometimes used to facilitate management buy-outs of corporations.

through innovative, capitalist methods. I strongly recommend this little book to everyone. Whether or not we agree with their answers, if we are to create a better economic system and avoid a serious class division we need to confront and respond to this and similar analyses of our current problems. Certainly the Kelsos' proposals are provocative enough to spur us to find new ways of addressing our situation within a capitalist framework.

The other class division that threatens our society is a division between what we might call the comfortable and the marginal. The "comfortable" include most of our workers, the large middle class—those who have sufficient resources to afford decent housing, a new (or recent vintage) automobile every so often, occasional vacation trips, and numerous little amenities around the home. These people are also likely to be covered by health insurance and a retirement plan at work. In most cases they work hard for what they have, but at least they have something to show for it: security and decencies and a lifestyle beyond the wildest imagination of their grandparents. Most of us are in the comfortable middle class, even if maintaining this comfort causes us great anxiety.

The "marginal", on the other hand, are in a different situation. They cannot afford their own house—at least not one that you or I would consider livable—and maybe not even a decent apartment. They are either underemployed or unemployed, continually on the economic fringe, perhaps unable even to feed their families without government assistance.

The challenge of equipping and training those on government assistance is an old challenge which we have yet to meet. We seem unable to move beyond ideology of the left and the right to find out what works, and our political lack of will is condemning yet another generation to hopelessness and poverty. We must not let this happen.

A newer challenge is the increasing number of people with jobs who fall below the poverty level. While there is (as always) some disagreement about the meaning of the statistics, it seems clear that the shift from traditionally unionized and higher-paying manufacturing jobs to lower-paying service industry jobs is a contributing factor to this. Whatever the complex of reasons, there are more families than before in which one or even both parents work full-time and yet they still remain financially marginal. And this situation is exacerbated by the fact that these people who are least able to afford medical bills or to set aside money for retirement are also the least likely to be covered by health insurance and retirement plans.

We must not let our society become one in which a relatively few professional, technical and managerial workers are well rewarded while the many struggle on the economic fringes, just as we cannot let our society become one in which wealth is so concentrated in the hands of a few that we lose our equal opportunity. We must confront both aspects of this problem with all the ingenuity and commitment we have, otherwise our capitalism will cease to be democratic, will cease to provide opportunity, will cease to be a supportable and defensible economic system.

Danger Number Two: Materialism

When our economic system is based on the incentive of material reward, and works well because of this, it also brings a great spiritual danger. There is a real danger that we might come to equate success in the economic system with a successful life, that we might come to identify the material rewards of the system as our goal in life and the source of meaning for us. In fact it is readily apparent in the lives around us that many people in our society have already made this grievous misidentification. And we in the churches have not done enough to make clear the difference between economic success and success as a human being.

I have already dealt at some length with this problem of money in Chapter 17. We need to understand that we cannot serve God and Mammon, that to set economic reward as our goal in life is to fail as a Christian and a human being.

Danger Number Three: Selfish Pseudo-Individualism

Individualism that is informed by integrity and compassion offers one of the great hopes of humanity, giving us the prophets and critics and dreamers which we so badly need, and giving us also the hope that some brave souls will lead us where we ought to go. However, an individualism guided instead by a desire for material gain and emotional ease is nothing more than selfishness—a heartless, sinful selfishness that exacerbates the dangers of division and materialism, eats away at the moral fiber of our society and threatens to destroy the fabric that holds us together. This is the kind of individualism that appeals to our great religious and political principles in name while turning its back on them in fact.

Individualism can be responsible. It can lead people to be concerned with the ethical implications of their actions and to accept responsibility for what they do. It can give us the ability not to go along with others just for the sake of going along, and so allow us to base our actions on what is right and what is wrong. It enables us to realize that our actions as individuals *do* affect others, that we as individuals can and must do our part.

On the other hand there is that selfishness which masquerades as individualism. In order to look out for themselves, this "individualism" leads people to go along with the crowd, or to acquiesce in the questionable practices of family, employer, or community. In the name of necessity, or security, or advancement, or just out of cowardice, these people abrogate their individual responsibility and take part in questionable or immoral or illegal activities because they are following orders, or because business demands it, or because if they don't somebody else will, or because it's the only way to get that extra dollar, or because it's simply easier.

And this is often done in the name of individualism, of "looking out for number one". In fact this "individualism" actually surrenders individual responsibility, giving it up to superiors or to society or to "the system" or to whoever we see as our peer group. It is a pernicious pseudo-individualism. To call it individualism is just a way of dressing up our base selfishness in high-sounding phrases.

When it comes to sharing of our own good fortune with others who are in great need, this selfishness continues to try to sound like individualism: "I take care of myself; others ought to do the same." But this is just a further evasion of personal responsibility. All of us have benefited from our education or our upbringing or our innate abilities (for which we can take no credit). Those of use who have received any measure of success have in fact benefited from our economic system, and we who benefit from a system have a personal responsibility to assist those who are unable to benefit from it. And we who are fortunate have a responsibility to assist those who are not. No amount of posturing about other individuals' responsibilities can remove our own responsibility here.

So in fact this pseudo-individualism—really selfishness masquerading as individualism—evades individual responsibility and by so doing sacrifices individual integrity. And in giving up individual integrity—whether for popularity or monetary gain or whatever—it gives up its right to claim to be individualism. It is after all nothing more than selfishness, the "antichrist" to real individualism.

There is an all-too-prevalent attitude which encourages this pseudo-individualistic abdication of responsibility: the blaming of individual or corporate actions on "the system." This is done both by some who oppose the particular system and by some who support the system but oppose individual responsibility.

Now it is of course true that any "system", any society or culture, will encourage certain ways of acting, both good and bad. It is true that some systems produce such horrendously ill effects that we are obligated to try to change them. It is also true that we must work hard to ensure that the laws which govern our own system protect the public health and welfare and provide aid for those who cannot make it on their own. Nevertheless, while this concern about systemic effects is absolutely necessary, in very many cases to blame "the system" is both whitewash and hogwash.

Decisions are made and carried out by individual human beings, acting alone or in groups. Whether it is a technician or company president, janitor or engineer, sales team or board of directors, each of the individuals involved is responsible for his or her actions to God. If any of these people make or carry out a decision to cheat or to steal or to pollute or to do something that threatens health or safety or the public good, they cannot escape their own personal moral responsibility by pointing to the corporate structure or the capitalist system. Those individuals are not robots; they have a choice. Those who choose loyalty to money or security over loyalty to God have sinned. They are personally culpable. It is time we quit excusing individuals because of "the system". The sooner we do, the sooner "the system" will quit producing some of its bad results which are after all nothing other than the cumulative effect of individual actions.[6]

These are the dangers that constitute the challenge to democratic capitalism: class division resulting from an inequitable distribution of our society's wealth; the spiritual emptiness of materialism; and the selfish pseudo-individualism that avoids personal responsibility. The challenge is not to an impersonal system. The challenge is to us—to you and me— the individual citizens who make up this system. Through our individual decisions on how to live, what to spend our money on, who to vote for and which policies to advocate, we will determine the nature of this society. We can't blame it on a central planning committee or a ruling elite. It's up to us.

If we accept our individual moral responsibility, if we are careful about how we use our money and how we share it, and if we make sure to extend our caring about others to our political and economic system, then we will be able to make this a capitalist economy that does what it ought to. But this will not be easy. It requires hard work. It means attentiveness and diligence and an openness to new ideas and new methods, for we must find ways to open the system to all.

If we are self-centered, if we act out of concern only for our own wealth and privileges, if we do not share as individuals and as a society, then we are sinful. And not only that, but we will find that we stand in risk of losing this system which we claim to value so highly. If this comes to pass—if we lose our capitalism and our freedom because we could not (or would not) make it work for the benefit of all, because it collapsed under the strain of class division and materialism and unrestrained selfishness—then we will have no one to blame but ourselves.

---

[6]We can take some comfort at the fact that finally, toward the end of the twentieth century, prosecutors have begun applying criminal statutes to corporate officers who make decisions that (for instance) cause death or injury to a worker or to the public, and charges brought against these individuals include manslaughter and homicide charges. This should have a salutary impact on people recognizing their individual responsibility.

CHAPTER 19: A NEW SPIRITUALITY AND THE WHOLE OF LIFE: THE SACRED, WORSHIP, PRAYER, WORK, THE CHURCH, AND WHERE WE GO FROM HERE

"Whither shall I go from thy spirit? And whither shall I flee from thy presence?" "The earth is full of the steadfast love of the Lord." (Psalm 139:7, 33:5)

We have covered a lot of ground in this book. We have seen that because of the change in our common sense over the last twenty centuries we find a number of traditional Christian views to be inadequate and no longer tenable: Biblical literalism, the idea of a God who goes "zap", the religious significance of miracles, and such doctrines as the Incarnation, the Trinity, and the sin and salvation complex. Perhaps more surprisingly, we have also seen that many of these traditional views are also incompatible with a proper understanding of our faith, with the love of God as preached by Jesus Christ.

But we have done more than just work at the demolition of traditional ideas. We have also suggested interpretations that are consistent with our modern common sense, with our understanding of how the world works and with our understanding of the physical sciences—interpretations that are also consistent with our faith. Thus we have suggested appropriate ways of talking about God, and a way of understanding Jesus the Christ in a functional manner, and ways of reinterpreting Christian Myth. We have done this in ways that address our deepest need, that for meaning in our lives. We have further pointed out the crucial difference between faith and doctrine and have examined the impact that our faith must have on our lives: on our character, on the way we live and the way we treat other people, on the way we deal with money, and on our economic system.

Throughout all this we have emphasized the need for integrity: a moral integrity that holds us to our principles in all areas of life. We *must* come to understand that if we sell out our selves we have lost the only thing that is truly ours. This integrity can be understood as right relation with oneself. We who profess Christianity have further grasped that this can only exist fully in partnership with right relationship with God and with others in line with the teachings of Jesus the Christ.

But integrity also includes intellectual integrity: an honesty with ourselves that includes a demand for consistency throughout the different areas of our life. We do not believe one thing in church and another in science class and another in our business. We do not deny our heart for the sake of our head, nor vice versa.

And in fact in the course of this book we have seen how we can develop a theology (which is an explanation of our religion, a conceptualization of that which gives real meaning to our lives) that is consistent with *both* our faith and our common sense. What we have done is to point towards the development of a new spirituality, one that is not restricted to "sacred" buildings or to one hour a week, one which rather encompasses all of reality. In this final chapter we will consider the nature of spirituality, the sacred, the role of worship, different forms of prayer, the integration of our work world into our faith, the nature and purpose of the Church, and where we go from here. These discussions will of necessity be brief, but it is my hope that they will nevertheless provide an adequate overview and point the way for further development of these ideas.

1. What Is Spirituality?

We must begin with the question of "what is spirituality?" It might be defined as the awareness of God and the recognition of the sacred in our life. It includes the understanding that our quest for meaning is our most important task in life and that this cannot be satisfied with shallow answers, cannot be fulfilled with possessions or status or wealth. Spirituality therefore means that our awareness of the sacred and our drive for meaning have an impact on our lives, on the choices we make and the way we live. We sensitize ourselves to the pull of God and try to align ourselves with this pull. If our spirituality is real it pervades all aspects of our life.

We have said that we need a "new" spirituality. This is because the traditional models are based on a theology that does not and cannot fit with our common sense (and all too often does not and cannot fit with our faith). Even if we were able to suspend our common sense in the area of religion in order to buy into this traditional theology—something which many people have felt forced to do because they saw no good alternatives—we would then have a spirituality that is unable to adequately fulfill its role. Because it is incompatible with our understanding of the world it is unable to inform the rest of our life. It is restricted to a sheltered corner, walled off and protected from reality.

Therefore a spirituality that is worthy of the name—one that is able to address and inform all the areas of our life—must be founded on a theology that is consistent with the common sense that undergirds all these different areas. The main purpose of this book has been to propose just such a theology so that we now have the foundation we need for this new spirituality.

We accept our modern common sense. We accept and even embrace the discoveries of modern science. But we do not stop there, and we do not postulate a God who is in conflict with these. Instead, we see God as greater, as *including* this scientific understanding of the universe. God includes and transcends the physical universe as we know it. This physical universe itself works as a result of such an improbably fine balance of forces as to be cause for wonder at the very least; it is certainly congruent with our conception of God. Furthermore, we see this God, we feel this God, in and through the processes of this universe, coaxing us and pulling us to love and to wholeness.

Spirituality is the recognition of this dimension of the universe, the recognition that God is the context within which we live out our lives. But spirituality is more: mere recognition, mere cognitive awareness, of this dimension is not enough. Besides a sensitivity to this dimension, spirituality also includes an aligning of one's life with it, a directing of one's self towards God in the way one lives. When this is given its focus and direction by Jesus of Nazareth then it is Christian spirituality.

2. The Sacred

The sacred[1] has often been thought of as that which is set apart because of a special closeness to God. But how can that be if God pervades the universe and the world around us, if God is the context for the whole of our lives? We cannot confine God to a particular mountain top or building or one hour a week. There is nothing we do that is not in the presence of God.

In Chapter 10 we did in fact describe the sacred as that which is special and set apart, that which is beyond question, that which is of such value that it inspires awe and reverence. But sacred things are not set apart because they are somehow closer to God. Rather, the sacred is that aspect of the world, those elements in it, that point towards God,

---

[1]For the purpose of this discussion I am considering "holy" to be synonymous with "sacred".

that help us to become aware of God and to direct our lives towards God. There is nothing in the universe that is intrinsically more sacred than anything else. To be sacred, a person or place or thing must be sacred *to* somebody. That which points us to God, that which emphasizes God's presence and makes clear God's love and reminds us of our need to respond to God—this is what is sacred to us. It is that which yields our deepest meaning to us, whether person, place, event or writings.

If we are Christians, if we are among those who try to order their lives according to the understanding of God, of love, of value and of true victory given in the life and teachings of Jesus of Nazareth, then we proclaim Jesus as the Christ: it is he who serves as the compass or focus for the meaning of our lives. And thus Jesus the Christ is for us the epitome of the sacred.

Certainly there are other people or places or things or times that are also sacred to us. Many of these are *derivative* from the sacredness of the Christ, associated with worship or meaning to which he is the central direction-giver. Included among these might be those parts of the New Testament other than the Gospels which are consistent with Jesus' teachings; other Christian writings; Christian places of worship or songs and prayers used in this worship; the sacraments; perhaps the life of a Christian we know or read about who exemplifies for us the way Jesus told us to live.

But there may also be other places or teachers sacred to us that are best described as *auxiliary* rather than derivative. That is, they have no particular connection with Jesus of Nazareth, so if we are Christians they must play a subordinate role, one that complements his role as central meaning-giver and direction-pointer. They point independently in the same direction as the Christ, much as we might use landmarks to complement our compass reading. If they assist our primary guide in pointing to the one God who is in all creation and who is pulling us to love, then they are auxiliary sacred for us. Such things might be included here as natural theology (the making of inferences about God from a study of the natural world); the teachings of other great religions—again, to the extent they are compatible; or even the Old Testament prophets, depending on how you view their relationship to Jesus.

So we see that "sacred" is not an independent characteristic of any person, place or thing. It is a relational concept. As we have said, to be sacred something must be sacred *to* somebody. It must help point them to God. And the sacred includes a variety of persons and things, writings and events, though necessarily of a quite limited number for any one person. For us as Christians the role of Jesus the Christ makes him the epitome of the sacred, but we also have other places and people whose sacredness is *derivative* from his and additional sacred things which are *auxiliary* to him.

Every one of these sacred persons or objects or events performs the same role for us: they are particular bits of reality that point to the God who is through all reality. They remind us that the whole world is full of the presence of God and that our lives are lived in this presence. Not just a portion of our lives, not just in certain times and places, but our whole lives.

3. Worship

Worship, whether public or private, involves the highlighting of the sacred and the reinforcement of spirituality. As a public activity worship also involves a reaffirmation of group identity, through shared creeds, hymns, and prayers and also through the reinforcement of human fellowship. The purpose of worship is not generally to give new information to people—after all, much the same group of people gathers regularly. In some cases worship can yield new insights as it helps people to gain a deeper understanding of religious truths. But more often it serves to remind us of what we already know and to encourage us to act accordingly. In our case, it reminds us of the presence of God in which our lives are lived, of our acceptance by God, of the pull of God towards love and wholeness, and of the direction to God pointed out by Jesus the Christ. Worship encourages us to live up to the commitment we have made (and are reminded of) to live according to Jesus' teachings.

If we are to worship privately then we must find ways to perform these functions for ourselves, by ourselves. While this is possible at times, private worship is best considered as an auxiliary to public worship; as such, it needn't fulfill the whole range of purpose that public worship does, but can be satisfied with lifting up one or two aspects. Private worship as a *substitute* for public worship is suspect and in grave danger of being one-dimensional. Not nearly as many people worship alone as say they do; even less do it well, and even in these cases it seldom (if ever) can suffice as a substitute for public worship. This is true even if one participates through radio or television in a public worship service. There is just no substitute for sharing the physical presence of other imperfect human beings who are also trying to be faithful, for we are called to support and encourage and love one another.

Another function of worship, whether public or private, is to evoke awe and wonder and to promote the attitude of worship as an appropriate response to God. Awe and wonder may be evoked by a number of facets of the universe—the sacred, beauty, the world, life itself—as well as by worship. But worship itself is appropriate only for God. We must remember that while the sacred may help us to worship God, we do not worship the sacred, but only God.

In the same way that the sacred points to the God who is in all reality, so worship—while it may be something we do in a separate time and place dedicated to this particular purpose—must point to a life that is lived towards that which we worship. The worship experience cannot be disconnected from the rest of our life. Rather it must be an epitomizing, a lifting up and making explicit, of the pattern that is present in all our places and times. So if our worship is successful and our life is successful, our life will take on the same pattern as our worship, the pattern of living towards God.

4. Prayer

If has long been recognized that people come in a broad range of personality types, that people approach the world and interact with others in different ways. In the past century this observation has become more refined. Perhaps the best known classification comes from four basic dichotomies noted by Carl Jung and further developed into a grid of sixteen different personality types according to whether one is extraverted or introverted, sensing or intuitive, thinking or feeling, and judging or perceptive.[2]

For each of these sixteen "types" there has been developed a description of how people of this type interact with others, what they enjoy, what kind of occupations they do well in, and so on, even what style of worship they find meaningful.

But all this is ignored or forgotten when it comes to prayer. For when it comes to prayer there is an apparently irresistible urge to proclaim that a particular method or style is *the* way—the one and only *really* right way—to pray. For everybody. It must be that either our way of praying is so closely tied to our own personality needs that we cannot conceive of another way, or else that our way of praying is so important to us that we cannot bear the challenge of any alternatives. But in fact there is no one right way to pray.

For one thing, there are several different styles of prayer: corporate and individual, spoken and silent, set written traditional prayers and "free" prayers. Consider just this last pair: some people find prayers written by others to be meaningless for them, and find traditional prayers to become empty with repetition so that they are nothing but noise or, at best, pleasing sounds with no significance. Other people find that these same prayers focus their minds for them and contain a beauty of form and meaning that lift their hearts towards God. The important thing to say is that this is fine. There's nothing wrong with either group of people.

---

[2]These types are best developed and most used in conjunction with the Myers-Briggs Type Indicator Test. See Isabel Briggs Myers, *Introduction to Type* (Palo Alto, California: Consulting Psychologists Press, 1976), and other material from this publisher.

They are different people. Why shouldn't they respond to different models of prayer? So we must expect differences in the way we pray just as we expect differences in our favorite hymns.

But still, even if we grant that different people should expect to use different styles of prayer, there are some important questions about prayer in general. What are we doing when we pray? What is its purpose? What is it supposed to accomplish? Does it make any sense to tell things to a God who already knows everything? Or to ask things of a God who doesn't go "zap", who isn't a specific interventionist? Or to give thanks to a God who didn't take any particular steps to bring about the specific things for which we are thankful?

To begin with, we do not think of prayer as communicating particular bits of information to God. God already knows. Rather than communicating, we are *communing* with God. The purpose of prayer is to put ourselves in touch with the God who is in all and through all, to reaffirm our own identities by confirming the meaning in our lives, and to verify whether we are living in the proper direction.

What about petitionary prayer, asking for help? If God isn't going to respond by making sure we win the lottery or by effecting a miracle cure then what can be the purpose in this? Well, if you want a God to pray to who will give you a red bicycle for Christmas or solve all your problems for you, what you're looking for is magic. God doesn't work this way. But petitionary prayer nevertheless accomplishes several important steps for us. In the first place, praying for God's help reminds us that we are not in control of the world or even of our own life, while reminding us that we are living in the presence of an infinite and eternal being. Besides being humbling—something that many of us need from time to time— this also helps us to take the first step toward solving a problem, namely that of admitting that we indeed have a problem and need help, even if we admit this only to God for now. And it also can accomplish the important step of putting our life and our troubles in proper perspective.

Furthermore, in praying for God's help in dealing with a certain situation or problem, we cannot help but consider God's will for us. If we pray with the right attitude, if we bring willingness to "listen" for an answer, this will make us more sensitive to the pull of God so we in fact may get an "answer" by becoming aware of the direction in which we need to go to live towards God. And lastly, this whole process prepares us to face our problems and to deal with them in the most constructive way by properly grounding us and focusing us and even energizing us.

But what about intercessory prayer, in which we pray for help for others? Will our interceding on their behalf with God lead to God's interceding on their behalf in the world? No. We must be consistent with our earlier conclusions about how God does and doesn't act. We are not dealing with magic when it comes to others any more than in praying for ourselves.

But what, then? What good does it do those for whom we pray for *us* to become better grounded and focused in prayer?

We cannot deny that there are some real possible benefits here. To the extent that our prayers do put us in better touch with the will of God, and to the extent that we are a part of the situation in which those for whom we pray find themselves, this can lead us to participate in some real improvements for them. And to the extent that we are serious in our prayers for justice or peace or healing for others we become allies with God in the struggle for these, and we proceed from prayer to right action. (Prayer is *not* meant to be in lieu of action.)

Certainly these are not inconsequential. They may at times prove to be decisive. But the fact is that in intercessory prayer we aren't praying for *us* to help the other person; we pray for God to help them. I must repeat: the conviction that God does not work as a specific interventionist requires us to conclude that God does not respond in this way. God is not a genie in a bottle who responds to the magic words. Nevertheless, I must admit to an uncertainty here. My understanding of the pull of God and the connections of this world causes me to wonder whether indeed there isn't more to it than this, more that can be said, more that can be experienced. Certainly intercessory prayer doesn't hurt: it can help you, it can help you help the one for whom you pray, and it may even do more.

As for prayers of thanksgiving: if God did not specifically cause us to be fed or clothed or housed or otherwise fortunate, for what should we be giving thanks? First of all, for a universe constructed in such a way as to make all these things possible. For creation itself; for life itself. Second, we give thanks to God for the pull to wholeness and goodness which results in so many particular concrete instances of good. And third, we give thanks not in order that God will know that we are thankful but precisely in order to *make* ourselves thankful: to help ourselves realize not only how lucky we are in comparison to so many others (which is part of it), but how fortunate we are just to be in this world; to help us appreciate the many blessings which each and every one of us enjoys; to rekindle in us the sense of wonder and awe and gratitude in response to all that we so often and so cavalierly take for granted.

So indeed these different types of prayer have purposes and meaning and can play an important role in our spirituality. And certainly there are other kinds of prayer that can have meaning for us: prayers for guidance, prayers of praise, prayers whose goal is meditation on God or a feeling of union with God.

But we must remember our differences. Just because a particular type of prayer *can* be an important part of our spirituality, and in fact is for some people, doesn't mean that it *must* be for everybody. And this brings us to another problem that is a hindrance to many people, not just in regard to a particular kind of prayer but in regard to the whole idea of prayer in general. This is the traditional idea of prayer as withdrawal from the world, as time set apart from our normal activities. Now it is true that we all need times of withdrawal, times of quiet and meditation, of solitude and reflection. (Those who do not recognize this probably need such times more than anybody.) But such times, as needful as they are, are not necessarily any more sacred or any more prayerful than other times. What we have here again is the error of making normative a particular style of prayer. John A. T. Robinson observes that "Our traditional forms of spirituality have been adapted from the monasteries for the millions,"[3] which doesn't make a lot of sense. The lives of most of us do not resemble those of monks. Robinson admits that he is one of those who never had much luck at praying in the set aside "empty spaces". Too often they simply remained empty. But in his activity, in his busy involvement with people, he found the addressing of God and the communion with God that we call prayer: "My own experience is that I am really praying for people, agonizing with God for them, precisely *as* I meet them and really give my soul to them."[4]

Surely Robinson makes a valid point here. We can fulfill the functions of prayer in our activity as well as in our "empty spaces". In our caring, our hospitality, our struggling along with others to find love and to do what is right, we can and must seek the guidance of God, trying to better sense God's pull; we can and must intercede on behalf of others, give praise and thanks to God, and try to focus our lives on living towards God. Since people are different, there is no one way of doing these that is right for everyone. Some will benefit greatly from traditional, set-apart prayer; others will do better at—and benefit more from—prayer as an aspect of their activity. Each of us must use that form that works for us. But shouldn't we all be trying to live in such a way that our whole lives can be offered to God as prayer?

5. Work

Work? What has work to do with the sacred and worship and prayer? The fact that this question can even be asked is good evidence of the problem we have had with a constricted spirituality. But in fact our spirituality cannot be limited to certain times and places. The sacred is special to us, but it points to the God who is in all places and times. Worship and prayer may take place in a time set apart, but they cannot be a serious endeavor on our part unless they give direction to the whole of our lives. And the place where this has been the most problematic is

---

[3]John A. T. Robinson, *Honest to God* (The Westminster Press, 1963) p. 92. See pp. 91–104.
[4]*Ibid.*, p. 99.

the arena of work. How does our faith impact on what we do to earn a living? How does our spirituality inform and give meaning to the hours and days and months and years we spend in our occupation?

You can relax: I'm not going to tell you that you ought to like the fact that you have to work, or that every bar of soap you sell or widget you make should give you a sense of fulfillment or should be understood as for the glory of God. Not that this would be bad; it just strikes me as unlikely. But apparently—judging from surveys—a majority of us actually do like what we do for a living. This is certainly something to strive for. And fulfillment in one's job is not only a hoped for satisfaction; it is a condition that employers need to work hard at bringing about through the sharing of planning and responsibility, for the sake of productivity and quality as well as for the sake of employees. But many workers still don't have this sense of fulfillment, and even those who do may not like the obligation of doing what they do to earn a living. I don't like *having* to work—why should you?

Of course there are some good points to the necessity of work. Civilization did not develop on this earth where the living was easy. Civilization developed where people were challenged, where they had to work together to bring food out of the ground, where without irrigation the earth would bring forth nothing. Certainly there is some analogy here to our lives as individuals. How many of us would cope well in character and accomplishment with not having to work? Some would, of course; but many would not. Many in those circumstances *do* not. Furthermore, much material progress is engendered by the necessity of work. But this still doesn't mean that we like having to do it.

Not only do the vast majority of us have to work for a living, but what we do in the course of our jobs is generally not up to us. It is determined by our bosses or by our customers or by necessity. And we need to do well enough at these tasks imposed upon us to support ourselves and our families. How can our faith, our spirituality, inform our decisions and our actions on the job?

The need for integrity comes up again. We must act in ways that are consistent with our principles. In the first place this puts a negative limit on what we can do. As followers of Jesus Christ we simply cannot engage in dishonest or deceitful practices. We cannot participate in any activity that may cause harm to others, such as producing or selling an unsafe product or dumping toxic wastes. We cannot cheat on our customers or even our competitors (though certainly we need to make a decent profit from the former and we can work like the dickens to outsell the latter). If we are given the option to make more money by going against our principles in any of these ways we must say, "No." Or else we must choose the money, in so doing deciding that we are not going to be Christians after all.

We can be thankful that we live in a country which has legally mandated respect for the rights of workers. We have substantial protection against dismissal for refusal to violate the law and for refusal to go against our consciences, and substantial legal recourse if this does occur. But the time still may come when we have to choose between our livelihood and our faith. This is a painful and difficult choice which we may hope never to face. But if we believe what we say we do, is it not also a clear choice?

This refusal to participate in unethical practices, while an important part of our faith and our integrity, is only a negative limit. Our spirituality means more than this. It recognizes that all of our life is lived in the presence of God. We are called upon to nurture the best in others, to show hospitality and acceptance, to put ourselves in right relation with others through caring and sharing. This doesn't mean accepting less than satisfactory performance from someone else: we must expect others, just as ourselves, to do their best and to contribute their efforts to the success of the enterprise. We have a right to expect—but we must also foster and enable—others to do their jobs adequately and competently.

But in the context of these minimum requirements we can and must add more. We must add the positive elements that come from our faith. At first sight this may seem difficult. We may not see how our responsibilities and routine tasks are at all connected with our faith, whether it be making parts on a production line or totalling numbers and billing customers, whether it be keying data into a computer or serving up hamburgers, selling real estate or planning the next step in company expansion. Quite often, except for the calling to do our job to the best of our ability and to do it honestly and ethically, the specific tasks of our job may not have much to do with our faith. Much that we do is religiously neutral. Whether we meet our production quota or design a better widget or cook a better hamburger may be important to us but matters to very few others. Only a few people are so fortunate as to do as part of their job something which has a positive impact on others.

But the rest of us still have the opportunity to make an impact—often a very big impact—on the lives of others. For most of us our daily work involves innumerable contacts with other people. It is impressive to see how an otherwise enjoyable job can be made miserable by the pettiness and immaturity of a few people—in fact, by just one person if he or she is good at it, or is the boss. But it is also impressive to note how an otherwise humdrum or tedious job can be made bearable, enjoyable, and even a place for growth when people of good will act cheerfully, courteously, kindly and caringly toward one another.

Courtesy is a good place to start, courtesy along with cheerfulness. You don't feel cheerful? That has nothing to do with it. Cheerfulness is a way of acting, not a feeling. We can make our part of any interactions pleasant and polite. And this is not just a matter of propriety or social etiquette. Rather it is an important ethical and religious question: what kind of environment do we create for our co-workers? What kind of atmosphere do we help make in which other people spend two thousand hours each year? By having respect for others, by cheerful courtesy, we can at least make our part of this environment a pleasant corner in which others feel built up instead of put down, sheltered instead of battered.

This means, too, refusing to take part in the all-too-common gossip and back-biting. Complaints about someone else—which so often are directed to everyone *except* that individual—must be shared, in private, with the person concerned. Certainly confrontation may be necessary at times—but it can be done as discreetly and lovingly as possible.

And we can do more. We can care about these people and not treat them simply as animate machinery that we use as needed to get our own jobs done. We can care about them *as* people: people who have families, people who have unguessed talents and interest, people who feel lonely or anxious or unfulfilled. We can rejoice in their triumphs and commiserate in their sorrows, whether these happen on or off the job. We can encourage growth by the way we interact with people—growth in maturity, growth in spiritual wisdom, growth towards God.

We may not be able to choose the tasks we do to earn our living, but we *can* choose how we treat other people. Does this seem small and unimportant? If you think so then you are part of the problem in this society. You had better go ask the people who come home and snarl at their spouse and children because of how they've been made to feel, or the people who suffer silently while stress mounts and ulcers and high blood pressure take their toll. The fact is that we can make our places of employment—where we spend more waking time than any place else—into environments that tear people down or that build people up. The cost of working in a place that tears us down is immense. But if we do not leave our faith at the front door of our workplace we each have substantial opportunity—and substantial responsibility—to contribute to the creation of an environment that builds others up, that reflects right relationship, and that will build up ourselves in the process.

6. The Church

We have seen that our spirituality is informed by the sacred and by worship, but that it cannot be limited to these arenas and that in fact our spirituality is directed by these into the whole of our life, to the God in whose presence we always are. Given the broad role and all-inclusive realm of spirituality, we need to ask: what is the Church? What is its purpose?

First, a preliminary note: by Church with a capital "C" I do not mean any one particular organization. Rather I mean the totality of all those groups and organizations that function self-consciously as Christian churches. (The fact that there are some organizations about which it is questionable whether they function as *Christian* churches is beyond the purview of this discussion.)

The Church is, of course, a human institution. As such, it has both the strengths and weaknesses that you would expect. It suffers at times from inertia and an unwillingness to change, from internal power struggles, from putting its self-preservation ahead of its mission, from the abuse of worldly power, from misinterpretation and misunderstanding, from persecution *by* others and (far worse) persecution *of* others. But it also has the ability to endure through the ups and downs of history and the comings and goings of individuals, to teach the message of Jesus to generation after generation, to inspire countless men and women to perform deeds of love and mercy, and even with all its failings is able to help a certain number of people choose to really focus their lives on love of God and love of others in accordance with Jesus of Nazareth.

What is the purpose, the function, of the Church? It proclaims that it is the Church of Jesus Christ. This must be the primary determinant of what it is about. It claims to be the body of Christ in the world today, that Jesus the Christ is its head. If this is to mean anything at all significant then the purpose of the Church must be to encourage people to adopt Jesus of Nazareth as the compass for their lives. It does this in a variety of ways: by teaching about Jesus of Nazareth; by teaching and preaching his values and his understanding of God; by providing regular reminders of these values which are so different from those promoted by Madison Avenue and the American Dream; by helping people experience the sacred in a way that reinforces the sacred meaning-giving role of these values; by providing an arena in which people can lend mutual support to each other in trying to live out a life based on these values; and by setting an example in the way the Church itself acts and treats people and deals with issues.

This is what it means to be the Church: enabling and leading people to follow Jesus Christ, not in their words alone but by *living* towards God, by putting Jesus' message at the center of their lives. At their best, individual churches can encourage the kind of small groups that can give us some of the benefits of the "radical response" discussed in Chapter 17 without the accompanying drawbacks. Caring groups can meet regularly to share, to create community with one another, to discuss how members are doing in their own struggles to be faithful, to make sure that each one takes the questions of faith seriously. People can be held lovingly accountable to one another as an aid and encouragement on this journey we call life,[5] as well as supported during the difficult times that we all have.

Of course the Church must also embody Jesus' message in its own life. In worship, in structure, in mission and in day to day activities it must show what it means to have Jesus' teachings as compass and focus. In every way it knows how the Church must stress the sacred importance not only of God but also of serving God in the right way—a way that stands in opposition to so much we are taught by our society which sometimes pretends to be Christian.

This will mean involvement in both personal evangelism and social justice. Sometimes it will lead to numerical increase and "success" in worldly terms, but sometimes it will mean taking unpopular stands and sacrificing this "success." But the Church's role is not to be successful. It is to be faithful. Indeed, being faithful is its only true success.

7. Where Do We Go From Here?

The purpose of this book has been to show that we do not need to adopt all of the traditional Christian concepts and beliefs in order to be Christian, to propose some alternatives in keeping with our faith and our modern common sense, and to make the point that being a Christian has more to do with *living* a certain way than with believing certain doctrines. Where do we go from here?

The purpose in doing all this is to enable each and every one of us to confront the message of Jesus of Nazareth. This needs to be our first step: to confront the message that the true meaning in life is found in loving God and in loving others, that the only true success is a life lived faithfully. We must face his challenge to not only believe this but to live this, to live our lives towards God.

Only you can decide whether you will accept this challenge or reject it. Do not consider it lightly. It is not a path of comfort and complacency. There is much at stake for you either way.

For those of us who have decided to try to live our lives towards God with Jesus as our focus, we can insist on our right and our obligation to develop a theology that makes sense to us and that is faithful to the message of the Christ. We must try to make our families, our churches, our communities, and even our world the kind of places they ought to

---

[5]A number of churches have fine programs along this line, but I am particularly impressed by the Covenant Discipleship groups recently being developed in the United Methodist Church. (See David Watson's *Accountable Discipleship* [Nashville: Discipleship Resources, 1984.])

be. We need to live responsibly, to put ourselves in right relationship with our selves, our neighbors, and our God. And we will find in this a joy, a freedom, and a wholeness of self that is unobtainable in any other way. And now we need to get on with it. There is much to be done.

APPENDICES

The two appendices are somewhat more technical in nature. Appendix A is on the canon, the Christ, and the historical Jesus, in which we consider how the authority of the Bible is related to the authority of Jesus. I argue that Jesus the Christ must serve as our "canonical principle," by which we decide which parts of the Bible are authoritative for us today.

In Appendix B I examine some of the current scholarly opinions about the nature of the resurrection, weighing carefully the arguments of those who I call the "minimalists," who maintain that nothing extraordinary happened. How persuasive is their reasoning?

Appendix A: The Canon, the Christ and the Historical Jesus

Since early in the Church's history the Old and New Testament have been recognized as its "canon", as authoritative over all other writings, beliefs and opinions. But in recent decades there has been an increasing tendency to try to go behind this, to reconstruct the traditions and writings as they existed before they were incorporated into the Bible in their present form. This has been encouraged by our knowledge of the different sources of the Bible, by the development of form criticism and its insights and speculations into the early stages of the formation of the Gospels, by questions about the "original" intent of passages before they were set in their present literary context, by questions of "what really happened", and by the attempt to unravel diverse strands of tradition in both Old and New Testaments. This has proceeded to such an extent that it too often seems as if the only alternative to a Scripture that is inerrant, and so not subject to this sort of analytic study, is a Scripture that is so analyzed and picked apart that there is no Scripture left.

Of late a movement has begun to correct this situation. Foremost in this campaign to consider the Scriptures as subject to modern critical analysis but at the same time to treat them *as canon* is Brevard Childs, professor of Old Testament at Yale. In fact he so strongly feels the need to press his point that he has crossed over into the field of New Testament studies to wage his campaign there as well.[1] And indeed Childs has performed a valuable and needed service in reminding us that what we have now is not just individual passages, nor is it just the "books" which as larger units give the individual pieces a place in the larger narrative. What we have now is canon, a body of work recognized as authoritative Scripture in its present complete form. This is a much

---

[1]See Brevard S. Childs, *The New Testament as Canon: An Introduction* (Fortress Press, 1984), and *Old Testament Theology in a Canonical Context* (1985), and *Introduction to the Old Testament as Canon* (1979). (I have one quibble: Childs' writings are not as accessible as one might wish to the non-specialist, a problem which I know he can overcome from my own experience with one of his lecture courses.)

needed corrective to those who have adopted the historical/critical method not only as a tool but also as their principle of interpretation (or "hermeneutic principle", in theological jargon). That is, some scholars have interpreted passages of the Scripture as we have it by speculating about their origin in oral tradition or by separating them into various earlier strands. But we cannot interpret a present literary passage by showing what it (perhaps) once was. Nor can we take an individual verse or story or "pericope" in isolation. The canon gives these a place in the whole, often balancing them with other elements. And the canon as we have it does not consist of separate historical strands but of the whole of the Bible as it now stands.

But as necessary and salutary as this movement is, this "canonical approach" in turn occasions some very basic questions itself. Childs and the others who promote this approach begin by assuming the fact of the canon. The Church has indeed recognized this particular body of writings as sacred and authoritative, not to be added to or subtracted from or tinkered with. And many people have had this recognition of the Bible's sacred authority confirmed when their faith was confirmed in their lives.

But we can no longer take this attitude for granted. Even many of those within the faith no longer recognize the whole Bible as authoritative (and even those inerrantists who claim to do this do not do it in fact). It is no longer sufficient to say that because the Church of eighteen or nineteen centuries ago decided that these writings are canon, therefore they are authoritative for us today. We must have more of a reason than this.

This may be due in part to our own democratic traditions. But other factors also give rise to our questioning. Those who established the canon had a common sense different from ours and viewed the Scriptures in a different way. We no longer recognize the apostolic authorship of the Gospels or believe that Moses wrote the Pentateuch; we no longer maintain the doctrine of inerrancy. We are much more aware of the differences among the Gospels, of the influence of editors and the early Church, of the various traditions and literary relationships. So it seems all the more difficult to accept the Bible as authoritative just because somebody—tradition or the early Church—says so, when in fact these somebodies did not know as much about the Bible's history and background and diverse elements as we do today.

So we recognize the importance of the canonical approach of Childs and others, with its question of "since this is canon, how do we go about interpreting it?" But before this question can even be addressed we have to ask first whether we do in fact accept the Bible as authoritative canon; and if so, why; and if so, do we accept the whole or parts of it; and if parts of it, which parts, and why?

Why the Bible?

In Chapter 13 we explored the question of "Why Jesus of Nazareth?" We concluded that there are several reasons that could be used to support an argument for choosing Jesus as our compass, for granting him a sacred role as meaning-giver: first, we are not aware of any especially good alternatives; second, his ability to serve in this role has been confirmed in many faithful lives; and third, in choosing him we align ourselves with a compass which is in the public domain, and as such our interpretation is subject to the correction of tradition and public debate. The importance of this in avoiding proprietary religions and perverse, demonic, idiosyncratic interpretations should not be underestimated.

We need also to remember, however, that while these three reasons demonstrate that it makes sense to choose Jesus as our compass, in the final analysis this choice is not one that is reasoned out. It is a question of meaning and value, a choice that each of us must make for ourselves, one that we can make only if we find in Jesus of Nazareth a key to value and to truth that is confirmed in our lives.

The question of "Why the Bible?" can be answered in very much the same way. We can adduce arguments as to why it makes sense to recognize the authority of the Bible—many others have accepted its authority; this approach can give direction to our lives; etc.—but it is ultimately a question of meaning and value. The difficult problem here is in the relationship between choosing Jesus as our focus and recognizing the authority of the Bible. Many people do not even recognize this as a problem: surely if we grant the sacred authority of meaning-giver to Jesus then we must also recognize the authority of the book which tells his story!

But the message of Jesus does *not* agree with all the parts of the Bible, particularly with some of the harsh understandings of God expressed in the Old Testament and implicit in some of its laws. And as we have seen, even in the New Testament there are sayings attributed to Jesus which very probably do not originate with him and there are interpretations of him which are not consistent with what he taught. We have to choose: is our primary authority the Bible? Or is it Jesus of Nazareth? (Those who think they treat the two as one unified authority generally do this by reinterpreting all contradictory passages to fit with their understanding of Jesus. But since not all parts of the Bible fit with Jesus' message as they stand, this involves a definite subordination of some passages of Scripture. Jesus Christ is in fact the primary authority for these people.)

So the choice is either to recognize the Bible as primary authority, and Jesus of Nazareth as just one aspect of it along with Moses and the prophets and the many Old Testament laws not specifically superceded in the New, or to recognize Jesus of Nazareth as primary authority. We have repeatedly made the point that to be Christian means to choose

Jesus of Nazareth as our compass, our focus. His life and message must be our primary sacred authority.

And if Jesus of Nazareth is the primary authority, the epitome of the sacred for us, then the sacredness of the Bible (as we point out in Chapters 10 and 19) is derivative from the sacredness of Jesus in his role as the Christ. What does this mean for the question of canonicity, that is, the Bible's status as canon?

The fact that its sacredness is derivative constitutes no argument against the Scripture as canon. Literature is always derivative, is always distinct from the reality to which it points. The Gospels were recognized as canonical in the first place because they witnessed to something else: to Jesus the Christ. So the Scriptures have a recognized sacred authority, a canonicity, based on their close association with the sacredness of the Christ. So when we acknowledge that as Christians we recognize primary authority in the Christ, this implies a derivative sacredness in the Bible that makes it our most sacred literature, and thus our canon. But at the same time this recognition of Jesus the Christ as our primary authority sets a limit to the authority of Scripture that raises questions about canonicity. Since it is the life and teachings of Jesus of Nazareth that are our compass, that by their presence in the Gospels and their relationship to the rest of Scripture give sacredness and canonicity to the Bible for us—what does this mean for those passages which are in conflict with Jesus' teachings and those which are merely irrelevant to his message and apparently unrelated?

Jesus as the Christ: Hermeneutic Principle or Canonical Principle?

Our first option is to adopt the message of Jesus as our hermeneutic principle—that is, the principle by which we interpret the Scriptures. This is essentially the approach used by those people we mentioned above who see no conflict between the Bible as a whole and Jesus' teachings, except that here we recognize the conflicts and consciously try to interpret them away. Certainly there are places where this must be tempting: the ten plagues visited on Egypt by God because God had hardened Pharaoh's heart, the "holy war" instructions to Joshua to kill all the inhabitants of Jericho and Ai, and other passages that reflect an understanding of God that is certainly not consistent with the God of love taught by Jesus of Nazareth. With a Christocentric hermeneutic we would somehow interpret these passages to render them consistent with Jesus' message, so that they reflect a God of love and not a God of vengeance and retribution.

There are, however, two serious problems to such an approach: First, it is difficult to see how some of these passages could possibly be interpreted in a way that is in keeping with Jesus of Nazareth; and second, even if this could be done, the process would necessarily do damage to the original intent and to the established scriptural meaning of these passages. We would be reinterpreting them so radically as to show no respect for their meaning or their context. I for one view this as a dishonest and unacceptable method of interpretation.

If we are to take seriously the fact that the sacredness of the Bible is derived from the sacred function of Jesus as the Christ, and if we cannot use Jesus' message as our hermeneutic principle to interpret everything in the Bible, then our only other option is to use Jesus' message as our canonical principle. We cannot and need not reinterpret everything in the Scriptures to agree with Jesus, which is what would be required if we claimed the Christ as our principle of interpretation. But we can and must use the Christ as our principle of canonicity: not to make everything agree with his message, but to rule as authoritative (canonical) those portions which agree and to rule as unauthoritative (noncanonical) those portions which are inconsistent with his teachings. We do not interpret the ten plagues in a way that enables them to fit with a loving God; instead we say that our belief in a loving God as understood through Jesus the Christ renders the ten plagues without authority for us.

If the canonicity of the Scriptures depends on Jesus' role as compass for us, on the fact that they contain the writings which gave us this compass, then it would follow that only those portions of the Bible that contain, support, cohere to or elaborate on this compass can in fact be granted the authoritative status of canon. Canonicity depends on a positive relationship to the Christ. Therefore those portions of Scripture which are not so related cannot be recognized as canonical. The Bible is not a monolith, and recognizing canonicity in one part does not automatically imbue the rest of it with this status.

We could then say that those parts of the Old Testament which show a primitive misunderstanding of God are just that: primitive misunderstandings that do not have canonical authority for us. But we also might find much of the Old Testament included as canonical. After all, it was the Scripture for Jesus; he grew out of this tradition and saw himself in continuity with the law and the prophets. There is much in these books that constitutes the foundation on which he built: the story of this people's search for understanding of God and the notable calls for justice and righteousness. Other parts of the Old Testament need to be retained as historical and literary background—but this needn't make them canonical.

Of course, the New Testament is not exempt from this same kind of examination. It is doubtful that all the theologizing in Hebrews, the remarks by Paul about women and slaves, or the apocalyptic horrors of Revelation will be found to be consistent with Jesus' message.

Even now I can hear outraged voices protesting that this is profaning the sacred. But it is not. If the principle that makes these writings canon for us—the message of Jesus the Christ—also rules out certain writings which we have considered "Scripture", this is not to profane the sacred but to uphold it, to defend it. To say that God really did slay the first-born in Egypt and really did need the blood of an innocent victim on the cross before we could be forgiven—in direct contradiction to the teachings of Jesus—*this* would be to profane the sacred.

And in reality, most of us already proclaim a lack of canonicity of certain Biblical passages in the way we treat them. When we confront the ten plagues or the massacre at Jericho or the laws in Leviticus we may find them to be of historical interest. But we do not say that God actually did these or ordered these. We do not treat them as authoritative.

But then what do we do with the Bible? Go at it with scissors? Recognize a reduced portion as canon and put the remainder in a much-enlarged appendix with the Apocrypha? This is the direction in which this reasoning seems to lead us, but the dangers of this are both obvious and overwhelming. We would end up with a fractured canon, with bits and pieces taken out of their Scriptural context, with a different body of canon for each theological point of view, and with those portions of Scripture which we find uncomfortable not only ignored but disposed of altogether.

The Canon and the Canonical

There is an alternative to this which both recognizes Jesus of Nazareth as our canonical principle and yet also preserves the canon intact. This is to recognize the Bible as it stands, Old and New Testaments, as our canon, but to recognize that only portions of it are in fact canonical.

What does this mean? How can the whole be "canon" but only parts be "canonical"?

The whole of the Bible is "canon" in the traditional sense that it constitutes our sacred Scriptures. It cannot be added to or subtracted from. It is that body of writings which contains the message of Jesus of Nazareth, who fills for us the sacred role of the Christ.

But not all of these Scriptures are "canonical" in the sense of being authoritative for us. The canon carries within it the principle that makes it sacred for us—the meaning-giving testimony of Jesus, which we as Christians recognize as primary authority. Therefore, to be true to this principle within the canon, we must consider as non-canonical (i.e., non-authoritative) those portions of the canon which are not in keeping with it.

In fact we find that this is what we do. Once we have grasped Jesus' message of God's love, those Biblical passages about divine plagues or holy war or retribution or sexist customs lose their authority for us. They do not cohere. They do not fit with our compass.

Yet we do not excise these passages from our Bibles. Why not? What sense does it make to have a canon that is not canonical in all its parts?

First, because there is a sense here in which the whole is greater than its parts. The search by the Hebrews for a true understanding of God, from Abraham to Egypt, from the Promised Land to exile, witnesses as a whole to the love of God and to the requirement for justice on our part, and forms the matrix out of which Jesus' teachings developed.

Second, and perhaps more important, because to keep as part of our canon those passages which we do not consider canonical (in the sense of authoritative) establishes a persistent healthy tension. We are not able to dismiss out of hand those passages we do not like. We are not able to erase them or put them away somewhere. They are *there,* demanding our attention, demanding to be dealt with. Thus each generation, each new interpretation, perhaps each person, must confront these passages as a part of the canon, must consider whether they are authoritative, and must give good reasons if they conclude that a passage is not.

This tension of having passages in our canon which are not canonical, which demand by their very presence a reconsideration of their authority, is a healthy tension precisely because it is uncomfortable. We cannot dismiss certain passages just because of personal idiosyncracies without having to face them again. And truths that we cannot see because our society's prejudices get in the way are able to keep confronting us until they get through. Thus, for instance, Paul's apparent support of slavery lost its authority for us only after eighteen centuries and seventy or so generations, as the full implications of Jesus' message of the worth of each human being finally sank in and became authoritative instead (at least with regard to slavery). Similarly European missionaries brought to other lands a Scripture which contained concepts of justice that eventually undermined European imperialism. No doubt our descendents will look back and wonder why we could not see the obvious implications of certain passages in regard to peace or justice or charity.

A Canon Within the Canon?

Do we then have a canon within the canon? Of course we do. Everybody does, though not everybody admits it. We cannot make sense of the Bible without a principle of interpretation, without a decision about hierarchy or priority within the Scriptures. Even Childs admits that "much of the debate over a canon-within-the-canon has been misplaced. The issue at stake is not whether one needs material criteria by which to interpret the whole, but rather what is the nature of the criteria."[2] The

---

[2]Childs, *The New Testament as Canon: An Introduction,* p. 42.

important step here is to spell out one's criteria and then to be consistent with them.

Of course there are many people who take the approach that the whole Bible is literally true, making it impossible to give priority to any portion of it. We considered the problems associated with this approach in Chapter 2. The additional point can be made that to the extent these people do in fact treat the whole Bible as equally sacred, they are using the whole of Scripture as their compass instead of Jesus of Nazareth. And if they also claim priority for him, which many do, they then create an interesting problem of interpretation which it is fascinating (when it is not painful) to watch them try to deal with.

The Historical Jesus

We have said that we have Jesus of Nazareth as our compass and not the whole of the Bible. We need to be more specific about this. Do we mean the picture of Jesus presented in the four Gospels? Or do we mean a "historical Jesus" which we can develop as a result of historical critical study of these Gospels? Or something else which is somehow in between, perhaps as in Chapter 5 where we ruled out only particular types of passages from the Synoptics and accepted only congruent passages from the Gospel of John?

There are problems with each of these. An unquestioning acceptance of everything the New Testament says about Jesus yields us a picture of Jesus that suffers from internal inconsistencies, that is clearly in a few places a construct of the needs of the early Church, and that will not stand historical critical scrutiny. On the other hand, attempts to construct a picture of the historical Jesus have been fraught with personal biases to the extent that Jesus the first century Palestinian often comes out resembling nothing so much as the ideal nineteenth century European liberal or twentieth century American conservative or twenty-first century third world radical, depending upon who is constructing this "historical" picture.

Another more recent problem with this approach is that the tools and techniques used by modern critical scholars to arrive at a historical construct are specifically designed to weed out teachings by or about Jesus that might be attributable to someone else, that might have originated with the early Church or the Gospel editors or contemporary Judaism. The "principle of discontinuity" thus recognizes as teachings of Jesus only those sayings which are "discontinuous" with the Judaism of his day and with the apparent interests and needs of the early Church. The whole problem with this, of course, is that while it may work well at showing us the irreducible core that was absolutely unique to Jesus, it can in no way give us a balanced picture of him. Every individual shares a great deal in common with his or her culture, with their predecessors and with those who follow. This would be especially true for an individual who exemplified the best in their cultural tradition in addition to developing some new insights, and who then passed on both old and new through a movement they started. To say that the only historical or important aspects of this person are those which are not inherited from the past and which did not meet the needs of their followers, would be patently absurd. To try to draw any sort of picture of this person without these common traits and ideas would give us so minimalist a portrait as to be useless at best and misleading at worst.

So if we can neither accept the whole Biblical testimony about Jesus nor reject most of it to construct our own "historical Jesus", this leaves us again the uncomfortable but honest middle. On the one hand, as we have seen, there are some apparent intrusions in the testimony by the early Church, by the conclusions of hindsight, and by the theology of John and others, that cannot be glossed over. On the other hand, within certain acknowledged limits we have a generally accurate representation of the teachings and actions of Jesus of Nazareth. There will be a constant tension at the edges of the picture: does a particular saying represent too neatly the needs of the early Church? Did Jesus in fact take this particular stand on this particular issue? Is it consistent with the rest of the picture?

This is as it should be as we continue to try to refine and improve our understanding of Jesus. But unclear details on the edge of the picture in no way affect the clear central image.

The Historical Jesus and the Christ

We have eschewed the traditional quest for the historical Jesus, with its tendencies to wander far afield from the text and to turn Jesus into a person after the interpreter's own heart. I suspect that it is nonetheless evident that we have in fact adopted a different form of the historical Jesus, the Jesus of Nazareth that appears in and through that portion of the Gospels that we have no good reason to doubt. It is this picture which confronts us powerfully with the choice for or against God and love, this understanding which serves as our focus, our compass, our Christ.

Yet there is a limit to how closely we can identify the historical person Jesus of Nazareth with the Christ, for two reasons: first, there is much we do not know about the historical person, and clearly it is not necessary to know this or to include this in the understanding that serves as "the Christ" for us. It is his message with which we are concerned, his message of the love of God and love for neighbors as expressed in the way he taught and in the way he lived. It is this aspect of the historical Jesus of Nazareth that functions as the Christ for us.

Second, for many people a picture of Jesus that includes unhistorical and mythical elements has served as their compass, has functioned as the Christ to bring them into right relationship with God and neighbor. We cannot say that this is not a valid picture of the Christ for them (see Chapter 8 on the validity of religious beliefs). But we can say that it is an unhistorical picture of Jesus of Nazareth, and since we are aware of this, and since we cannot violate our own common sense, this unhistorical and mythical picture will not work for us.

Jesus of Nazareth as portrayed in the Synoptic Gospels, with the qualifications noted above, can function as the Christ for us. He challenges us to accept or reject the message. If we accept the message, if we focus our understanding of God and life around this message, if we live toward God and in right relationship with others with Jesus as our compass, then for us he is indeed the Christ.

ACKNOWLEDGMENTS FOR APPENDIX B

Grateful acknowledgment is made to Random House, Inc., for permission to reprint excerpts from *The First Coming: How the Kingdom of God Became Christianity* by Thomas Sheehan. Copyright © 1986 by Thomas Sheehan. Reprinted by permission of Random House, Inc.

Grateful acknowledgment is also made to The Crossroad Publishing Company and William Collins Sons & Co. Ltd. for permission to reprint excerpts from *Jesus: An Experiment in Christology* by Edward Schillebeeckx. English translation copyright © 1979 by William Collins Sons & Co. Ltd. Reprinted by permission of The Crossroad Publishing Company in the United States of America and by permission of William Collins Sons & Co. Ltd. in the British Commonwealth.

APPENDIX B:
BIBLICAL SCHOLARSHIP AND THE RESURRECTION: DID HE OR DIDN'T HE?

Anyone who wishes to propose a hypothesis for "what really happened" on Easter is taking on a difficult challenge. Besides the fact that this is an emotionally charged subject, we have no evidence except for accounts written down fifty or more years later by people who had a particular point to prove. Nevertheless over the past couple of decades "form criticism" has been able to learn much about the pre-Gospel sources that contributed to the New Testament, and scholars have put forth a number of hypotheses.

Let us state right here at the beginning that any hypothesis about the resurrection or the resurrection appearances must meet several criteria: (1) First, it must be consistent with the results of modern scholarship; (2) Second, if it is proposed as a conclusion based on the evidence, and not just as speculation, the evidence must in fact be persuasive enough to lead to this conclusion; (3) Third, it must be consistent with the Biblical evidence about the post-Easter Church; that is, it must explain the dramatic turnabout in the disciples and it must fit with the proclamation of the very early Church.

The purpose of this appendix, then, is to summarize the results of modern Biblical scholarship concerning the resurrection, to look at the conclusions reached by those whom I will call the "minimalists", and to evaluate their arguments and proposals.

Who are the minimalists? First of all, we must say that *no* serious exegetes propose that the resurrection accounts as we have them in the Gospels are accurate representations of events that took place two thousand years ago in Palestine. It is generally acknowledged that the post-Easter appearance narratives are the end result of much elaboration. Some would maintain that these accounts point to after-death appearances of Jesus to the disciples, the precise nature of which is lost to history. The minimalists are those who do not think that these narratives point to any analogous historical event, who maintain that in fact there were no post-mortem appearances of Jesus at all, no experiences of Jesus after his death by the apostles.

We need to note that these people are not necessarily enemies of the faith. Some of them are exegetes and theologians who after careful consideration have felt compelled to conclude that this is what the weight of the evidence points to. As representatives of the minimalists I will consider Edward Schillebeeckx's *Jesus: An Experiment in Christology* (Crossroad Publishing Co., 1979), a long and weighty study of current New Testament scholarship, and Thomas Sheehan's *The First Coming: How the Kingdom of God Became Christianity* (Random House, 1986), a more accessible argument based on the results of Schillebeeckx and a number of others. (Perhaps we should note a warning here, however, that another of Sheehan's views—that Jesus' purpose was to end religion by preaching that God is in our midst—is an idiosyncratic position not representative of modern scholarship. However, I confess a strong sympathy for what I see as his underlying purpose: to get people away from the teachings *about* Jesus and back to the teachings *of* Jesus.) Before we examine their arguments, though, we should remind ourselves of what the Gospel record is.

The Resurrection Appearances in the Gospels

All the Gospels agree that on the first day of the week Mary Magdalene, either alone (John) or with another woman named Mary (Matthew) or with her and also one or more other women (Mark and Luke), went out very early to the tomb and found that the stone had been rolled away from the entrance. They may have been taking spices with which to annoint the body (Mark and Luke). She (they) encountered either one angel (Matthew and Mark) or two (Luke and John). In the Synoptics the angel(s) tell them that Jesus has risen, and in Matthew and Mark that they should tell the disciples that Jesus is going before them to Galilee, where they will see him. Mark then says that the women "said nothing to anyone"—and this is the end of what we have of the original version of this Gospel. (More on this later.)

Matthew alone mentions that guards had been posted at the tomb and that they were bribed to spread the story that Jesus' disciples had stolen his body.

Then Jesus appeared to the women (Matthew) or apparently did not (Luke) as they went to tell the disciples, or else appeared to Mary Magdalene after she told Peter (John). The disciples either responded by going directly to Galilee where Jesus appeared to them once, though some still doubted (Matthew), or they experienced appearances of him in Jerusalem (Luke and John), perhaps not leaving for Galilee because they did not believe the women (Luke).

So only Luke and John report appearances to the apostles in Jerusalem. Luke tells of Jesus walking to Emmaus with two of his followers, who do not recognize him during the journey but only when he breaks bread with them, at which point he disappears. They return to Jerusalem and find the eleven gathered together, are told that Jesus has appeared to Simon, and then Jesus appears among them. He eats a piece of fish to prove that he isn't a spirit, preaches to them, and then goes out with them to Bethany from where he ascends into heaven. (In the Book of Acts, though, Luke says that Jesus appeared among them for forty days.)

In John, Jesus also appears to the disciples, passing through locked doors, then appears again a week later to a group which this time includes Thomas, who previously doubted but now believes. Then John (unlike Luke) also includes a detailed account of an appearance in Galilee. Seven of the disciples were out fishing and were directed by a person on the beach to try on the other side of the boat, at which point they made a great haul of fish and realized that this person must be Jesus. Returning to the shore, "none of the disciples dared ask, 'Who are you?' They knew it was the Lord." (John 21:12) (This strikes one as a strange way to describe *recognizing* someone as familiar to them as Jesus). Then Jesus passed out bread and fish and gave instructions to Peter.

All of this, of course, leaves one puzzled. Did he appear to the women or not? Did he appear to the disciples only in Galilee, only in Jerusalem, or in both? Why do the disciples have trouble recognizing him at times? Why does Mark mention no appearances at all? And why are we told nothing about the specifics of his appearance to Simon Peter when this is generally credited with being the formative event of Christianity?

While the defenders of a resurrection can point to a unanimity that Mary Magdalene discovered an empty tomb and (including Mark by inference) that Jesus appeared to the apostles, those who argue against it can point to all these inconsistencies. And while some discrepancies should perhaps be expected in descriptions of very unusual events that were written down in the form we have them some fifty years after these events, this can hardly serve as an argument for their accuracy.

At this point we will look at the arguments based on (1) the empty tomb; (2) the absence of appearance narratives in Mark; (3) the testimony of Paul; and (4) the evidence of the oral traditions. We will attempt to evaluate the various arguments as we proceed, before summarizing the evidence and then examining the hypotheses put forward by the minimalists.

1. The Empty Tomb

Even the minimalists grant there may very well be a historical basis to the account of the discovery of the empty tomb. There seem to be two separate traditions that point to Jesus' body being put in a grave by Joseph of Arimathea. If it were a new tomb (Matthew, Luke and John) this would have met the requirements of Jewish law that the body of one who had been hanged on a tree not be buried with anyone else. Even Sheehan admits (p. 148) that the women may have seen where this was and that Mary Magdalene (either alone or with other women) visited the tomb early on Sunday morning and found the stone rolled away and the tomb empty. Schillebeeckx further acknowledges what is to me the obvious conclusion about Matthew's story about the guards being bribed: if Matthew is refuting a story that Jesus' body was stolen, then even the Church's enemies who spread this story acknowledged that the tomb was empty.

But it is generally accepted that an empty tomb didn't prove anything. It certainly didn't prove or even imply a resurrection in first century Palestine. The picture of Mary weeping outside the tomb because "they have taken away my Lord" is the kind of reaction one would expect. In fact, the disappearance of the body wasn't even *necessary* for a resurrection according to many of the contemporary ideas.

Some scholars suggest that the account of the empty tomb was passed down by the early Christian community in Jerusalem, who may have known the location of the tomb and used it as the focal point in periodic commemorations, perhaps as a shrine. It is further suggested that the empty tomb was not even originally connected with the appearance narratives. Sheehan uses this to argue that Mark knew about the empty tomb but not about the appearances (see below), and that Paul may not have known of the empty tomb.

There is an interesting aspect to the minimalists' argument here. Because the empty tomb is the most historically defensible element of the resurrection narratives, they point out all the reasons why this would *not* imply a resurrection. But this also deprives them of one anticipated hypothesis—that the fact of the empty tomb gave rise to the appearance stories—and it also explains very well why Paul would not bother to mention it when he had resurrection appearances to point to. It also corroborates the reactions related in the Gospel accounts.

Meanwhile we are left with no answer as to who rolled the stone away and why the body was missing. Did Joseph change his mind and want his tomb back? Did grave robbers or enemies of Jesus steal the body? Did his disciples? (This seems unlikely as it seems to have been only the women who knew where it was.) We shall never know. But since an empty grave does not a resurrection make, it doesn't really matter.

2. The Gospel of Mark: No Appearances?

It is generally accepted that Mark 16:8 is the end of what we have of the original version of this Gospel and that verses 9 to 20 were added sometime in the middle of the second century AD to compensate for the lack of appearance accounts. It is also generally accepted that Mark is the oldest of the Gospels, dating from around 70 AD. Sheehan argues that the lack of resurrection appearances in the oldest Gospel indicates that in fact there *were* no resurrection appearances (pp. 98, 131–146). That is, the stories in the later Gospels (15–25 years later) are not just accounts that have become more specific, more physical and more elaborate over the years (which all scholars would admit), but they are in fact mythical stories not based on real events at all. While we cannot prove this one way or the other, there are several serious problems in arguing this based on Mark.

First of all, even though it is the oldest ending we have, we cannot be sure that 16:8 was the original ending of the Gospel of Mark. The majority opinion seems now to be that it was. I suppose one might ask, how does one lose the end of a book (or scroll)? However, I can see some strengths in the persistent minority view that what we have is *not* the original ending of Mark: even for a Gospel that tends to be abrupt in nature, the ending is *very* abrupt. The women told no one? It ends that way? It doesn't make sense. And as for losing the end of a book—I have done this myself, and with bound books, so I am sure that it is possible to lose the last piece of a scroll. (But see Schillebeeckx's argument below and Sheehan's on narrative structure.) In any case, one must be somewhat tentative in making conclusions based on the end of a Gospel that may not have been its end. We shall never know.

Second, Schillebeeckx argues that the reason that Mark mentions no resurrection appearances is not that he wasn't aware of them, but rather because they didn't fit with his theology. "If the assertion is correct that in associating exaltation with Parousia (thus not with resurrection) Mark does not see the celestial Jesus as presently operative, but affirms the complete absence of Jesus from his sorrowing and suffering Church, it then becomes possible to understand his not accepting the tradition of Jesus appearances: 'appearing' is what Jesus will do at the Parousia, not before" (p. 418). Thus, "he is going before you to Galilee" (Mark 16:7) does not in this understanding refer to a resurrection appearance (either implied or in a missing original ending), but rather to the Second Coming. If this is the correct interpretation of Mark then he may very well have been aware of resurrection appearance accounts.

Third, we have the insightful study of the narrative done by Sheehan himself. He points out that "the rhetorical structure of this narrative is calculated to hold the reader within the tale and, from within the tale, to confront the reader with the possibility of believing in the resurrection. The narrative effects that purpose in part by allowing the listener to understand more than the subjects of the story do. . . . It would seem, then, that the story is confronting you with a decision and inviting you to do precisely what the women did not do: to believe that Jesus has been raised rather than to flee in confusion." (p. 141)

This may explain how 16:8 could have been the original ending of Mark, but it also points directly to a shared knowledge of the resurrection and so by direct implication to the resurrection appearances. The empty tomb was not enough. Therefore the readers, who know this was not the end of it, are indeed impelled back to their own faith and their knowledge: "we know what happened next, and why this was not the end of it!", they say to themselves.

Sheehan, however, conjectures that the pre-Marcan oral version of this account was "content to leave the question unanswered" (p. 145) as to where belief in the resurrection came from. But this is to ask us to believe that Jesus' followers in Jerusalem didn't know about the appearances—with Simon Peter in their midst for a while? And Sheehan also claims that "it is clear that the narrative does indeed point beyond itself"—not, however, to an alleged happening in the past, since "the story's purpose is precisely to show that such past 'events' do not bring about faith" (p. 144). But is not the opposite clear? The story's point may be to show that the specific past event of the empty tomb did not bring about faith. But it then very clearly forces us to ask ourselves, "If the women said nothing to anybody, then how do we know he was raised? Then what happened next to change this, for here we are being told about it? What event transpired?" This is what the structure of the narrative impels us to do.

The minimalists *could* use Mark to argue against any resurrection appearances in Jerusalem, since he points to Galilee if he indeed implies this kind of appearance. In this understanding, Mark may have the women be silent either to explain why the apostles hadn't heard of the empty tomb, or more likely, to emphasize that the empty tomb was not enough, that something else needed to happen. However, we must remember Schillebeeckx's argument that Mark simply wasn't going to admit resurrection appearances, no matter how many he knew of. (One also can't help but wonder—if Mark is so careful to play down any causative role of the empty tomb, are we perhaps being too naïve in agreeing that it played no role in belief in Jesus' resurrection?)

Fourth, the final clincher against using Mark to argue that the appearance accounts were not known at the time of this earliest Gospel is the simple fact that Paul, writing two decades before Mark, makes specific mention of resurrection appearances. Not only that, Paul quotes what is recognized to be an earlier creed in I Corinthians 15:3–5: "For I delivered to you as of first importance what I also received, that Christ died for our sins in accordance with the Scriptures, that he was buried, that he was raised on the third day in accordance with the Scriptures, and that he appeared to Cephas [Peter], then to the twelve." He then goes on to mention appearances to more than five hundred brethren, to James, and then to all the apostles (which may be part of the creed passed on to him or else may be Paul's own addition) before adding "Last of all, as to one untimely born, he appeared to me." (15:8)

So there can be no doubt that resurrection appearances were known of by about 55 AD, at least fifteen to twenty years before Mark was written. If this creed was passed on to Paul near the time of his conversion then we are talking about a possible dating as early as 32–34 AD, only a couple of years after Jesus' death.

But there are a number of questions about Paul's testimony and the conclusions that can be drawn from it. We will turn now to consider this.

3. Paul's Testimony

"He was raised on the third day . . . and . . . he appeared to Cephas, then to the twelve." (I Corinthians 15:4)

> To judge from Paul's early formulations of faith, then, the raising of Jesus from the dead has no chronological date or geographical location ascribed to it and no connection with an empty tomb. In fact, the raising of Jesus seems to be no event at all, but only an expression of what Simon had experienced in Galilee. And as regards the appearance to Simon, the text in First Corinthians, upon closer examination, calls into question the notions (1) that such an appearance was an 'event' that occurred after Jesus had physically left his tomb and (2) that Jesus was made manifest to Simon in any visible or tangible way. (Sheehan, p. 117–118)

On what basis does Sheehan make these claims, and how persuasive are the arguments that he and other minimalists put forth in regard to Paul? We will look at (A) the question of chronology (does "the third day" mean "the third day"?); (B) the accounts in the Book of Acts of Jesus' appearance to Paul; (C) inferences from these accounts about the resurrection appearances; (D) Schillebeeckx's view on Paul's relation to the classical "conversion model"; and (E) inferences as to location and "event".

(A) Paul's Chronology: Does "The Third Day" Mean "The Third Day"?

Paul says (quoting a creed) that Jesus "was raised on the third day in accordance with the Scriptures". (I Cor. 15:4). Both Sheehan (p. 112) and Schillebeeckx (pp. 526–532) argue strenuously that Paul did *not* mean by this that Jesus was raised on a particular day which happened to be the first day of the week. This is one of the few areas in which it seems apparent that the minimalists have let their conclusions determine their assessment of the evidence instead of the other way around, but we will examine their arguments.

Sheehan supports his assertion only by assertion and by reference to the conclusions of several exegetes, so we must examine Schillebeeckx to discover the line of reasoning here. He points out first that the Gospel Easter narratives never mention "the third day", but always "the first day of the week", even when elsewhere these Gospels include earlier predictions of a rising on the third day. Therefore, he concludes, these were two different traditions.

But does that mean they don't refer to the same day? Schillebeeckx argues that "on the third day" doesn't refer to a particular day at all. He points out that in Jewish tradition "the third day" had special significance. It was the decisive and critical day, "the day of important, salvific events or of sudden overwhelming calamity" (p. 259). It indicates a decisive event after a short period of time. "On the third day" is a scriptural term, and may have been used by Jesus as part of his self-understanding. Thus, he says, to say that Jesus was raised "on the third day" affirms that God's rule has come in Jesus (p. 531) and "is charged with immense salvific implications. It tells us nothing about a chronological dating of the resurrection" (p. 532). Sheehan even states that it "took place outside space and time" (p. 112), an argument often used by defenders of the resurrection to shield it from historical inquiry!

There are two problems with the minimalist position here. First, like Bultmann, they show a lack of appreciation for the flexibility of language (see Chapter 4). It is quite possible for a phrase to connote a great and decisive day and also to denote a specific date. Consider, for example, "Independence Day"—for citizens of the United States this means the signing of our Declaration of Independence, the victorious struggle for freedom and the beginning of the noble experiment of democracy; it also means fireworks and family picnics and a long weekend. But it also means, with no doubt whatsoever, the fourth day in the month of July in the year 1776. So even if Paul, and the creed he quotes, use "on the third day" to mean a great and decisive day, no one can show any reason to doubt that they also meant to pinpoint a particular day shortly after the crucifixion.

Second, one feels compelled to ask whether the minimalists are claiming that Paul and the Gospel writers couldn't count. "On the third day"—not the third day *after*—does happen to be the first day of the week when they went to the tomb. And in fact one can see very clearly in Matthew's version of the predictions of the Passion that he could count and that he has changed Mark's "after three days" to his own "on the third day" in *order* that this would correctly designate the first day of the week. So for Matthew (and Luke), who were much closer to the thoughts of the early creeds than you or I or the minimalists, "on the third day" did refer to a particular chronology. Otherwise, they would have left Mark's wording unchanged, which in Matthew's case would have fit better with his reference to Jonah. One of the problems here was to get "in accordance with the Scriptures" to be compatible with the chronology that they knew. Mark apparently gives preference to the Scriptures, perhaps with Jonah in mind (who was in the belly of the whale three days and nights *before* being rescued). Either that or we must admit that Mark—unlike Matthew and Luke—is *not* concerned with chronology. But since these latter two never even allude to Hosea 6:2 ("on the third day he will raise us up"), and since Matthew would otherwise have remained consistent with the "after three days" of Jonah, we must stay with our conclusion that it was precisely their concern with chronology that caused them to say "on the third day" instead of "after three days". To deny that any concern of this type is reflected in Paul's use of this same phrase is to make a conclusion which there is no rational basis to make.

Meanwhile, of course, the point could be raised that what happened on the third day was the discovery of the empty tomb. The resurrection itself is not dated in the Gospels. Rightly or wrongly, Matthew and Luke seem to assume that if it had happened sooner the disciples would have heard about it sooner, or they simply fall into the common human habit of equating an event with our knowledge of it.

(B) Jesus' Appearance to Paul: The Accounts in Acts

All Paul says in I Corinthians (and elsewhere) is that Jesus appeared to him. To get any details about this appearance we have to turn to the Book of Acts, where accounts are found in Chapters 9, 22, and 26.

The account in Acts 9 relates that as Paul was on his way to Damascus to continue his persecution of the early Christians, suddenly a light from heaven flashed around him, he fell to the ground, and heard a voice saying, "Saul, Saul, why do you persecute me?" "Who are you, Lord", asked Paul, and he was answered, "I am Jesus whom you are persecuting." He was then told to go into the city where he would be told what to do. (Acts 9:3-5)

A virtually identical account is attributed to Paul himself in Acts 22. In both accounts he was led into Damascus blind. The only difference is that in the first account Paul's companions heard the voice but saw no one, and in the second they saw the light but could not hear the voice. (We ought to note that in Acts 9 it doesn't say they didn't see the light, but that they saw "no one".)

The third account is related by Paul as part of his speech to King Agrippa in Acts 26. Again, he says he saw a light—"a light from heaven, brighter than the sun" (26:13)—and he and his companions fell to the ground, and he heard Jesus' voice. There is no mention of blindness, though this would be a not unusual temporary effect of a light brighter than the sun, and he was given his commission to bear witness to the Gentiles right then and there.

Now, we must ask: since these accounts were not written down by Luke (the author of Acts) until about fifty years after the event they describe, should they be treated as any more accurate than the resurrection appearance accounts in the Gospels? In spite of the similar distance in time, exegetes give much more credence to these accounts of Paul's experience, for some obvious and not-so-obvious reasons. What is obvious is that these accounts in Acts are much less elaborate—there are no physical appearances of Jesus, for instance—and much more consistent. In addition, Schillebeeckx argues that we have two separate traditions represented here and that the account in Acts 26 is somewhat contrary to Luke's own viewpoint, so that it probably represents "an already extant, authentic Pauline tradition" (p. 377). So perhaps we can conclude that Paul himself related his experience in terms such as those found in Acts.

(C) Jesus' Appearance to Paul: Like the Easter Appearances?

Here is the crux of the argument from Paul. In Paul's own words he links Jesus' appearance to him with the Easter appearances to Peter and the twelve (actually the eleven). In Acts we have accounts of this appearance which may go back to Paul himself which make it clear that this appearance of Jesus was not an "appearance" as we would think of it. (There certainly is no reason to think that Paul claimed a more physical apparition than described in Acts; these accounts tend to grow in the telling, not diminish.) So if the appearances to Peter and the eleven were like the appearance to Paul, as Paul seems to imply, then we can infer that the Easter appearances were not "appearances" at all. The minimalists then go on to conclude that there was no "event" or at least no experience of Jesus. We must now examine this argument.

First, we have to acknowledge that in accepting the description of Paul's experience in Acts we must do so with some tentativeness. It is at least possible that Luke, in telling the story, has exaggerated the difference between the Damascus event and the resurrection appearances in his Gospel in order to maintain a distinction between the original apostles and Paul. (But see Schillebeeckx, below.)

Second, even if we accept the accounts in Acts, it is quite possible that Paul exaggerated the similarity between the appearance to him and the appearance to the apostles in order to authenticate his claim to be also an apostle, one called independently by Jesus. Certainly this is an underlying theme of Paul's. Did it have no effect on his claim for a similar experience of Jesus?

But suppose we grant that Paul is correct in implying that the other appearances were similar in nature to his. After all, he met Peter and others who had experienced these, and no doubt heard about what had happened. And Schillebeeckx argues that Luke presents the Acts 26 version of the appearance to Paul as "really an 'Easter' appearance of Christ, in the same sense as the formal, official appearances of Christ to Peter and the Eleven" (p. 377). So let us grant that Paul not only claimed but was indeed correct in claiming that his appearances and the Easter appearances were similar—we need to ask, similar in what way? Surely Paul means to say that in both cases they experienced the risen Jesus and that in both they received their official charge as apostles. But on what basis can we assume that Paul meant to claim any more similarity than that? It is indeed *possible* that Paul meant to imply that Peter, also, saw a bright light and heard Jesus' voice speaking to him. But this is only one possible hypothesis which could be affixed to this chain of tentative conclusions. If we proceed any further we must recognize that we are well into the realm of speculation.

(D) Further Speculation: Paul's Conversion

Let us grant for the sake of argument that Acts is accurate, that Paul is correct, and that Paul meant to imply that the Easter appearances were similar to his in content as well as in function. This could explain the uncertainty and doubt of some of the disciples and the fact that they did not recognize Jesus at first. However, this would still constitute an experience of the risen Christ of such force that it would also explain the dramatic turnabout of the disciples and the content of their preaching. The minimalists, however, wish to take us further.

Schillebeeckx says that in Judaism conversion was often called illumination and was "represented by what has become the classic model of a 'conversion vision': the individual concerned is suddenly confronted with a brilliant light and hears a voice" (p. 383). He may be right, but he does not support this assertion with any references. It is true, as he notes, that Paul may have viewed conversion as enlightenment just as we often do, as "seeing the light". I see no reason that Paul should have taken that any more literally than you or I, but Schillebeeckx proposes that what we have in Acts 9 is Paul's conversion "expressed in the model of a conversion vision" (p. 384).

Schillebeeckx's conjecture, then, is that what Paul experienced was a conversion, that this was expressed as a "conversion vision" (even though, he implies, Paul really didn't experience Jesus), and that this evolved into the "Easter appearance" type of account in Acts 26. (This in spite of the fact that Schillebeeckx says that Acts 26 represents an older tradition than Acts 9 [p. 377].) You will have to judge for yourself whether it is reasonable to conjecture that Paul would relate his conversion, his experience of "seeing" that Jesus is the Christ, as an "appearance" to him of the risen Jesus. If this seems reasonable to you, then you have no good reason not to go along with Schillebeeckx's next hypothesis: that this is also what happened to Peter and the eleven. They had a conversion experience. "Jesus was [not] made manifest to Simon in any visible or tangible way" (Sheehan, p. 118). We will consider this hypothesis again below and examine whether it satisfies the criteria that we set out at the beginning, in particular the need to explain the turnabout of Jesus' disciples after the crucifixion and the content of their message.

Schillebeeckx would have a stronger argument if there were an established cultural tradition of a specific type of conversion experience such as can be found in certain Christian denominations, particularly in "evangelical" sects and in the southern United States. People growing up in these churches are taught to expect a "born again" experience that makes them really Christians. As a consequence they tend to have these experiences. But I know of no information that would lead us to believe that a faithful Jew of the first century would have been prepared to have such an experience.

(E) Location and Event

We have not yet addressed Sheehan's contentions that we can conclude from Paul that the resurrection had no geographical location or connection with the empty tomb, and that neither the resurrection nor the appearances were "events". First, as we noted previously, there was no reason for Paul to mention an empty tomb that—as everybody agrees—meant nothing one way or the other about a resurrection. Second, Paul gives us no hint whatsoever as to his thoughts about the location of the resurrection, either where or whether. He may well have thought he didn't need to, that people knew.

Third, while he does not directly address the question of whether the resurrection itself was an event, this is so curious a question that I would not expect him (or anyone) to address it unless this question were directly posed to them. And if the accounts in Acts are at all correct, Paul certainly considered the appearance to him to be an event that happened at a certain time in a certain location on the road to Damascus.

4. The Oral Tradition: Early Christologies

We noted earlier that form criticism attempts to go back behind the Gospels and the letters to infer the earlier traditions and strands. Some scholars who use this method believe they can discern four early Christologies. We must point out that these are very early indeed, antedating not only Paul's letters (just over two decades after the crucifixion), but also antedating a consensus on the creed which was received by Paul (cf I Cor. 15:3–5)—and if Paul converted in 32–34 AD or shortly after, would one not think that this creed was delivered to him reasonably close to this time? So if in fact the form critics can discern Christologies that existed before this, what they have given us is a window on the turmoil of the first few months and years right after the crucifixion, as Jesus' early followers were struggling to find ways to explain what had happened. (To be fair: it is possible that Paul received this creed later, or that it did not yet represent the consensus view, but both of these seem unlikely to me.)

With this in mind, let us examine what Schillebeeckx has to say about these earliest creeds:

> Of four ancient credal strands . . . only the various Easter Christologies make Jesus' resurrection explicitly an object of Christian proclamation; in the other three early Christian creeds the resurrection is at any rate not an object of *kerygma*. This is broadly admitted by a good many scholars, but with the proviso: the resurrection is of course presupposed; yet not a single argument is ever advanced for this; it is simply postulated (apparently on the strength of the resurrection *kerygma* present everywhere in the New Testament, which is indeed the unitive factor of the canonical New Testament). But it is another question whether for some Jewish Christians the resurrection was not a "second thought", which proved the best way to make explicit an earlier spontaneous experience, without their initially having done so. (p. 396)

While on the one hand we need to recognize the tentativeness of any conclusions about these very early pre-Gospel strands, on the other hand we do not wish to underestimate the work of the form critics. They have indeed accomplished a great deal. So let us grant Schillebeeckx his point, at least for the sake of argument. Let us suppose that not all of the earliest Christians explained the Easter experience(s) by concluding that Jesus had been raised. Some may well have thought in terms of exaltation: Jesus had been exalted to God, by God.

What implications would this have for the Easter appearances? It would mean that those aspects of the Gospel accounts which make it so clear that this was a resurrection (and not something else) were probably later additions and elaborations—but we had already concluded this anyway. Take away the angel(s) who said he was raised, Jesus' exposition on the way to Emmaus on how a resurrection was according to the Scriptures (and his earlier predictions of the resurrection), the ascension into heaven, perhaps the eating of fish and showing of his wounds. We are still left with some pretty unusual appearances: to Mary, to Simon, to the eleven (though with fewer details). Since there was no universal expectation of an immediate resurrection, it would not be at all surprising if an experience of Jesus' presence after the crucifixion were interpreted in some cases as an "exaltation" instead.

But I cannot see how it bears on our interpretation of the Easter event either way. Whether those who experienced this interpreted it first as a Jesus raised by God or as a Jesus exalted by God, in either case this is to make a remarkable claim: Jesus, who was dead and buried, made himself known to them! If this is indeed what happened, it would be surprising if they had *not* had some difficulty in interpreting this!

And in any case, as Schillebeeckx himself points out, "early Christian local churches did nevertheless all have an experience of Easter, that is, knew the reality which other churches explicitly referred to as 'resurrection'." (p. 396) And the general adoption of this explanation for what had happened, of the name of "resurrection" for this reality, took place very early on—as Schillebeeckx also says—"precisely because it so aptly articulated" the reality. (p. 396)

In conclusion, then, while there may have been some early Christologies that interpreted the Easter experience as "exaltation" instead of "resurrection", this would not be a surprising response to "appearances" of Jesus after the crucifixion, and so does not address the nature or the probability of these appearances nor the question of whether the exaltation interpretation somehow evolved separately from the appearance traditions. Furthermore, within a very few years, those local groups who began with the "exaltation" interpretation had joined the consensus behind "resurrection".

Summary

The minimalist case that there were no resurrection appearances, and in fact no post-crucifixion experiences of Jesus at all, rests on several lines of argument. But the strength of these arguments must be determined by examining each of them separately, not by lumping them together as if that would overcome any weaknesses. At this point we will review the evidence:

(1) The Gospel accounts of the resurrection appearances are confused and contradictory. In addition, elements such as angels, teaching by Jesus, and his physicalness appear certain to be myth.

(2) There is, however, a general agreement in the Gospels on the empty tomb and on appearance(s) to Simon Peter and a group of apostles.

(3) The "empty tomb" may have originally been an independent tradition, but seems to imply nothing about a resurrection.

(4) *If* we have the original end of the Gospel of Mark in 16:8—of which we cannot be sure—then Mark did not include an account of any appearances. But this may be a result of Mark's theology (Schillebeeckx), or Mark may assume the reader's knowledge of appearances (narrative structure). In any case the appearances were certainly known much before Mark, in a creed made known to Paul. So we can draw no conclusions here.

(5) Some doubt has been expressed whether the creed quoted by Paul meant "on the third day" to be a chronological reference to an event.

This argument is not credible, however. Even if it were, there is no reason adduced to think that Paul did not think of the appearances as events
that happened in a particular time and place.

(6) Form criticism has discerned evidence of four different early Christologies, only one of which seems to have included "resurrection". But
no argument can be made from an "exaltation" interpretation of the
Easter experience that it did not involve appearances of Jesus, and
within a short time the adherents of "exaltation" had subscribed to resurrection as the proper interpretation.

(7) Finally, this leaves Luke's account in Acts of a Jesus appearance to
Paul (which may have originated with Paul himself), and Paul's classify-
ing this with the appearances to Peter and the eleven. If we grant that
Paul meant to claim a similarity in the *nature* of the appearance, and
that he was correct in doing so—both of which are far from certain—
then we have here the first evidence that addresses the nature of the
resurrection appearances, aside from the unbelievability of the Gospel
accounts themselves. But even if we acknowledge our tentativeness here,
what sort of conclusions can we make? We will look at the minimalist
proposals, at whether they are inferable from Paul, and then at whether
they meet the criteria we adopted at the beginning of this appendix.

The Minimalist Hypothesis

Perhaps we should call this the "minimalist hypotheses", for Schillebeeckx and Sheehan present somewhat different proposals as to what
likely constituted the Easter experience for Simon Peter. Neither of them
allows for actual resurrection appearances, but Sheehan is rather more
minimalist than Schillebeeckx. He begins by allowing for an ecstatic
vision:

> In his despair, when he felt like a drowning man pulled to the bot-
> tom of the sea, the Father's forgiveness, the gift of the future which
> was God himself, had swept him up again and undone his doubts.
> Simon 'saw'—God revealed it to him in an ecstatic vision—that the
> Father had *taken his prophet into the eschatological future and had
> appointed him the Son of Man.* (p. 105—italics Sheehan's)

But then Sheehan begins to back away from the idea of a vision: "It
was an experience that could have been as dramatic as an ecstatic vision,
or as ordinary as reflecting on the meaning of Jesus." (p. 108)

And two chapters later he completes his denial of a special experience
by Simon:

> After his failure, Simon 'turned again'. He did see Jesus again—but
> only in the sense of remembering, re-seeing, the present-future that
> Jesus, by living out his hope, had once become. (p. 124)

What Simon experienced—both before and after Jesus' death—was not a 'vision' but an insight into how to live. (p. 124–125)

But Sheehan has now gone from an experience—an ecstatic vision—that he could have argued was paralleled by what actually happened to Paul, to a remembering or an insight, to nothing dramatic at all. Whatever else you may say about the appearance to Paul, it was certainly dramatic, for Paul could name the time and place of this event that caused (or was) his conversion. So Sheehan has gone beyond arguing from the evidence to simply stating his own hypothesis: Simon remembered. Sheehan, of course, is free to do this, but we will see below it does not meet the requirements we set for a credible hypothesis, besides not being consistent with Paul.

Schillebeeckx, on the other hand, agrees with us that "something happened". After Jesus' death and the disciples' loss of nerve and before we find these disciples "boldly and confidently proclaiming that Jesus was to return to judge the world or had risen from the dead . . . something must surely have happened to make this transformation at any rate psychologically intelligible." (p. 380) "That the New Testament bases itself on specific experiences after Jesus' death (however they might be interpreted) seems to me, on the strength of the foregoing analysis, undeniable." (p. 394)

What does Schillebeeckx then propose as these specific experiences? He follows his argument from Paul: that Acts 26 is an "Easter appearance", that this developed from the account in Acts 9 and 22 which is a "conversion vision", and that what lay behind this was Paul's conversion experience, expressed here according to the classic model. So he proposes the same scenario for the disciples: conversion experiences that later, over time, developed into the official resurrection appearances that we have in the Gospels:

> These disciples did of course come to realize—in a process of repentance and conversion which it is no longer possible to reconstruct on a historical basis—something about their experience of disclosure that had taken them by storm: their 'recognition' and 'acknowledgment' of Jesus in the totality of his life. This is what I call the 'Easter experience' . . . And then we may indeed say: at that juncture there dawns the experience of their really seeing Jesus at last. (p. 387)

This is at least arguably consistent with the evidence from the appearance to Paul. And it certainly avoids the problems of the Gospel accounts and the demands that we believe in the supernatural appearances of a dead man. It is also consistent with the results of modern scholarship.

But it there not something missing? Does it meet our other criteria? Is this persuasively consistent with Paul? And does it explain the dramatic turnabout of the disciples and the content of their proclamation?

The Argument from Paul (Again)

Is it credible to argue that a process of conversion is what Paul alludes to in I Corinthians 15? We can infer that Paul himself would disagree. Whether "appearance" means "visual" or not, it certainly refers to the intrusion of something outside oneself. Schillebeeckx himself says "The four differentiated instances in I Cor. 15 relate to Jesus; what is called the 'appearing', therefore, is obviously not to be characterized as an occurrence deriving merely from human psychology; on the contrary, it is described as an initiative of Jesus himself." (p. 347)

A further problem with Schillebeeckx's hypothesis that in Acts we see an Easter appearance account develop from a conversion experience account (aside from this problematic interpretation itself) is that Schillebeeckx himself recognizes that Acts 26 is based on an older tradition, not a more recent one.

Therefore, neither Schillebeeckx nor Sheehan can support their own hypothesis with an argument based on Paul. The most we can say based on I Corinthians 15 in conjunction with Acts is that the earliest accounts of the resurrection appearances may very well have been less explicit and elaborate than the present ones in the Gospels (which we had already assumed), and were perhaps analogous to the accounts of Paul's experience on the road to Damascus as we find them in the Book of Acts.

How Do We Explain the Conversion and the Content?

We said at the beginning of this appendix that any hypothesis about the resurrection appearances, besides being consistent with modern scholarship and arguable from the evidence, must also explain the dramatic turnaround in the disciples and the content of their preaching. By postulating that the Easter experience of the disciples was the conversion process, how does Schillebeeckx explain this conversion? That is the big gap that I see in Schillebeeckx's hypothesis (and of course also in Sheehan's even more minimalist proposal). The question is, "what happened after Jesus' death and before the conversion that we see evidenced in the bold and joyous preaching of the disciples? What brought about this conversion?" To this question, Schillebeeckx can only answer: the conversion itself. Under the circumstances, in the wake of a crucified, dead and buried—and apparently failed—prophet, Schillebeeckx's answer does not meet his own requirement of making this transition "psychologically intelligible". I cannot avoid the conclusion here that something else had to happen to occasion this conversion.

What was this something? And what hypothesis would explain the content of the post-Easter preaching of the disciples? Even Sheehan points out that there was a dramatic shift between the content of Jesus' preaching and that of the disciples shortly after Easter. As Sheehan puts it, "Simon and the first believers . . . focused not on Jesus' way of living but on Jesus himself." (p. 125) The content of their preaching was an exalted or raised Jesus, one who was not defeated on the cross but who was instead victorious.

What could the "something" be that not only brought about the turn-around in Jesus' disciples—for surely something happened to do this—but which also changed the content of the proclamation from the message of Jesus to the message *about* Jesus, the message that he was triumphant, was exalted and/or raised from the dead? Is not the answer obvious? Only a modern minimalist over-reaction against the resurrec-tion accounts could prevent us from seeing this: Simon Peter and the apostles experienced something that they could—and did—understand as the presence of Jesus.

What was this something? I don't know. Certainly we owe a debt to form criticism and the minimalists for pointing out that this experience was probably more akin to the accounts in Acts of Paul's experience than to the appearance accounts in the Gospels. (This would also explain the attendant confusion and doubt mentioned in the Gospels.) But the evi-dence does not allow us to agree with the minimalist thesis that nothing extraordinary happened. It is clear that something very extraordinary did happen to propel the apostles and to transform the content of their proclamation. Other than that it signified Jesus' presence and so his resurrection to his disciples, I doubt we shall ever know the nature of what it was that transpired—but, as we concluded in Chapter 6, what-ever it was is not of theological significance to us today.

INDEX

SCRIPTURE REFERENCES

Occam Publishers
18 Frank Street
Cortland, NY 13045

We welcome your comments on this book. If you wish to order additional copies, make a copy of this page and use it for an order form. (If you want to order ten or more copies, write to us about our group purchase discount.)

Name _____

Address _____

_____

Please send me _____ copies of *Common Sense Christianity* at $19.95 each.

Total _____

New York State residents add sales tax _____

Shipping and Handling _____
($1 for the first copy, 50¢ for each
additional copy.)

– or –

First Class Postage _____
(If you wish quicker delivery include
$3 per book.)

TOTAL _____

☐ check enclosed

☐ charge this to my credit card   ☐ MasterCard   ☐ VISA

Acct number _____

Exp. date _____

Signature _____